UNLEASHING THE STRANGE

UNLEASHING THE STRANGE

TWENTY-FIRST CENTURY SCIENCE FICTION LITERATURE

by

Damien Broderick

THE BORGO PRESS

An Imprint of Wildside Press LLC

MMIX

*I.O. Evans Studies in the Philosophy
and Criticism of Literature*
ISSN 0271-9061

Number Forty-Seven

www.wildsidepress.com

FIRST EDITION

CONTENTS

To the Memory of

CHARLES N. BROWN

These days, SF and fantasy storytelling is a vast, sprawling city, and creators and readers of prose fiction form what is merely one of that city's older neighborhoods.

—Patrick Nielsen Hayden

CHAPTER ONE

CONCEPTOIDS IN A TIME OF SINGULARITY

The value of a book of criticism for a thriving field, genre, mode depends on how *au courant* the critic is, how insightful or insipid, whether there is an axe being ground, or a theory being driven through the work under examination like a Mack truck into the front of a heritage-listed house. If most reviews are instantly disposable, certain informed reviews and critiques stand at such magisterial elevation that they risk being read as a substitute for the book—I'm thinking here, in the context of science fiction and fantasy, of Stanislaw Lem's and John Clute's work especially—or at any rate there arises an oppressive imperative to swallow these readings as definitive. Luckily, many commentators clash with each other, as insights from diverse and different angles are brought to bear. For a writer, critical response to a novel can be highly valuable, in showing how readers skilled or naive have responded to the external trace of that complex and strictly incommunicable journey the writer has been pursuing for months.

Most of my work in the last four and half decades, since I was nineteen or twenty, has been science fiction writing and criticism, or futurist theory and reportage. No conflict of interest there. *Writing* fiction and *thinking about* fiction are profoundly intertwined, of course, but with this fluent instrument we call science fiction, writing and theorizing the *fiction* is profoundly intertwined with thinking about the *science*, learning about the science, speculating about where the science might go next, for good or ill. *Science fiction* has been a recognizable marketing term for less than a century, although *scientific romances* of various kinds—stories informed by the spirit and methods of empirical and theorized investigation of the world—can be found as far back as the first stirrings of science proper. I will use the standard abbreviation "sf," which also stands for Robert A. Heinlein's somewhat more dignified term, "speculative fiction."

"Sci-fi" is a gauche journalistic and now popular idiom disdained by sf aficionados; appropriated to mean bad or incompetent science fiction, it is sometimes playfully mispronounced "skiffy."

If there are three sf-theoretical concepts that I am known for deploying and promoting, these would be the sf *megatext*—my borrowing from Christine Brooke-Rose, who got it from French theorist Philippe Hamon; *transrealism*—the useful coinage from writer and mathematician Rudy Rucker; and the *Singularity*, part prospective science, part science fiction trope, advanced more than twenty-five years ago by Vernor Vinge and only now percolating out into the global community. If there's a common element in the trio, it might be unleashing the fantastical and strange into ordinary life.

"Ordinary," at any rate, as life is experienced by those for whom the strange *is* increasingly ordinary. It surely will be so for the transhuman or posthuman folks living somewhere up there in the future—perhaps only twenty-five, perhaps fifty, perhaps a thousand years hence—and those for whom the ordinary already *is* fantastically strange, like transrealist Rudy Rucker and his heroes Kerouac and Breughel.

Since my previous theoretical book about sf was *x, y, z, t: Dimensions of Science Fiction* (to which this volume is a kind of freestanding companion, rather than a sequel), let me once again adopt the perspectives of space and time, my two favorite dimensional realms...if you leave aside the rolled-up ones conjectured by physicists. These days I have a sharpened awareness of both time and space, living as I now do in Texas, very far from my native territory in Victoria, Australia. The six years I have lived in the USA do not just make up your ordinary, humdrum lump of duration. As I'm increasingly conscious, they are a large segment of what is either the last decade or two of my life (on the three-score-and-ten-or-twenty model), or the final scary interval bridging traditional mortal life and some epochal transition into endless life...if all goes right, if the rate of medical advance keeps roaring along at its exponential pace, if the world does not go down first into blood-thirsty grievance and counter-grievance, or environmental ruin.

For an Australian, as I can attest, America—the dominion of science fiction for at least eighty years—is another country, another space, almost another time, as well as another time-zone and season; things are done differently here. But not all *that* differently. After all, Aussies have been exposed, from infancy onward, to a world seen through American eyes—or, at any rate, through a kind of caramelized Hollywood version, simultaneously hyped up and smoothed out, violent and schmaltzy. The world seen through

American eyes is usually America itself, even when the portion we are watching is set back in the Biblical past, when dinosaurs and women in fur bikinis roamed the earth, or a galaxy far, far away. That astute critic H. Bruce Franklin even titled his (Marxist but American) study of the most influential body of sf in just that way: *Robert A. Hein-lein: America as Science Fiction.* I made a similar point half my life ago in the anthology *The Zeitgeist Machine:* "the genre is, after all, an instrument for amplifying American accents." That's not *everything* sf is, of course, so I added: "but more deeply it is a transducer of the technological experience: the myth of the *man-transistor interface*.... We all press our mouths to the grease-nipple; for us, pity and terror are newly shaped, and can benefit from new means of expression."

Today's twenty-first century myth, by contrast, is the *human-microchip* interface, soon to be the embedded *human-nanochip* link, and that, too, is profoundly American, even though many U.S. companies are hectically shoveling as many of their electronics and computer-related jobs as they can, out of the Homeland, and into the low-paid margins of America-as-the-world. Places like India and the many South-East Asian nations to the north of Australia. So the world grows ever more like America, even as America grows more like Mexico and post-communist Russia. It is an odd experience to be immersed inside, a pressure cooker with the dynamics of one of those old lava lamps the Aussie writer Terry Dowling likes to place in his fantastical stories.

Most of the writing discussed in this book is science fiction, although some ventures into science fiction-flavored fantasy (such as John Wright's and Mary Gentle's) or fantasy-flavored sf (like Charles Stross's). I choose not to explore the rich and often powerful, artfully wrought work of the New Weird or horror writers and their companions in adjacent fantastika (China Miéville, Kelly Link, Jeffrey Ford, K. J. Bishop, Jeff VanderMeer, Kathe Koja, many others). By and large, the last decade has seen the triumph of commercial fantasy in print and film product, a retreat from future shock, to some extent, even when it is implemented using the most amazing computer technology. But the popularity of magic-imbued medieval fantasy and erotic or frightening tales of vampires and zombies is also an understandable reaction to the placid, controlled, white-collar urban desperation of lives as clerks, checkout chicks, bank tellers, McFood dispensers, mothers and sometimes fathers stuck at home with 1.3 babies, Ph.D. students.... People want stories that embed their imaginary deputies in grit and discomfort, and then release them from that allegory of throttled tedium into exalted estate, high romance, tragic loss, deep passion, everything our flattened world seems to have squeezed out of our experience.

Is this contemptible or embarrassing? Well, while "doorstopper trilogy" fantasies rely on fairly simple and gratifying fairytale identification with secret princesses, magic powers, and alpha males (or Xena-style females) with big swords, such fantasies do enact a kind of mythology of growing up, finding one's place in the world, experiencing heightened emotion, tragedy, love.... Much classic science fiction did the same thing, of course, in its way—Robert A. Heinlein often told tales of rite-of-passage, looming responsibility, the enjoyments and burdens of exercising maturity. His young men became farmers in the sky, or citizens of the galaxy. There has been a rash of gung-ho space battle novels by women as well as men that seem pitched at US forces stationed overseas or getting ready to leave, or former service personnel. Many thousands of space military books donated by the late Jim Baen and his partner Toni Weisskopf were shipped to soldiers and sailors overseas for free distribution as leisure reading. I doubt the Pentagon would welcome donations of science fiction raising questions (as Joe Haldeman's *The Forever War* did during the Vietnam conflict) about the joy or honor of war.

Meanwhile, recent novels by Bruce Sterling and William Gibson are set closer and closer to the present day. It gets ever more difficult to make up believable, artistically satisfying stories about a star-spanning future in which folks just like us, but tougher and more resourceful and almost certainly more beautiful, deal thrillingly with aliens and galactic empires faster than light. Those imagined realities are insufficiently strange. The future is simply not going to be like that, any more than our world is an imaginable extrapolation from the life of hunter-gatherers. So it is easier to turn to a kind of heightened near-future techno-political fantastika—or retreat to rampaging zombies or to a magical version of a medieval world that never existed, tearing along through it without the unfortunate discomfort of fleas, no hair shampoo or conditioner, no flush toilets, no dentists, and, oh, that's right, no antibiotics or reliable contraceptives.

Our marvelous time of escape from real Dark Age deprivation has been all but fatally wounded by the power jackasses running the planet—yet, ironically, their stupid, bottomless greed is a serious factor in pushing along the technologies that could make life increasingly prosperous for *everyone*, not just the wealthy First Worlders. That's an unfashionable view, though, and if it were a matter of belief rather than rational analysis I'd have to admit to moments when faith wavers. Sociologists and economists have noted the paradox that even as everyone runs around with cell phones and people gorge and wallow in front of the TV or computer until their bodies bulge like bags of horsemeat, we also feel that things are getting worse. The supersizing culture is certainly nose-diving. Here in San Antonio it is hard to find streets with decent sidewalks where one can set out for a stroll without fear of being mown down by an SUV, and too many of the roads flood when it (rarely) rains.

But in fifty years, if not sooner, it is possible that people will only have to age and die if they choose to, or if some power-mad or god-smitten psychopath kills them. Right now, plenty of people depressed about the state of the planet seek consolation in dreams of magic kingdoms and demonic wars. What of science fiction, though, in such a world? The overload of change, the tsunami of ceaselessly accreting knowledge, can be crushing. Immersed in Charles Stross's, Greg Egan's, Vernor Vinge's density of reference, half the time one has no exact idea what they are talking about. We must read it as poetry, take what we can from context and by osmosis. I hope readers of my own science fiction and criticism do the same when I go off into an apparently incomprehensible aria. As a child, I had a dictionary next to me when I was reading; now I have Google. If the internet is murdered by spammers or the thought police, we are going to feel as if one half of our brains has been amputated. As if we had been flung back into flea-scratching Fantasyland, without the magic. That would be a catastrophe.

* * * * * * *

In the late 1960s, when science fiction finally matured, the brash, ambitious British editor Michael Moorcock famously asked, on the cover of *New Worlds:* "What is the Nature of the Catastrophe?" Mike Moorcock figured entropy was to blame. Running down, burning out, giving up. Perhaps it was a premonition of the dreadful Thatcher years, when Britain did just that. But Moorcock himself didn't give up, certainly not. When *New Worlds* and its surrealist community of New Wavers yielded up the ghost, finally, after heroic battles with marginality, weariness and public indifference, this archetypal Londoner moved to...Texas. A little town called Bastrop, an hour and a half up the freeway from where I am sitting right now in downtown San Antonio. His wife and mine met after starting women's shelters in central Texas, trying to deal with victims of the catastrophe. Small world. Science fiction as America.

When I was young and science fiction seethed in my blood, Moorcock took over *New Worlds* at the age of twenty-four. Now he is a grandee in Texas, when he is not enjoying Paris and the comforts of Europe. I am nearly as old as Moorcock myself, and science fiction in Australia is deep into its third generation. Or maybe its fourth, or even fifth, if you wish to count the yellow peril thrillers from the start of last century; I don't. Rather, I tend to count the start of real sf in Australia from the late 1950s and early 1960s, when writers you have probably never heard of such as Wynne Whiteford (b. 1915), Lee Harding (b. 1937), David Boutland (b. 1938), and John Baxter (b. 1939) started to break into *New Worlds* several years before Moorcock's New Wave slammed over it, capsizing the canoes and stranding most of the Aussies. They helped comprise the non-US wing of what we might call the Second Wave of modern science fiction.

Let me propose that the First Wave was the epoch stretching between Jules Verne and H. G. Wells, and Hugo Gernsback. The Second was marked by the great US magazine editors John Wood Campbell (*Astounding/Analog*), Anthony Boucher and J. Francis McComas (*The Magazine of Fantasy & Science Fiction*), H. L. Gold (*Galaxy*), and, in the UK, John "Ted" Carnell (*New Worlds* and *Science Fantasy*). The great proportion of "masculine" science fiction was intensely, ideologically conservative in manner as well as hard shelled, despite a powerful resistance to McCarthyism, racism, and anti-intellectualism. One of the astonishments of writers like Theodore Sturgeon and Edgar Pangborn emerging in the 1950s was, in addition to their poetic voices, and surely not by accident, their concern for human difference, variety, sensibility, and emotion. Fortunately, the best science fiction today seems to me to combine all of these characteristics, as the best fiction always has. When I was twelve or thirteen, I was besotted by science fiction comics and magazines, and then a little bit later by wonderful paperbacks of the classic 1950s' sf by Second Wave writers such as Arthur C. Clarke, Alfred Bester, Robert A. Heinlein, Theodore Sturgeon, James Blish. I wanted to grow up and write fiction like that. Nobody wanted me to. (I suppose nobody wanted me to become a bank robber, either, so it's probably just as well that I never did.)

The Third Wave was the modernist convulsions of Michael Moorcock (his revitalized *New Worlds)*, Judith Merril (editor of the eclectic *Year's Best* anthologies), Harlan Ellison (*Dangerous* and *Again Dangerous Visions)*, Damon Knight (his *Orbit* new fiction anthologies), Cecilia Goldsmith (*Amazing* and *Fantastic*, which discovered such brilliant innovators as Ursula K. Le Guin, Thomas M.

Disch, and Roger Zelazny), and Terry Carr, the founding editor of the Ace Specials series of novels that introduced Ursula K. Le Guin's *The Left Hand of Darkness* and William Gibson's *Neuromancer.* Thus, the "New Wave," in both the UK and USA, was really just the most flamboyant part of the Third Wave of maturing sf, followed most recently by a Fourth Wave inaugurated by cyberpunk and now richly exfoliating into the New Space Opera and the New Weird. (These "New" sub-genres get old fast, inevitably, and any day now we might see a true Fifth Wave of science fiction bursting forth from the keyboards of the grandchildren of the New Wavers.)

As it happens, the last gasps of that Second Wave coincided with Australia's first substantial sf generation, if we leave aside the immigrants already established in the field (A. Bertram Chandler, most notably, and Nevil Shute). The margins between Second and Third waves saw the first serious critical work starting to seethe in Australia, dealing not so much with local sf—there wasn't very much of it—but with the great landmarks of the rest of the planet: Brian Aldiss, Philip K. Dick, J. G. Ballard, Stanislaw Lem, Cordwainer Smith, Ursula K. Le Guin. We were young, as sf writers often are, or used to be, most of us in our twenties. With the British genre boat overturned, few of us managed the move to the major U.S. markets, and those who did took a long time getting reestablished. Nobody was getting any younger. George Turner arrived like a lion in 1978, with *Beloved Son,* a novel well-received in the U.K., and the astonishing thing was that he was already sixty-two-years old, a decade older than Brian Aldiss, four years older than Isaac Asimov for heaven's sake, who was even then twenty or even thirty years past his peak when Turner surfaced. Turner had first made his mark, of course, as a ferocious critical commentator, and as an award-winning mainstream novelist. So the clock was reset. As time passed, as the Third Wave ebbed, a strange thing became noticeable. Australian sf writers, and perhaps readers, were becoming *old.* Jack Dann, now an adopted Aussie, was born in the same year that Hiroshima and Nagasaki made sf hideously real. I had shown up the previous year, and Terry Dowling in 1947. Sean McMullen is only four years younger than I am. But even the formerly new kids on the Aussie sf block are not kids any more, not at all. Lucy Sussex was born in 1957, Margo Lanagan in 1960, Greg Egan, that marvel of nineties' innovation, was born in 1961, Garth Nix in 1963, Cat Sparks in 1965, and Sean Williams (whose email address is lad@chariot.net.au), hit forty, the statutory mid-life crisis, in 2007, as did Australian fantasy star Kate Forsyth.

This was not just some terrible affliction of the southern continent. Science fiction everywhere, once marked by the striking prodigiousness of its creators, and the adolescent freshness of its fans' cheeks, had grown up, and then grown downright elderly—even those of the Fourth Wave. William Gibson had been born in 1948, less than three decades after the typical birth date of the Second Wave or "Golden Age" innovators, who tended to cluster around 1920. Bruce Sterling, former boy gadfly of cyberpunk, now a sort of international gray eminence, was born in 1954, John Kessel in 1950, Lois McMaster Bujold in 1949, Connie Willis in 1945.

Consider the winners of the John W. Campbell Award for Best New Writer: In 2001, this honor went to Kristine Smith, who has a BS in Chemistry, and after a brief stint in a retail clothing distribution center has had a working career in manufacturing and R&D, with twenty years at a large pharmaceutical manufacturer. Campbell awards for the rest of the century so far went in 2002 to Jo Walton (b. 1964), 2003 to Wen Spencer (b. 1963; but her books deal with vampires and werewolves), in 2004 to Jay Lake (b. 1964), in 2005 to Elizabeth Bear (b. 1971), in 2006 to John Scalzi (b. 1969), in 2007 Naomi Novik (b. 1973; her enjoyable, *faux* Napoleonic sequence of novels proposed an aerial fleets of dragons in a complex alternative history), in 2008 to Mary Robinette Kowal (b. 1969), and in 2009 to David Anthony Durham (b. 1969). As I write, then, the "youngest" of these new writers is thirty-six-years old.

Other notable Fourth Wave writers include Jeffrey Ford (b. 1955), Mary Rickert (b. 1959), Charles Coleman Finlay (b. 1964), Alastair Reynolds (b. 1966), Ted Chiang (b. 1967), Jeffrey Vander-Meer (b. 1968), Kelly Link (b. 1969). Of course, there are other new writers (are these, perhaps, the first of the Fifth Wave?) who were not born until the 1970s and1980s—for example, Paolo Bacigalupi (b. 1972), Nick Mamatas (b. 1972), Tobias S. Buckell (b. 1979), Tessa Kum (b. 1981), Sara Genge (b. 1983)—but the mean age of the new frontrunners seems to be a bit over forty, where once the innovators might have been fifteen or twenty years younger when they made their mark.

I take heart from these facts. Yes, the Second Wave Golden Age writers of the 1940s and 1950s were frightfully young when they blazed into the skies of speculative fiction, lifting it from pulp repetition to exciting innovation. Some few of them are still with us, but by and large their work slowly grew staid and respectable, as you'd expect from the elderly. But the shift from sf as disposable commodity to an art (at least at its best) means that experience—both in writing and in living—pays off in richer, more rewarding work, or at least it holds that promise. The graying of sf world-wide need not imply any failing of its impulse, the pressure it can bring to bear on our expectations of the future.

It is a familiar argument that only sf is capable of dealing imaginatively and fully with the kinds of accelerating and monumentally disruptive changes that technology is insidiously pressing into the core of our lives, including our very life spans. Sixty is the new forty (and as Rudy Rucker has pointed out, zero is the new minus-ten), and sometime in the next few decades an accumulation of biological advances will allow us to slow, then still, then even reverse the ticking of the body's evolved clock. That is a very American dream, of course, brought to us from the land of the Extreme Makeover (as advertised on TV!). I wouldn't be surprised to see it first in the medical laboratories and clinics of San Antonio, where I now live.

That promise or threat of indefinite lifespan was an early science fictional idea, of course, not to mention a mythological and religious obsession. Interestingly, it never became one of those crochets that have driven sf's development: those odd little bees in bonnets that capture editors and writers alike, turning sf into a weird form of propaganda for the futuristic, the blue-sky-unlikely, and the frankly ridiculous. It is generally agreed that H. G. Wells invented science fiction as a medium for thought experiments. Thirty years later, when it became a commercial publishing format with the Second Wave, and began to be regarded as a genre, science fiction was a blend of rousing adventure tale, fabulous spectacle, and rude scientific speculation: "Extravagant fiction today," as Hugo Gernsback promised, "Cold fact tomorrow."

Bit by bit, these primitive speculations—drawn to some degree from science and perhaps in equal part from legend, mythology and wish—grew routine and stale. Editors began to seek out what one of them, Orlin Tremaine, called "thought variants". SF had started down the path to the valorization, or at least the eye-catching exploitation, of what I'll call *Conceptoids*.

* * * * * * *

"Factoids"—the term from which I adapted the Conceptoid of Conceptoids—are little bundles of what people *claim* to be facts, but usually aren't: urban legends, rumors, detritus from old advertising or political campaigns. Conceptoids are something like that: empty signifieds coupled to handy signifiers, waiting to be filled by theory or practice, and slyly or heavy-handedly promoted by someone in a position of authority or influence. (I could have called them *signe-foids,* but that might seem a heavy-handed pun on Sigmund Freud or, in another sense, on the strange semiotics of psychoanalysis exemplified by Jacques Lacan.)

As the decades passed, these graspable but potless handles seem to have become both a convenient marketing tool and a versatile device that editors could impose upon a magazine's writers and their unwritten stories, lending the fiction a kind of quasi-real or substantial unity or focus. Let me enumerate some of these Conceptoids, which have something in common with tropes or with Rucker's appropriation from rock, "power chords."

Perhaps the most conspicuous—once we get past the early years of the last century when simply deploying television and aircraft was sufficient to provide heady thrills for the reader—are space travel or rocketry, and atomic power and nuclear weapons. The horrible realization of both these ideas in the Second World War, and then again a decade later with the deployment of nuclear power plants and the first space satellites and ICBMs, made science fiction briefly seem prophetic indeed. For a time the nightmare scenarios of post-atomic holocaust, recycled to the point of vapidity, entered the popular consciousness, both through people's awareness of the real political threat of the Cold War, and via science fiction movies.

But those Conceptoids, while joining the general discourse or shared megatext of science fiction, became, by virtue of their very success—of their reality or threatened reality—too tame to excite regular science fiction readers. And so editors like John W. Campbell and Ray Palmer plucked from the aether, or from the muddled minds of some of their pulp writers, one crude but fertile Conceptoid after another: hidden underground deros from lost Atlantis and Mu, flying saucers, symbolic and multi-valued logics as key to advanced thinking, general semantics as an even more advanced form of just such logic, Asimovian algorithmic robotics with deeply embedded fail-safe routines, Dianetics (supposedly an engineering approach to the human mind), parapsychology, wild talents and ever more fanciful psi powers, space drives that laughed at Newton and Einstein alike, although the laugh, of course, was on them, parallel or divergent worlds and histories, and eventually, rather late in the day, the triumph of miniaturized electronics (*Astounding* foresaw *really tiny* vacuum tubes), cryonic suspension of the dead, astrology messing up radio reception, symbolic machines with no internal parts except inked wiring diagrams, cyberspace and virtual reality, dreams embodied at last in machines, and in people become machines. And finally in the most recent decades—as the impact of accelerating microtechnology deepened—gene engineering, nanotechnology, and the Vingean singularity.

Oddly enough, the more recent grand Conceptoids don't appear to have been sponsored by specific editors, of either magazines or original books. They've arisen spontaneously out of the vacuum fluctuations of popular science journalism, or, arguably, in the case of the Singularity, out of the singular mind of Vinge himself. Certainly the singularity was anticipated by others, as a vague notion, and these predecessors have been acknowledged by Dr. Vinge. Nonetheless the recent contamination—or fertilization—of the science fiction meme pool by the trope of singularity, or what I sometimes call the Spike, reminds me of nothing so much as the impact of Campbell's own varied and distinctive Conceptoids.

* * * * * * *

I hope it is clear that I am not automatically disparaging such Conceptoids, since few ideas are so fraught with long-term human significance as nuclear war, post-nuclear or other global devastation, the exploration and exploitation of outer space, the emergence of artificial intelligence whether in robot form or as an adjunct to our own minds, and now this final grand conceit which, if taken seriously, subverts the very possibility of any future science fiction: that accelerating technologies will zoom upward exponentially, or even hyper-exponentially, on the chart of change, and converge in some unimaginable cataclysm or Parousia, at any rate forming an opaque wall beyond which our best minds can't track the future's likely course.

It is worth comparing these narrative rallying points with the canonical tropes of the sf mode, the kind of archetypes catalogued and examined by Professor Gary Wolfe, who discerned certain icons that overlap with Conceptoids but are not always identical with them: the spaceship, the robot, and the monster, as well as classic loci such as the city, the wasteland and the barrier. Some important tropes aren't Conceptoids in the sense I mean, although they share many aspects in common and might become such at any time, should an editor choose to orchestrate a promotional program around their alleged reality and imminence, or their special narrative allure. They include engineered immortality (or negligible senescence, as biogerontologist Dr. Aubrey De Grey puts it); suspended animation of the *living*—long a trope, but never, to my knowledge, claimed as something you could sign up for, unlike postmortem cryonics, promoted in the 1960s by editor and novelist Frederik Pohl;

demonstrable life after death, a favorite at a church near you but not any sf editor's hobbyhorse. Psychohistory is a wonderful sf trope, and even has a parallel academic sub-discipline by now, but no editor actively promoted its real-world development. Cloning has featured often in sf, but no editor has adopted the Raelian faith and urged readers to clone their way to redemption.

Is my neat little schema breaking down so soon? If cloning isn't a Conceptoid, just because nobody at *Galaxy* or *Analog* or *Nebula* took up its cause, what is it? Well, cloning is certainly a *conception.* By now cloning is an established sf *icon,* or narrative device, a firm element in the megatext armamentarium, but of course it is also a barnyard reality. Has a medically contrived human clone been born yet? We don't know, but surely it won't be long, despite the hand wringing of ethicists. (Justifiable at this time, I hasten to add, given the current safety limitations due to our continuing partial ignorance.) So—might society, preparing for that day, learn anything other than outright prohibition from science fiction's exploratory games with what we now call *nuclear transfer reproduction*?

In 2005, *The New York Review of Science Fiction* published a talk Robert J. Sawyer gave at a symposium on sf and social change. He had some sharp words to say about the failure of social thinkers to pay attention to sf's long advance notice of cloning and its implications. Had our meditations been heeded? Alas, no. Instead, hysterical know-nothings rushed into print and ranted on TV deploring this novelty, unaware that it had been dissected and anatomized for decades. "Fifty years of serious dialogue had fallen only on the ears of sf fans," Sawyer noted with regret. Meanwhile, he said, "The public was running around spouting garbage about whether human clones were really people, and fearing that they might have psychic abilities. Our enlightened sf dialogue had utterly failed to have an impact upon human consciousness" (Sawyer, 13).

This reproachful lament is oddly wrongheaded. Think of the notable sf tales about cloning, beginning with Aldous Huxley's great founding act of imagination: cloning as a recipe for a society rigidly segregated by innate ability and temperament. *The Boys from Brazil* cloned Hitler, and a number of more recent sf books cloned Jesus. Ursula K. Le Guin's "Nine Lives" not only has male and female cloned identical siblings (which of course is impossible without special tinkering), but these people are linked by telepathy. Psychic abilities in clones! Clone kin share a sort of group mind in the award-winning novel by Kate Wilhelm, *Where Late the Sweet Birds Sang.* In the same novel, for no justifiable reason, the clones become sterile after several generations, as if cloning were a kind of iterated

Xeroxing. In Arthur C. Clarke's *Imperial Earth,* cloned generations mysteriously inherit an acquired disorder that was not in the original parent-brother's DNA. Robert A. Heinlein's *Friday* dealt with a smart, able woman generally despised because her mother was a test tube, her father was a knife. True, Heinlein showed that this was a ridiculous prejudice, but he knew that there'd be a lot of idiots running around saying that clones can't have souls. On the other hand, he also wrote novels where it was deemed admirable for an old man to clone femalized versions of himself for sexual purposes. I'm not necessarily objecting to this, if all the parties are agreeable, but I can see that Leon Kass (former President George W. Bush's high-tech morals czar) might get a bit squicked.

How about Michael Marshall Smith's *Spares* (1997), which—absurdly—has cloned twins of the rich and careless kept in filthy conditions as they're repeatedly mined for spare parts. Would you accept a replacement organ from someone (literally your time-lapsed twin, remember, your own physically compatible flesh and blood) who struggled for life in foul squalor, operated on without anesthesia? It makes zero sense, but this is the kind of catchpenny or witless nonsense that too much sf has dumped into the minds of people with no great interest in learning the fairly prosaic facts. A similar critique can be made of Booker Prize winner Kazuo Ishiguro's more air-brushed *Never Let Me Go* (2005). It is not at all clear to me that these fictions, however allegorically enjoyable and beautifully written some of them are, have advanced human understanding one whit, at least as far as the moral and social status of cloned people is concerned.

* * * * * * *

The social utility of sf is an old, old topic, and so are several other conundrums that keep teasing me. *Obsessing* might be a better word. How *does* sf work? What sets it apart from other forms of what we might call made-up writing—that is, fiction that does not present itself on its face as portraiture of the quotidian, especially of the exquisite consciousness. Consider the Old Space Opera that Brian Aldiss lovingly anthologized thirty years ago, when the gaudy texts he chose were themselves only twenty or thirty years old. Here's his justification:

> One can be fairly sensible and still get pleasure
> from reading about armored chaps with flambeaux,
> drinking out of bellarmines and leading warhorses

into starships before they dash across the parsecs at many times the speed of light.

You can, in other words, take these stories seriously. What you must not do is take them literally. The authors didn't. There's a way of reading everything. (Aldiss, 1976, viii)

Aldiss found one key to the appeal of this sort of fiction in the playful precedence of *Homo ludens* over workaday *Homo faber*:

A galactic empire owes more to Cecil B. de Mille than Einstein: it is the Spectacular of SF.

Quite right. But he wasn't finished; he had a stronger claim to make:

This unashamed escapism is not incompatible with profundity of thought. (Aldiss, 1976, vii-viii)

Is that true? Is it even *thinkable*? Was Aldiss pandering, perhaps, in the nicest possible way, to a readership craving nothing more than hot starship fumes and bare-breasted goddesses in chain mail? (One of whom was displayed, most attractively, on the cover of his anthology.)

Not at all, or at least not entirely. In Arnold Toynbee, the Slavoj Žižek of his day, Aldiss found this claim: "With the increase in our power, our sense of responsibility and our sense of distress increases." The real and the ideal become sundered. Even more saliently, perhaps, with the increase in *their* power (whoever they are), *our* sense of powerlessness and distress increase. In any event: "If this is so," Brian Aldiss suggested, "then the galactic empire does make a contribution to one of the central problems of our time, sharing as it does both the real and the ideal; that it manages this via swordplay, suppurating aliens, and gadgets is an indication that philosophers are not being addressed."

Well, then, what makes some people read sf and others turn away in amusement, disgust or simple boredom? It is not enough to say, "A modicum of good taste," as snobs might. But as Carlo Rotella, director of American Studies at Boston College, noted in the *New York Times* in July, 2009, "When applied to literature, 'adolescent' does not only have to mean pedestrian prose that evokes the strong feelings of emotionally inexperienced people. 'Adolescent' can also mean writing that inspires the first conscious stirrings of literary sensibility...if under that heading we include the transformative experience of falling in love for the first time with a beautiful sentence." He was speaking specifically of the *sui generis* work of Jack Vance, but one might expand that to "falling in love for the first time with a beautiful or dazzling idea."

When we were young, we gulped down just about anything that offered a thrill. I think of those baby birds with their heads flung back, eyes clamped shut, beaks wide open, waiting for Mama to drop anything at all into their starving throats. Hard to maintain that omnivorous appetite beyond adolescence, I suspect—and just as well, really. But then our tastes do tend to harden if not sclerose as we age.

More baffling, how can we explain the astonishing triumph in the movies, during the last three decades, of all sorts of sf tropes and spectacle, simultaneously with the continuing lack of interest in written sf, even hostility, on the part of those hundreds of millions of movie-goers? *Locus* showed in February 2009 that *The Magazine of Fantasy & Science Fiction* in 2008 had a monthly average total paid circulation of a bit over 16,000 copies. *Asimov's* moved a little more than 17,000 copies, and even *Analog* struggled to shift 26,000 copies. (Fifteen years earlier, it had been 75,000; in 1939, according to its editor, the number for *Astounding* was allegedly an...astounding...300,000.) I'm informed that the newly revived *Realms of Fantasy* approaches *Analog*'s circulation. These are grim figures. It is possible that the cadre of loyal readers is literally dying off, and that the new readers either do not know the magazines exist (traditional distribution outlets and processes having almost gone for good) or do not read them, being satisfied with free or pirated wares on the internet.

True, the Harry Potter books and movies sold prodigiously, but I doubt that many besotted children rushed from Hogwarts to *Red*, *Green* or *Blue Mars*, let alone the dazzling confusions of M. John Harrison's *Light* or the equally dazzling clarities of Geoff Ryman's *Air*.

Might it have something to do with the kind of peculiar mind that dreams up Conceptoids, and the adjacent minds that lock on to these conceptual attractors, blood racing, perhaps, glazed eyes turned to an interior landscape far, far away from this time and place? But that, too, is a highly selective slice through the readership. Many enthusiasts dote just as much on sf's whimsy, its sharp rebuking or embracing glance at the here-and-now as rendered into the strange, the sideways or the almost-here. Consider the bitterly funny little scene in Cory Doctorow's novel *Someone Comes to Town, Someone Leaves Town* (published by Tor in their science fiction list, although closer in some ways to high-tech Gothic horror), where the youngish crustypunk dumpster diver Kurt tried to sell a seventeen-year-old jaded reporter on the virtues of a free WiFi network in Toronto. This caustic child is the very spirit of youthful take-no-prisoners sf-ishness. Here is Doctorow's reporter:

> The kid rolled his eyes. "Come off it. You old people, you turn up your nose whenever someone ten years younger than you points out that cell phones are actually a pretty good way for people to communicate with each other—even subversively...Yet every time someone from my generation talks about how important phones are to democracy, there's always some old pecksniff primly telling us that our phones don't give us real democracy. It's so much bullshit."
> Kurt's mouth hung open.
> "I'm not old," he said finally.
> "You're older than me," the kid said.... "Look, I'm not trying to be cruel here, but you're generation blind. The Internet is great, but it's not the last great thing we'll ever invent. My Pops was a mainframe guy, he thought PCs were toys. You're a PC guy, so you think my phone is a toy." (268)

Kurt is aghast. He bursts into an aria of self-justification, like Lester del Rey faced by the New Wave, like cyberpunks drowning under the New Weird:

> "We're trying to put it on every corner of the city, for free, anonymously, for anyone to use. We are doing it with recycled garbage, and we are paying homeless teenagers enough money to get off the street as part of the program. What's not to fucking like?"
> The kid scribbled hard on his pad. "*Now* you're giving me some quotes I can use. You guys need to work on your pitch. 'What's not to fucking like?' That's good." (270)

I think we have a clue here. Sf is becoming, perhaps has been for a decade or two, a literature of nostalgia, for what critic John Clute calls simply "ago". Even those endless *Star Trek* franchise yard-goods are ripe with nostalgia for their founding epoch, the mid to late 1960s, which of course was only a decade or so later than the true Golden Age of grown-up science fiction, the mid-1950s. The fabled Golden Age is often said to extend from the late 1930s to the mid-1940s, but its true fruition was achieved in 1953, in the Third Wave, now a full half century and more ago.

Nostalgia is a virtue oddly overlooked in most moral catalogues. For the traditional science fiction fan, it is an unlikely key to the fullest enjoyment of this fertile mode of story-telling. One might think that sf should push into totally unexpected territory, seeking novelty as its prime virtue. Yes, but what's also true is that sf should not cast off the best lessons, painfully learned, of the past, or the great works where those lessons were learned. All too often, though, today's sf readers are cheated of our quite lengthy tradition, for many classic texts have been allowed to fall out of print. For those who do know and love the old wonders, and not just the currently valorized texts of Philip Dick and Bill Gibson, today's best science fiction can rekindle fond memories as well as forging fresh paths. As a writer, I was surely influenced by Roger Zelazny, and Fritz Leiber, by Arthur C. Clarke and James Blish, Robert A. Heinlein, "Cordwainer Smith," and those of the following literary generation, Ursula K. Le Guin, Samuel R. Delany, Thomas M. Disch, many more scarcely remembered. At their best, which was attained often, these were witty poetic geniuses who placed their stamp indelibly on the development of the field. They stand above us, beckoning; we look back a trifle mistily, despite the keen edge of our critical suspicions, our hermeneutic ferretings.

It is notable that 2009, when I am writing, marked the fortieth anniversary of humankind's first landing on another world, and, by happy coincidence, the seventieth birthday of the Second Wave, that approximation of real grown-up commercial US sf—taking the usual marker for the start of the Golden Age as July 1939's *Astounding Science Fiction*, under editor John Campbell. And what a long strange trip the genre has seen. Robert A. Heinlein's once epochal story "The Roads Must Roll" (from 1940), re-read today, is dreadful on the simplest technical narrative level, as well as for the absurdity of its central conceit. And yet...well, Heinlein did anticipate strip malls alongside the monstrous freeways, the war-level annual death tolls from traffic accidents, the depletion of oil and coal, the rise of solar power. But this is supposed to be the advent of a new sophistication of sf writing under Campbell's tutelage...Granted, Heinlein presents "hard-bitten, able" trained working men, and union machinations, and other aspects of the real world that one didn't find, I suppose, in most gaudy slipshod skiffy entertainments prior to 1939.

Later Heinlein stories and novels showed the true path to successful science fiction as a kind of knowing literature of the strange, especially in the better juveniles. What surprises one about that 1940 story was how *un*lived-in its world was, how much guided walk-through and excruciating "As you know, Bob, back in the '60s—" crusts up the pages, alongside slabs of undiluted exposition. It is only barely Heinlein. And the surprise isn't that alone—after all, everyone has to learn how to do it, especially those who are inventing it on the fly; it is the extent to which this primitive botch *did* galvanize the mode, did show people there was another and better way to unleash the strange.

In that context, it is no less a shock to realize that the best of Blish and Knight and Budrys and Sturgeon and Disch and Zelazny were then only a couple of decades away, or less.... And now it has all been done, the roads have been rolled up and packed away back into writing competent enough to be understood outside the science fiction ghetto. Ironically it seems nobody much under the age of twenty-five is reading this new improved model, either, apparently, certainly not very many reading it in slender digests on cheap paper. Is this sad, or just what happens at the age of seventy? Achievement brings its own bitterness, as well as its recollected satisfactions.

Traditions do need refreshing, as those good writers and their peers, decades ago, renewed the imaginative narrative forms bequeathed by both the science and the fiction of sf's first Golden Age. This is no longer such an innocent time. We cannot take a step without casting a theory ahead of us. And once more I find myself in a curious position. Aside from Samuel Delany and a few other high-theorist sf novelists, I might be one of the Anglophone world's most heavily encrusted post-poststructural novelist-theorists of sf. After such knowledge (as C. S. Lewis and then in sardonic echo James Blish asked), what forgiveness? Where might so simple a virtuous vice as *nostalgia* feature in a definition—or better, recalling Samuel Delany's strictures on the pointlessness of attempting definition, a *description*—of a century of sf? Here is what I said about sf in my attempt at a sort of synoptic summary in *Reading by Starlight*, an attempt quoted by British critic Adam Roberts with the wry proviso that "the sheer complexity of this definition enacts the pseudo-scientific discourse that is also at the heart of much SF":

> SF is that species of storytelling native to a culture undergoing the epistemic changes implicated in the rise and supersession of technical-industrial modes of production, distribution, consumption and

disposal. It is marked by (i) metaphoric strategies and metonymic tactics, (ii) the foregrounding of icons and interpretative schemata from a collectively constituted generic "megatext" and the concomitant de-emphasis of "fine writing" and characterization, and (iii) certain priorities more often found in scientific and postmodern texts than in literary models: specifically, attention to the object in preference to the subject. (Broderick, 1995, 155)

I was quite serious in compiling those differential attributes, and trying to compress them down so they'd fit into a single brown paper bag. The question upon which I muse these days is whether sf *is* still native to a culture in the epistemic crisis of just such *supersession*, which many of us are experiencing, as the technical-industrial modes of the last century are swallowed up by newer ways of dealing with the material world and human desires. I confess that my own discourse twenty years ago, when I framed that description-slash-definition, was seriously influenced by the monstrous dialectical concatenations of Fredric Jameson—to whom we shall return—and Samuel R. Delany, although I was not a Marxist and have never hung out on the dangerous and crusty margins as Delany did. Well, I got better, as you can see.

Perhaps Delany has, too, without abandoning his genuine political edge—his and sf's commitment to saying new things in new ways. In a *Rain Taxi* online interview, he observed:

> Certainly there's new content to write about.
> As certainly we are all drawn to some content—emotional, political, sexual—more than others.
> But over time we can all watch what once seemed inescapably pressing, *because* of the strident relevance of its content, lose more and more of its interest till it's nothing but a formal arrangement. (2000)

Nowadays, I am more likely to become infected with tropes such as transrealism, seeing evidence everywhere for its canny and hallucinatory composite of the fantastical and the toe-jarring stony. But is transrealism a description only, or also a sort of prescription? Of course, Professor Delany was there, too. Asked about identity politics, the presence of the self in the art, he offered a prescription that enfolded its analysis:

Fantasize—and fantasize in modes that allow our most cherished and forbidden inner worlds to peek out (and speak out) here and there. Fantasize. Analyze.... In order to negotiate the unknown with any precision and intelligence, analysis has to become speculative. It's scary to talk about your own fantasies—to plumb that part of one's inner autobiography.... Bring analysis—rather than blanket acceptance or rank dismissal—to *those* thoughts, and you'll find out how the world, dark or light, might figure itself under passion's stress.

It might be argued that transrealism is indeed a Conceptoid, and that Rucker and I have been elected *by the meme* to spread it far and wide. That would be doubly mistaken, since, firstly, transrealism is Rucker's *invention* and not his *discovery* (although, good mystical Platonist that he is, he might disagree with me about that), and second, I have no Campbellian bully pulpit or power to enforce or even advise its adoption as a practice of writing and reading. I shall return to this topic in detail in chapter 3, but let me quickly note Rudy Rucker's own statement:

> Transrealism means writing about your immediate perceptions in a fantastic way. The characters in a transreal book should be based on actual people and hence richer and more interesting...(writing about your immediate perceptions in a fantastic way) ("Transrealist Manifesto")

This approach to imaginative fiction runs the risk, in consequence, of slamming straight down into the pit of the Intentional Fallacy. Rucker might tell us that he bases his characters on himself and his friends, but we cannot really be sure that this is so. Nor, I think, do we really care—except for the voyeuristic pleasure of peering behind the white page into another human's biography, however gaudily transmuted. Still, I found myself oddly attracted to Rucker's perspective.

It is the grittiness, the circumstantial density and chaotic unpredictability of lived reality that is absent in most speculative fiction, science fiction, magical fantasy, even some magical realism. As noted, in the last few years, we have started to see an increased quotient of gritty realism in works more often at the margins of science fiction than at its center: rich texts such as Geoff Ryman's *Air,* and China Miéville's work in general. One might add Kim Stanley Robinson's highly researched and detailed novels, but perhaps they seem more like Hal Clement's invented alien puzzle-worlds conducted by other means. This is not to disparage them, of course, but it does suggest that most of what Kim Stanley Robinson is doing is not transrealism. Books closer to Rudy's prescription are Jamil Nasir's *Distance Haze* and John Barnes' metafictional *Gaudeamus* (discussed in Chapter 4), which is altogether closer to autobiography than academics in provincial towns are likely to find comfortable.

It might surprise you, though, to learn that the book I read recently that seemed closest to the spirit of transrealism looked at first *not* to be strictly science fiction at all, nor even slipstream, but a sort of middlebrow romance: *The Time Traveler's Wife*, best-selling debut novel by Audrey Niffenegger. Until you read this elaborate time-twisting invention, you might well dismiss it as confectionary for book club readers and fans of Oprah. It is considerably more than that, despite all the flaws one could tediously enumerate. In particular, it is precisely a realist novel grounded in a strange premise, a fantasy enriched by copious detail drawn from the real world of the author.

That, at any rate, is one's impression, as another middle-class reader/writer recognizing certain telling aspects of the world. Luckily, we can test this hunch by chasing down some of the numerous interviews with Niffenegger archived on the Internet. Here is a revealing quote:

> I like science fiction, but it's not really what I read. So I wasn't trying for science fiction… what I was initially interested in was having one fantastical or strange thing and then regular reality. There's this idea that you change one thing about the world and everything else moves around it. This idea that you're allowed to play with reality somewhat. In my art, I'm somewhat surrealistic…. I like changing things. (bookslut, 2003)

What Ms. Niffenegger was reaching for, quite obviously, was not "surrealistic" but *transrealistic.*

Sf is all about changing things, but what happens when you are telling a contemporary story—even one where a six-year old girl is likely to be visited by her forty-something, stark-naked future husband—and an external event overwhelmingly intrudes into your own life, into history, into your book. "The part that happened around 9/11 was interesting," Niffenegger said,

> because, of course that happened when I was almost done with the book and I thought, wow, I can't really let this go un-addressed. For the most part real world events don't really make it into this book because I didn't want to date it and I didn't want it to be about the world. It's really about this relationship. I figured, you have this gigantic thing and if you don't at least nod at it, it's going to seem glaring in its absence. (Ibid.)

This is one version of the insistence of the empirical, the return—not of the repressed—but of the quotidian, in this case amplified into gritty terror that serves in the narrative, for a brief moment, as an icon of the traveler's uncanny, dreadful, fated, powerless standpoint, ever moving, never moving.

What distinguishes *The Time Traveler's Wife* from, say, a clever traditional sf entertainment like Poul Anderson's *There Will Be Time* (1972) is its very ordinariness, its refusal, by and large, to use this paranormal irruption as an opportunity to showcase the time traveler's technical prowess, political *nous* or prejudice, trans-historic destiny. Niffenegger says, "It's something that bugs me about actual science fiction, this effort to provide all the answers and make everything work out very neatly." But of course her novel *is* "actual science fiction," at least if *Flowers for Algernon* is sf. She is right to feel qualms, however; more than *actual science fiction*, her novel is *actual transrealism*.

* * * * * * *

Can we imagine a fertile mating of transrealism and science fictional nostalgia, in a time of imminent Singularity? I believe we see it increasingly. A provocative story like William Barton's "Off on a Starship" (2001), which enacts the uncensored fantastical sf-driven yearnings of a sixteen-year-old nerd, is at once transrealist—grounded intimately in Barton's own lived truth (or so I imagine)—and profoundly nostalgic. Editor Gardner Dozois positioned it as the opening story in his 2004 *Year's Best* volume. As Barton's character's alien robot companion becomes first a UFO Gray with large black eyes, then a naked eleven-year-old girl reconstructed from his first pre-pubescent yearnings, and at last a naked and extremely horny young adult, as their odyssey through a wasteland galaxy places them in charge of ten thousand mothballed interstellar warships "bristling with missile launchers and turrets and ray projectors," which they bring to Earth and deploy in absolute adolescent fantasias of omnipotence, we are drenched in the sort of poignant longing, loss and despair that Brian Aldiss discerned in the ripest space opera of the 1940s and '50s.

Despair, Gregory Benford asserts, is just another way to pronounce Diaspar, Sir Arthur C. Clarke's ancient unchanging city at the end of time in his *The City and the Stars* (1956). Yet beyond Diaspar's walls, as its first new child in ten million years observed, "along the path he had once followed, Man would one day go again." They don't mint nostalgia like that any longer. I love its paradox of the purple afternoon and the hinted glow of long summer morning, its dying fall optimism. I disagree with Benford about the hidden hermeneutics of the name "Diaspar": it is not despair, it is *diaspora*—the outflung promise of an endlessly open and ancient universe, the kind we know we inhabit. The kind most science fiction inhabits.

That is what science fiction speaks to us, perhaps ironically, since all will be changed, including humankind, in a time of Singularity. That is the largest and most enthralling Conceptoid of all. A universe that we will fill to its limits, changing and growing as we go. That, I think, is a large part of what powers the New Space Opera of the most recent decade, quite as much as its political, subversive savvy. It is a magical, quite exhilarating fusion of nostalgia and hope, indeed of determination. Maybe there'll be a Spike in the next twenty-five or fifty years. Maybe everything will go lightshot exponential, the flowers will open to the sun, the Sun will wait for us to work our will upon it; maybe we'll live forever, as the new advocates of an engineered technology of negligible senescence are claiming (I am one of them), but probably we early twenty-first century sf readers won't make it, will miss out on the escalator to the Eschaton. It seems altogether too likely, alas.

But *toujours gai*, there's a dance in the old genre yet, the old mode of future past. Strap on your transparent fishbowl helmet and your brass tights, loose the nanobots, and step on to the spinning galactic wheel with me. We will go out there to where the stars hang like jeweled Brownian dust, even if we take the trip inside our heads, where the real becomes fantastical and the fantastical real, and we don't just dutifully suck up the drab gray entropy anymore. "What's *not* to fucking like?" That'll do me.

CHAPTER TWO

WHERE WE CAME FROM: THE THIRD WAVE

Before we turn to a sampling of the fiction of this millennium's Fourth Wave, it will pay dividends to recall in some detail the trajectory of the Third Wave, the upheaval that swept across the complacent golden age sandcastles of the Second. This was, of course, sf's New Wave, detested by many, besotting many others, whimpering away, at last, into a backwash, but leaving nothing unaltered.

The 1960s—like the turn of the twentieth century, and the apocalyptic, futuristic millennial years 2000 and 2001—carried a special freight of nervous expectation. Atomic weapons ringed the world, and people daily suppressed their anticipation of radioactive doom from the skies. That terror had been manifest, in disguised form, in earlier sf tales and movies of monsters, horrific transformation and alien invasion. By late 1962, the world actually faced just such a science fictional threat—the Cuban missile crisis—and saw it narrowly averted. Two images epitomize this turbulent, paradoxical era: the brief, grainy film frames of President Kennedy's assassination in November, 1963, and the equally indistinct television coverage, live from the Moon, of Neil Armstrong's first step into the lunar dust on July 20, 1969. These were beamed about the planet via a medium, television, that just forty years earlier had been, in the contemptuous phrase journalists love, "*mere* science fiction."

After the generally straitlaced, vapid fifties, and despite repressed dread, the sixties would be a metaphor and icon for psychic unbuttoning (which Marxist guru Herbert Marcuse decried as "repressive desublimation," diverting insurrectionist rage into self-indulgence). Obsessed with style, teens and twenties reached first for simple raunchy pleasure in popular music and other entertainment media—to the distress of an older generation—and then for complexity and engagement. The growing moral crisis of the Vietnam War was not resolved until American defeat and withdrawal from Southeast Asia in the early 1970s; partisans in the conflict would find literary expression, in part, through upheavals in the way science fiction was written, published and read. In this chapter, the emphasis will be almost entirely on sf from the West—Britain, the USA, Australia, and other Anglophone outposts. Significant work was being done in the USSR and its satellites—by Stanislaw Lem in Poland, especially, and by Russians such as the Strugatsky Brothers—but despite efforts to translate and publish the best work, it had little effect on sf's main trajectory until more recent decades.

While it is not entirely absurd or arbitrary to view history as a succession of decadal tableaux, alternative perspectives are equally valid. A human generation is roughly twenty-five years long, birth to parenthood. Certain punctuations leave their generational mark on a whole culture, especially disruptive warfare or atrocious natural catastrophe. In the West, the two global wars created just such markers. By 1918 and 1945, many young men in their prime were dead; millions more had been separated from home for years. The routine cycle of marriage and childbirth was disrupted. Both wars were followed by a baby boom, particularly the second, which coincided with a period of feverish technical growth and new abundance.

One might expect the children of those epochs to make their cultural mark *en bloc*, in their late teens or early twenties. So it proved with the emerging field of science fiction in the 1940s, although military service disturbed the expected pattern somewhat, delaying the full flowering of Golden Age sf for several years. A raft of the most brilliant Western sf writers of that period was born around 1920, from Fred Pohl (1919), Isaac Asimov (1920) and James Blish (1921) to Judith Merril (1923). Roughly a generation later, we find another loose cluster: John Clute, Thomas M. Disch, Norman Spinrad (1940), C. J. Cherryh, John Crowley, Samuel R. Delany (1942), Joe Haldeman, Ian Watson (1943), Michael Bishop, Ed Bryant, M. John Harrison, George Zebrowski (1945). Some of these war years' prodigies would blossom in their teens—Delany's first novel was published when he was nineteen; others, like Haldeman, would be delayed by a new war.

Perhaps this generational claim is falsified by a representative scattering of equally brilliant, consequential names from between the wars: Brian Aldiss (1925), Philip K. Dick (1928), Ursula K. Le Guin (1929), J. G. Ballard (1930), Gene Wolfe (1931), John Brunner, and Harlan Ellison (1934), Robert Silverberg (1935), Joanna Russ, John Sladek, Roger Zelazny (1937), Michael Moorcock

(1939). Still, few of these important figures came to true literary fruition until the early or mid-1960s, as did, say, Carol Emshwiller (1921)...perhaps because the *Zeitgeist* had not yet condensed into a favorable configuration able to bring their interests and technical skills to an appropriate convergence. It is plain, even so, that in some important ways the emerging concerns and techniques of Dick and Zelazny have far more in common with those of Delany than they do with the narrative tools of Robert A. Heinlein (1907), A. E. van Vogt (1912), Arthur C. Clarke (1917), or that golden *wunderkind*, Isaac Asimov.

This new postwar generation had great expectations, and chafed under them. Education, especially to university level, increased many-fold, with a post-Sputnik scare boost for the sciences and engineering but also seeing vastly increased places throughout the West for humanities students. Paperback books filled every back pocket; early, beatniks declaimed rough, angry and sensual poetry, and later, The Doors broke on through to the other side. So if politically it seemed in some ways the dreariest of times, it was also hopeful, striving, experimental. A high point of kinetic sf modernism in the 1950s, the vibrantly knowing science fiction prose of Alfred Bester (and other savvy, literary writers such as Theodore Sturgeon and Cordwainer Smith) was one goal for emulation by the smart kids who went through college in the late fifties and early sixties, wolfing down John Webster, Arthur Rimbaud, James Joyce, and Jack Kerouac alongside their astronomy or physics classes. Ambitious in ways unknown to most meat-and-potatoes sf readers, they thrilled the innocent with vivid language, bold imagery and a profoundly skeptical analysis of the world even as they unsettled an old guard who found these modernist experiments a betrayal of everything in sf's established rules.

The emergent movement, a reaction against genre exhaustion but never quite formalized and often repudiated by its major exemplars, came to be known as the New Wave, adapting French's cinema's *Nouvelle vague*. Film *auteurs* such as Jean-Luc Godard and François Truffaut broke with narrative tradition at the start of the sixties, dazzling or puzzling viewers with tapestries of jump cuts, meanderings, all-but-plotless immersion in image. Christopher Priest appropriated the term for an sf almost equally disruptive, existentially fraught and formally daring, that evolved around the British sf magazine *New Worlds* in the mid to late 1960s.

* * * * * * *

Alfred Bester had provided a kind of advance imprimatur. In February, 1961, fiction reviewer for the most literary of sf venues, *The Magazine of Fantasy & Science Fiction,* he boiled over in a scornful denunciation of his peers. "The average quality of writing in the field today is extraordinarily low." He meant not stylistic competence—"it's astonishing how well amateurs and professionals alike can handle words"—but thought, theme, and drama. "Many practicing science fiction authors reveal themselves in their works as very small people, disinterested [sic] in reality, inexperienced in life, incapable of relating science fiction to human beings, and withdrawing from the complexities of living into their make-believe worlds... silly, childish people who have taken refuge in science fiction where they can establish their own arbitrary rules about reality to suit their own inadequacy" (Bester, [1961] 2000, 400, 403).

It is undeniable that by the early sixties much sf had become complacent, recycling with minor modification a small number of tropes and ideas. The previous decade's sf had suffered in microcosm just the sort of preposterous, trashy pseudo-ideas that would blossom as the "Age of Aquarius" and go on to form the basis of an ever-expanding retreat from Enlightenment science and values, what would become known as the New Age movement—eerily, a feature of the end of the twentieth century predicted and deplored in Robert A. Heinlein's Future History as "the Crazy Years."

Most of these loony tunes—Dianetics, the allegedly psionic Hieronymus Machine that worked even better if you took out the resistors and left only the circuit diagram, even a sophistical advocacy of slave-holding—were warbled by John W. Campbell, Jr., usually regarded as Golden Age sf's founding father and fearless proponent of science and gung-ho technology in an era of renewed superstition. During 1960, his famous and influential magazine, *Astounding,* changed its name to the less ludicrous *Analog,* in a bid for respectability and lucrative advertising, but his irascible editorials pressed on with the promotion of strange ideas, deliberately against the liberal grain. His magazine slowly lost popularity among the young even as its bizarre quirks foreshadowed the flight from reason that would go hand in hand, among hippies and housewives alike, with chemical self-medication in the quest for existential meaning and transcendence in a cruel world where, as even *Time* magazine noted in a famous cover story of 1965, God was dead.

Alexei and Cory Panshin (in *The World Beyond the Hill,* 1989) have argued that the driving impulse of Second Wave sf had been a "quest for transcendence". That quest did not falter in the sixties, with the rise of the Third Wave; if anything, it intensified. By the seventies, its febrile flush was fading, and a kind of rapprochement emerged between the New Wave's radical stylistics, and those arduously won techniques of the "lived-in future" that Heinlein and others had devised, if not yet quite perfected. Perhaps surprisingly, the earliest index of this continuing hunger for transcendence was Heinlein's own award-winning *Stranger in a Strange Land* (1961), which by the sixties' end was a best-selling cult novel on campus and beyond, as was J. R. R. Tolkien's trilogy *Lord of the Rings* (1954-56; in one volume, 1968), the canonical twentieth century fantasy yet one developed with the rigor of an alien-populated science fiction landscape. In mid-decade, Frank Herbert's *Analog* serials *Dune World* and *The Prophet of Dune* (1963-65) appeared in revised book form as *Dune* (1965), perhaps the most famous of all sf novels (if we leave aside forerunners Mary Shelley, Verne, Wells, Huxley, and Orwell). It manipulated superbly that longing Bester had mocked so ferociously: an adolescent craving for imaginary worlds in which heroes triumph by a preternatural blend of bravery, genius and psi, helped along in this case by a secret psychedelic drug, *melange*. The deep irony of *Dune*'s popular triumph, and that of its many sequels, is Herbert's own declared intention to undermine exactly that besotted identification with the van Vogtian superman-hero. It is in this crux, as much as in the stylistic advances and excesses of the New Wave, that the sixties made its mark on sf, and the strangeness of sf made its even greater mark on the world.

Critic John Clute, in an essay with the deliciously absurd New Wave title "Scholia, Seasoned with Crabs, Blish Is" (1973), diagnosed James Blish's central sf texts as *Menippean satires*, a borrowing from Northrop Frye's *Anatomy of Criticism* (1957). Third century BCE philosopher Menippus, on this reading, prefigured a kind of seriocomic idea-centered fiction quite unlike the character-focused novel perfected in the nineteenth century and taken by literary scholars of the mid-twentieth century (and by many even today) as almost the only allowable version. Heinlein's *Stranger* is a clear candidate. Its characters are stylized, not naturalistic, acting as mouthpieces for systems of ideas paraded and rather jerkily dramatized. In this case, the ideas advanced included "free love"—still rather shocking in the early sixties—a sort of relativist "Thou-art-God" religiosity, and scornful hostility to such established doctrines as democracy. Young Valentine Michael Smith had been raised in isolation by aliens and hence with altered access to reality (in accordance with the now unfashionable linguistic theory of Benjamin Lee Whorf) due to unique Martian semantics, now a redemptive gift to humanity. The novel's cast were at once collective (sharing a

"Nest," bonded near-telepathically and given miraculous powers by the inscrutable Martian language), authoritarian (happily serving under their whimsical "Boss," Jubal Harshaw, one of the great figures of sf and surely a skewed portrait of Heinlein), yet libertarian: an unstable compound. Efforts by stoned hippies to put those ideals into practice came predictably unstuck—as the novel's paradigms, primitive Christianity and Mormonism, had done. Unfortunately, none of them could think in Martian. Still, the wistful fantasy filled a void left by the death of God, if only for a giddy semester.

Presumably Heinlein did not really believe that changing your linguistic habits could give you miraculous powers, although more than one of his stories used this trope. By contrast, it seems clear that Frank Herbert did intend his ornate, baffling sequence about the Atreides supermen and women of the year 10,000 to induct readers into a sort of advanced consciousness. L. Ron Hubbard, a Golden Age hackmeister, had made just that claim in his self-help cult Dianetics (enthusiastically supported by Campbell and van Vogt during the fifties). Happily, Herbert did not seek followers; like a Sufi or Zen master, he wished to prod his readers toward an enlightenment of their own, a moment of *satori* or insight that would free them from mechanical adherence to routine, habit and the dull complacency of the previous decade. Regrettably, his technique served better as a hypnotic. Hundreds of thousands of readers, probably millions, reveled in the glorious adventures of Paul Muad'Dib, embattled heir to the desert planet Arrakis or Dune. The books overflowed: female Jesuits, the Bene Gesserit, with their centuries-long eugenics breeding program, the mysterious Arab-like Fremen, blue-eyed from the drug *melange* and driven by visions and artful myth, the great savage worms like sand whales, Mentat supermen with enhanced minds able to think as fast as the forbidden computers, galactic intrigue and warfare....It remains a heady blend, if rather clunkily wrought, and carried the main vector of Golden Age sf toward a kind of apotheosis.

Except that Herbert had hidden a hand-grenade in his wish-fulfillment—so artfully that it blew up in his editor's face. Declining the sequel, *Dune Messiah*, Campbell complained with forthright coarseness:

> The reactions of science fictioneers...over the last few decades has [sic] persistently and explicitly been that they want *heroes*—not anti-heroes. They want stories of strong men who exert themselves, inspire

others, and make a monkey's uncle out of malign
fates! (cited O'Reilly, 188

Slyly, Herbert had meant exactly to subvert that facile template,
and his secret instinct resonated with the writers of the emerging
New Wave if not with older sf fans. "What better way to destroy a
civilization, society or a race than to set people into the wild oscilla-
tions which follow their turning over their judgment and decision-
making faculties to a superhero?" (O'Reilly, 5). That was nearly a
full generation, of course, after several self-declared supermen and
their viciously subhuman regimes were toppled in Europe at the cost
of millions of lives. It was a lesson that sf never quite learned until
New Wave writers began to peel open the ideological myth of supreme scientific competence and galactic manifest destiny. The first
begetter of this heretical tradition, or at least most prominent, is often held to be J. G. Ballard, whose uprooted childhood in wartime
Shanghai, brought to a close by the distant science fictional flash of
a nuclear weapon bursting over Japan, would be filmed by Stephen
Spielberg in 1987 as the movie *Empire of the Sun.*
     J. G. Ballard was launched in an unlikely venue: the venerable,
dull pages of John Carnell's *New Worlds* and *Science Fantasy,*
which against the odds were also responsible for Brian W. Aldiss,
John Brunner and several other brilliant autodidact harbingers of the
revolution. Strictly, these few slick British innovators were fifties'
writers, but each came into his own (or very, very rarely hers) during the ferment of the sixties' New Wave. With his achingly dry surrealist wit, clarified prose, and devotion to recurrent "properties"
(empty swimming pools, damaged astronauts, catastrophic and numinous landscapes), Ballard was from the outset a goad to traditionalists. By that very token, he was a gift to the quirky US anthologist
Judith Merril, whose *Year's Best SF* series featured his work, together with an increasingly agitated propaganda for new ways of
writing something she dubbed "speculative fiction"—new ways that
were generally, in the larger literary world, rather old. Alongside
unnerving tales by Aldiss, Ballard, and Cordwainer Smith, Merril
paraded pieces by Borges, Romain Gary, dos Passos, Lawrence Dur-
rell, plus the usual literate-to-brilliant sf suspects: Asimov,
Bradbury, Clarke, Zenna Henderson, Algis Budrys. In 1960, impec-
cably, she selected Daniel Keyes' superb "Flowers for Algernon," a
gentle emergent superman story with a bittersweet twist; today, it
seems scarcely sf at all, more like Norman Mailer's account of the
Apollo Moon landing. By 1965 Merril had Thomas M. Disch's
bleak, absurdist "Descending," the louche poetry of Roger Zelazny's

"A Rose for Ecclesiastes," and Ballard's paradigmatic "The Terminal Beach':

> In the field office he came across a series of large charts of mutated chromosomes. He rolled them up and took them back to his bunker. The abstract patterns were meaningless, but during his recovery he amused himself by devising suitable titles for them.... Thus embroidered, the charts took on many layers of cryptic association. (Merril, *10th Annual SF*, 259)

As, indeed, did Ballard's ever stranger body of work. When *New Worlds* expired under Carnell in 1964 of terminal blandness, a youthful Michael Moorcock tore in to its rescue, changing the magazine utterly as its backlog cleared. Now, with Ballard as house patron saint, under the sign of William Burroughs, the New Wave began to roll relentlessly toward science fiction's crusted shores. Donald A. Wollheim found Norman Spinrad's gonzo novel *Bug Jack Barron*, serialized in *New Worlds*, a "depraved, cynical, utterly repulsive and thoroughly degenerate parody of what was once a real SF theme" (cited Harrison, 1971, 170). Still, the undeniable detritus carried along with the New Wave was not necessarily welcome even to devoted surfers. (A usefully analytical, admirably waspish study of New Wave and *New Worlds*, emphasizing Moorcock's role, is Colin Greenland's *The Entropy Exhibition*, drawn from his Ph.D. thesis.) Half the names on *New World*'s contents pages are now forgotten—Langdon Jones, Michael Butterworth, Roger Jones—and some were pseudonymous ("Joyce Churchill" hid M. John Harrison, a fine artist who grew disenchanted with sf's mode). That is also true, of course, of many regular writers for *Analog, Galaxy* and other US magazines—Christopher Anvil, William E. Cochrane, Jack Wodhams. What is striking in retrospect is how enduring, even so, the impact of the major New Wave writers has been, the longevity of its biggest names: Ballard (although he had largely abandoned sf), Aldiss, Moorcock himself, and sojourning Americans during the swinging sixties: brilliant funny, caustic John Sladek (who died in 2000), Pamela Zoline, Samuel R. Delany, Thomas Disch, Norman Spinrad. The work of Robert Silverberg, formerly a prodigious writing machine, deepened markedly in a New Wave direction after 1967, winning him a special Campbell Memorial award in 1973 "for excellence in writing". Still, another important writer-critic, disenchanted by the hype, declared the Wave washed-up by the decade's close (Blish, 1970, 146).

Its brief moment is displayed in raucous glory in several anthologies: Merril's proselytizing *England Swings SF* (1968; in Britain, *The Space-Time Journal*), Harlan Ellison's immensely ambitious fusion of New Wave and American can-do, *Dangerous Visions* (1967), Spinrad's *The New Tomorrows* (1971), and Damon Knight's important long-running not-quite-New Wave series of original anthologies, *Orbit* (1966 and later), showcasing such offbeat and consequential talents as R. A. Lafferty, Gene Wolfe, Joanna Russ, Kate Wilhelm, and Gardner Dozois. The mood of bewildered antagonism from the old guard is caught perfectly in Isaac Asimov's bitter remark, cited by Ace Book's editor Donald A. Wollheim on the jacket of Merril's showcase: "I hope that when the New Wave has deposited its froth, the vast and solid shore of *science fiction* will appear once more." Wollheim had already taken care to distance himself, to comic effect. On the back jacket, in bold red capitals, he shouted:

**THIS MAY BE THE MOST IMPORTANT
SF BOOK OF THE YEAR**

and underneath, in black and a smaller font:

(or it may be the least. You must judge for yourself!)

By 1968, however, Wollheim had proved himself an editor of some courage, if little discrimination, publishing amid a constant drizzle of mediocre consumer product several exceptional novels at the margins of the New Wave: Delany's romantic, flushed *The Jewels of Aptor* (1962), *Babel-17* and *Empire Star* (1966), and *The Einstein Intersection* (1967). Ursula K. Le Guin's first Hainish novels (*Rocannon's World*, 1964; *Planet of Exile*, 1966; *City of Illusion*, 1967) appeared under the dubious Ace imprint. Le Guin's triumph at the cusp of the seventies as the thoughtful, elegant anthropologist of sf and fantasy, begun with *A Wizard of Earthsea* (1968), was established with *The Left Hand of Darkness* (1969) under a revitalizing Ace Special imprint by New Wave-sympathetic editor Terry Carr, and confirmed by *The Dispossessed: An Ambiguous Utopia* (1974).

An error readily made when considering these several trajectories is to suppose that one literary movement follows another in a parable of progress, dinosaurs giving way to eager young mammals—or, in an allegory of regression, gains accumulated arduously are lost to the onrush of barbarians. Neither image is valid. In part, this is because writers, publishers and readers are always somewhat out of step. By the time a "fashion" is visible, built from the latest work available to readers, a year or more has passed since those texts were created and sold. Unless a movement is geographically concentrated—as the London *New Wave* scene largely was—mutual influence straggles.

Even more importantly in a marginal mode like sf, read most enthusiastically by the penniless young, genre history is piled up indiscriminately in libraries and secondhand book stores. Near the start of the 1960s, fresh inductees to the sf mythos could read the latest coolly ironic Ballard whack at bourgeois prejudice or Zelazny MA-trained gutter poetry—"where the sun is a tarnished penny, the wind is a whip, where two moons play at hot-rod games, and a hell of sand gives you the incendiary itches…." ("A Rose for Ecclesiastes," 1963)—then turn at once to a paperback of "Doc" Smith's tone-deaf *Lensmen* series from the Golden Age and earlier, meanwhile soaking up scads of Asimov, Heinlein, annual "Year's Best" gatherings, and comic book adventures. We must apply Stephen Jay Gould's evolutionary insight: in every era, most species are simple life forms, fitted almost from the outset to a range of environments and tremendously persistent. So the classics of sf, at least until fairly recently, have always remained alive in the humus. Certainly that was so in the 1960s and 1970s, when the backlists of many publishers formed a reliable backstop to their annual income.

Nor is the distinction between New Wave and Old as simple as pessimism versus triumphalism. Several sets of coordinates overlap, to some extent by accident. It is true that much of the "experimental" sf of the 1960s took a gloomy cast, while the continuing mainstream of commercial sf was distinctly upbeat, constructing a universe in which technological salvation comes through virtuous human efforts. Was that distinction *necessarily* echoed in the contrast between a disruptive textuality seeking to enact its ideas in richly modernist symbol and vocabulary, versus traditional sf's adherence to a "clear windowpane" theory of writing?

It is more likely that stylistic differences derived from the filiations (and education) of its writers. Even if the science of classic sf was often laughable or wholly invented, it did borrow something structurally important from the lab: scientific papers, after all, are meant to rid themselves of any taint of the subjective, uttering their reports in a disembodied, timeless Voice of Reason (even as those findings are acknowledged to be fallible, provisional, awaiting challenge). New Wave writers—and those signing up as established middle-aged veterans, like Philip José Farmer—took, as their model, narratives drenched in artful subjectivity, even when, as in Ballard's remote constructs, personality seemed willfully denied. From the outset, it was impossible to mistake Ballard's dry voice and curious obsessions: "Later Powers often thought of Whitby, and the strange grooves the biologist had cut, apparently at random, all over the floor of the empty swimming pool." ("The Voices of Time," 1960, in Ballard 1965). Or in his pungent, non-linear "condensed novels': "**Narcissistic**. Many things preoccupied him during this time in the sun: the plasticity of forms, the image maze, the catatonic plateau, the need to re-score the C.N.S., pre-uterine claims, the absurd—*i.e.*, the phenomenology of the universe...." ("You and Me and the Continuum," 1966).

At the same time, the brilliantly iconoclastic Philip K. Dick forged a powerful new vision from sf's generic trash, which he dubbed "kipple." Dick was no less driven than his more routine peers by commercial urgencies, but something wonderful happened when his hilariously demented tales ran out of control inside the awful covers of pulp paperbacks. Australian critic Bruce Gillespie has posed the central quandary, not just of Dick's *oeuvre* but for sf as a maturing yet weirdly shocking paraliterature: "how can a writer of pulpy, even careless, prose and melodramatic situations write books that also retain the power to move the reader, no matter how many times the works are re-read?" Part of his answer is that Dick repeatedly takes us on an "abrupt journey from a false reality to a real reality...," or, in the extreme case, "a roller coaster ride down and down, leaving behind ordinary reality and falling into a totally paranoid alternate reality. By the book's end, there is nothing trustworthy left in the world" (Gillespie, 2001).

Just that existential vertigo is arguably the key to New Wave textuality, sometimes masked as an obsession with *entropy*, the tendency of all organized matter and energy to degrade toward meaningless noise and inanition. Certainly that is how many traditionalists viewed their rivals, and who could blame them when faced with an exultantly transgressive cut-up collage from Thomas M. Disch's *Camp Concentration*, serialized in *New Worlds* in 1967:

The Parable of the Sun and the Moon

The king arrives unaccompanied and enters the parenchyma.... The dew Pia watering it, dissolving layers of trodden gold. He gives it to the toadstools. Everything comes in. He divests himself of his skin. It is written: *I am the Lord Saturn.* The epithesis of sin. Saturn takes it and careens (Hoa). All things are Hoa. He, when once it has been given Him, illapses into prepared matter. O how fall'n. (Squab, upon a rock.) (Disch, 1969, 102)

This delirious passage runs on for pages at a pivotal point in Disch's superbly crafted evocation of a sanctimonious genius growing much smarter, and bleakly insightful, under the baleful influence of a genetically-engineered syphilis virus. It left conventional sf readers cold or outraged, even as Samuel R. Delany found it "far and away *the* exemplar" of Disch's work, and by extension of the gathering New Wave project (Delany 1978a, 181). So Disch was entirely ignored by voters for the Hugo Award (hundreds of self-selected fans at the annual World SF convention) and even the Nebula (chosen by other sf writers). He would achieve no recognition until 1980, by which time his interests had moved elsewhere, to the genre's loss.

Still, such awards did recognize works of talent as well as less interesting candidates: Nebulas (started in 1965) went in the sixties to Herbert's Hugo-winning *Dune*, Keyes' *Flowers for Algernon*, Delany's *Babel-17*, and *The Einstein Intersection*, only to offer the 1968 prize to Alexei Panshin's competent but not extraordinary *Rite of Passage* rather than Delany's bravura *Nova* and Keith Roberts's *Pavanne*, now credited as the finest of all "alternate histories." Hugos were won by Walter M. Miller, Jr.'s *A Canticle for Leibowitz* (1960, but parts published in the 1950s), a mordant cycle tracking the recovery, after nuclear war, of technical knowledge guarded by monastic "bookleggers," by Heinlein's *Stranger* and New Wave-influenced *Lord of Light* (Zelazny's mythopoeic reworking in 1967 of Hindu and Buddhist imagery), as well as by Clifford Simak's sentimental, pedestrian *Way Station* (1963) rather than another nominee, Kurt Vonnegut, Jr.'s exquisite and funny *Cat's Cradle*. In a different medium, though, both old and new combined dazzlingly in Stanley Kubrick's 1968 movie from an Arthur C. Clarke script, *2001: A Space Odyssey* and Kubrick's 1971 *A Clockwork Orange*, both Hugo winners. It seemed for a moment as if sf might be about to come in from the cold.

Everyone agrees that it is inappropriate to judge a book by its cover, although for most of sf's commercial existence it has been shudderingly difficult to do anything else. Might we more reliably judge a book by its title? The shift from the lurid action-adventure 1950s to more polished, sensitive 1960s' sf might be gauged by considering some gauche short story and book titles from the earlier decade: "Lord of a Thousand Suns" (1951), "Sargasso of Lost Starships' (1952), "Captive of the Centaurianess" (1952), *War of the Wing-Men* (1958), *The Enemy Stars* (1959).

Contrast those with several measured titles by Poul Anderson, who in 1997 would be selected a Grand Master of the SFWA: "Deus Ex Machina," "World of No Stars," "The Road to Jupiter," *The Man Who Counts*, and a graceful, elegiac borrowing from Rudyard Kipling, *We Have Fed Our Sea*. These titles are more typical of a later generation, one senses, shaped by the revolution of the mid-1960s. The odd reality, though, is that the second set of titles is just Anderson's original choice for these somber, haunting tales brutally retitled by editors who figured they knew how to titillate 1950s' patrons. Surely those editors were wrong, since customers for "Captive of the Centaurianess" were not dissatisfied by Anderson's lyrical if sometimes thumping prose. One apparent transition from the fifties to the sixties and seventies, then, is more illusory than real, a tactic of crass marketing adjusted to a somewhat less barbarous newsstand ambience.

In the 1960s, popular taste—as registered in the Hugo awards for shorter fiction—favored a kind of excessive or hysterical posturing, mostly marked in several Harlan Ellison titles (matched by the overwrought contents): "'Repent, Harlequin!' Said the Ticktockman" (1965) through to "Adrift Just Off the Islets of Langerhans: Latitude 30° 54' N, Longitude 77° 00' 13" W" (1975). Such titles reveal the market's mood as plainly as "Sargasso of Lost Starships." In a fit of verbal thrift, Ellison won a 1978 Hugo with "Jeffty Is Five." Things were calming down.

After the flash and filigree of the sixties, the next decade can seem rather docile, even disappointing. It is widely regarded as an interval of integration and bruised armistice. David Hartwell, scholar and important sf editor (he bought both Herbert's *Dune* and, fifteen years on, Gene Wolfe's incomparable *Book of the New Sun* and its successors), declared: "There was much less that was new and colorful in science fiction in the 1970s and early 1980s, given the enormous amount published, than in any previous decade...a time of consolidation and wide public acceptance" (Hartwell, 1984, 182). At the end of the seventies, in the first edition of his magisterial *Encyclopedia of Science Fiction*, Peter Nicholls ran the two preceding decades together, noting an on-going and complex generic cross-fertilization. "The apparently limitless diversity opening up is an excellent sign of a genre reaching such health and maturity that paradoxically it is ceasing to be one" (Nicholls, 1979, 287).

This bursting open of a previously secluded or mockingly marginalized narrative form happened on the largest possible scale in

1977. Two prodigiously successful movies were released: *Star Wars* and *Close Encounters of the Third Kind,* vigorous and even numinous (if equally set at child's-eye level), unabashedly revived and exploited the sense of wonder known until then mostly to the few hundred thousand devotees of print sf—and the many who watched bad monster movies and clumsy early episodes of *Star Trek*, which premiered in 1966. In part this success was enabled by technical advances that finally came close to matching the immense spectacle of space travel, physical transformation, and sheer luminosity of metaphor that had always worked at a dreamlike level in classic sf. That impulse has not yet faltered, carrying sf/fantasy (of a rather reduced, simplified kind) to the point where it accounted for most of the highest-grossing films of the last two and a half decades.

Meanwhile, though, the generic hybrids of Old Wave and New, enriched by techniques drawn from modernist general fiction, myth, art and movies rose to broad popularity among sf readers. As with most scientific experiments, it was granted that many had failed (one might say that their hypotheses had been falsified), yet they led toward genuine improvement. Ursula K. Le Guin's stately, beautifully rendered and felt fiction had little in common with the thumping adventure tales that characterized early commercial sf, but neither did many polished routine tales. As in the greater world, political issues continued to bubble and deepen: feminism, renewed in the mid-1960s, found utopian and critical expression in sf, from sex-role reversals and other simple adaptations of standard patriarchal commonplaces through to the authentically subversive novels and stories of Joanna Russ (especially her technically dazzling *The Female Man*, 1975). It is arguable that Anne McCaffrey's endless Pern sequence, begun with 1968 Hugo winner "Weyr Search," resembles Herbert's Dune setting, remaking fairy tales into ecological planetary romances. Otherwise unremarkable women writers such as McCaffrey, Joan Vinge, and Marion Zimmer Bradley, Brian Attebery has commented, become more interesting if you ask of their work such questions as "what is a female hero?"

At the same time, gay writers such as Samuel R. Delany, who was also black and hence doubly alienated from the established order, used sf to confound prejudice and illuminate otherness—something sf had prided itself on doing since the 1950s, yet had rarely managed to achieve. Delany's most ambitious novel of the period, *Dhalgren* (1975), became a million-selling success, but not, by and large, among sf readers. His *Triton* (1976) was even less congenial, featuring a bitterly misogynistic man whose lack of insight into his woes within a diversified utopia are only worsened after a total sex change.

Adjustments to fresh possibilities are found on many of the Hugo, Nebula and Campbell Memorial Award ballots of the 1970s. Few remained untouched by a drenching from the New Wave, by then ebbed. Brunner's *Stand on Zanzibar* (1968), technically adventurous in borrowing formal devices from Dos Passos, was a kind of New Wave hybrid, and had been sampled in *New Worlds*. Le Guin's *The Left Hand of Darkness*, searchingly testing the nature of gender, won both Hugo and Nebula, but the following year so did Larry Niven's far less subtle *Ringworld*, in some ways a direct descendent of Heinlein and Pohl in the 1950s yet marked, arguably, by Hemingway's minimalism. Hemingway's influence could be seen five years later in Joe Haldeman's *The Forever War*, also a dual winner, which interrogated Heinlein's contentious *Starship Troopers* from the basis of Haldeman's own brutal experience of the Vietnam War. Yet old-timers were not absent either: Arthur C. Clarke won Hugos for both *Rendezvous with Rama* (1973) and *The Fountains of Paradise* (1979), each an exemplar of just what his old friend Asimov had hoped to find after the foam settled. So too, in its way, was Asimov's own *The Gods Themselves* (1972), Hugo and Nebula winner; his uneasy blend of satirical naturalism—portraying the practice of real science—with a truly alien (and even sexy) universe adjacent to our own was applauded more in affectionate tribute than for its true merits. (In 1974, Thomas Pynchon's *Gravity's Rainbow* was nominated for a Nebula, but had to settle for a National Book Award.)

The same drift toward convergence can be seen in several awarded novels at the end of the seventies: Kate Wilhelm's *Where Late the Sweet Birds Sang* (1976; Hugo), a cautionary tale of global pollution and human clones when those ideas were still new, Pohl's *Gateway* (1977; Hugo, Nebula, Campbell), told with sidebars and divagation, Vonda McIntyre's feminist wish-fulfillment *Dreamsnake* (1979; Hugo and Nebula), and Gregory Benford's masterful *Timescape* (1980; Campbell), probably the best sf novel combining plausible science and politics, wrapped around a fascinating idea: causality disruption via signal to the past.

None of these prize-winners was as radical in form as their New Wave antecedents, although the superb, cryptic fiction of Gene Wolfe, trialled during the 1970s in Damon Knight's anthology series *Orbit* and elsewhere, finally blossomed into full maturity at the very cusp of the 1980s with the opening volume of his *Book of the New Sun*. Inevitably, even insiderly popular taste missed some of the most profound or innovatory works of the period: Disch's *On Wings of Song* (1979) caught a Campbell Memorial Award but was otherwise scanted, as had Barry N. Malzberg's dyspeptic *Beyond Apollo* (1972), scandalously. Lucid, enameled and—let's not forget—very enjoyable essays in world-building, now apparently forgotten, include M. A. Foster's *The Warriors of Dawn* (1975), which introduced the mutant Ler, and the saga of their coming, *The Gameplayers of Zan* (1977). An increasingly detailed and delicious transhuman solar system—Heinlein as wrought by a post-New Wave hand—was introduced by John Varley in 1974. Jack Vance's *Demon Princes* sequence (1964-81) was quirky, ironic space opera sprinkled with mock-authoritative footnotes. Ian Watson's impressive debut, *The Embedding* (1973), was runner-up for a Campbell; the mandarin density of its mix of Chomskyan linguistics, radical politics and alien invasion made it one of the finest novels of the decade. Another runner-up was John Crowley's *Engine Summer* (1979); disregarded by fans, Crowley was fated, with Wolfe, to be one of the enduring talents in the new, enlarged hybrid form that was now science fiction.

Theorized criticism of science fiction from the academy, previously almost unknown, opened the sixties with spectacular ructions over British novelist Kingsley Amis's laid-back Princeton University lectures on sf, *New Maps of Hell* (1960), and closed the seventies with Professor Darko Suvin's formidably formalist and Marxist *Metamorphoses of Science Fiction* (1979), and a batch of other studies variously intelligible or obscure. None, of course, reached the paradoxical contortions and laborious *faux*-Francophone discourse familiar in subsequent decades, except perhaps Suvin's own, Fredric Jameson's (whose Marxist-structuralist essays provided dense, darkly illuminating insight into Dick, Le Guin and others), Delany's critical collection *The Jewel-Hinged Jaw* (1977), and his intensively close reading, influenced by Roland Barthes' proto-deconstruction, of a Disch story, *The American Shore* (1978b). Positioned midway was Robert Scholes (coining a term dead at birth, "structural fabulation"), a structuralist sliding relentlessly toward semiotics and deconstruction. With Eric Rabkin, he combined essays and exemplary stories in *Science Fiction: History, Science, Vision* (1977).

At the farthest extreme from these academics were several sadly lame works of advocacy by speakers for the Old Wave, especially editors Lester del Rey (*The World of Science Fiction*, 1979) and Donald A. Wollheim (*The Universe Makers*, 1971). M. John Harrison's wickedly accurate dissection tells how vile and misjudged Wollheim's efforts seemed at the start of the seventies: "Its awful prose style, rising like thick fog from the depths of its author's private grammar, permits only brief, tantalizing glimpses of subject matter and intent" (Harrison, 1973, 236). Wollheim stood firmly against the dismal entropic embrace of the New Wave, with its artsy nay-saying and repudiation of mankind's glorious galactic destiny. It was hard to reconcile with his early support for Delany, Le Guin, Zelazny, and even Merril.

Academic journals began to appear—*Foundation* in the UK (1972-) and the US *Science-Fiction Studies* (1973-); argument over the New Wave flourished in the major ephemeral US fanzines, especially Dick Geis's *Science Fiction Review* and Frank Lunney's *Beabohema*. Perhaps as importantly, shrewd essays in fanzines from the rest of the world began to puncture sf's complacency, by Australians John Foyster and Bruce Gillespie on Aldiss, Ballard, Blish, Dick, Cordwainer Smith; German Franz Rottensteiner on Heinlein and Stanislaw Lem (until then unknown beyond Poland); Lem on Dick, much of this translated initially for Australian fanzines such as *Science Fiction Commentary*.

One way to understand the long, slow eddies of those two decades, and the two generations they represented—one fading (but due for a startling resurgence in the 1980s, as Asimov, Clarke, Heinlein, Herbert, and Pohl reached toward belated bestsellerdom), the other growing into comfortable dominance—is to adapt Professor Scholes's simplified analysis of literary theory in his *Textual Power* (1985). He detects three primary ingredients in every encounter with texts: reading, interpretation and criticism. Strictly, none of these has priority over the others, but in a sense we can see them as a rising sequence of proficiency.

Reading is pushing a key into a lock. Meaning is stored inside a story's sentences, with agreed codes and procedures for unpacking it. Writer and reader are assumed to share access to those codes. In reality, texts are always gappy; we miss some things, and read in our own conjectures, a step one can call *interpretation.* "We may *read* a parable for the story but we must *interpret* it for the meaning" (Scholes, 1985, 22). Beyond interpretation, no text speaks with a clear, pure voice deflecting every misunderstanding: so the final step, *criticism*, must challenge in-built assumptions buried inside text and reader alike—ideological, political, ethnic, or gender biases inscribed subtly within the shape of the sentences and the story they tell, and lurking within our own prejudices in unpacking the literary experience.

A theorist might summarize these three moments of reading as *positivist* or *empirical* (accepting what is given), *epistemological* (questioning *how* we know), and *ontological* (interrogating what *is*, or is assumed to be). These can serve as a useful window into major forms of literary endeavor of the last couple of centuries: naturalist realism, modernist symbolism, and postmodernist deconstruction. This last is not as user-unfriendly as it sounds—it is embodied radiantly in all those reeling reality-disruptions of Philip K. Dick's novels and stories which form the core of several highly popular movies (including some, like 1998's *Pleasantville*, that fail to acknowledge his influence, now pervasive). A somewhat similar model is Joanna Russ's *naive, realist*, and *parodic* or post-realistic (Russ, 1972).

On this three-phase analysis, it is arguable that sf before the 1960s was predominantly *readerly*: however gaudy or galactic its venue, you accepted what was on the page as if seeing it through clear glass. With the New Wave, sf convulsed belatedly into the crisis of modernism that half a century earlier had shaken mainstream high art, opening its texts to a radically *writerly* invitation to endless re-interpretation. Beyond the end of the seventies, the prescient spirit of Philip Dick invited a new generation of sf innovators toward a postmodern gesture: deep ontological doubt, a profound questioning of every reality claim.

Obviously this does not apply to most science fiction of the eighties, nineties and later. The seductive rise of mass-media "sci fi" has torn sf away from its elaborated specialist roots, carelessly discarded its long, tormented history. Science fiction and its consumers now start again from scratch, again and again. For the best sf, though, accepted or consensus versions of reality have become the landscape, the postulate, to explore or explode with corrosive and hilarious doubt. Without the frenzy and exhilaration of the New Wave experimenters, this aperture might not have opened, and without the diligent consolidation of the subsequent decade it might have remained where Philip Dick's penny-a-word genius found it: eating dog food at the foot of the rich man's table.

CHAPTER THREE

POSTMODERNISM, TRANSREALISM, AND THE FOURTH WAVE OF SCIENCE FICTION

Before Philip Dick and some of his colleagues more or less stumbled into postmodern ways of unleashing the strange, most science fiction was resolutely pre-modern, or modernist at best, though often with a fatal patina of sentimentality (Sturgeon, notably). "Modernism" remains a useful umbrella term for the art that followed the collapse of Romanticism, especially in the first half of the twentieth century, but postmodernism was not simply its more recent replacement. In fact, most contemporary serious writing remains insistently modernist. *Postmodernism* implies a theory of the world as well as of art, and a shift in emphasis and method.

In literature, postmodernism implies showy playfulness, genre-bending, and denial of neat aesthetic or moral closure, but also, above all, writing that knows or even struts itself as writing, rather than as innocent or emotionally insinuating "true-to-life" portrayal. Postmodernists whose inventions edge close to sf include John Barth, Jorge Luis Borges, Christine Brooke-Rose, Italo Calvino, Angela Carter, Don DeLillo, Umberto Eco, Raymond Federman, and Thomas Pynchon. Within the sf genre or mode one might name Third Wavers J. G. Ballard, Samuel R. Delany, Philip K. Dick, Michael Moorcock, Joanna Russ, John Sladek, Kurt Vonnegut Jr, Ian Watson, and Robert Anton Wilson, as well as Norman Spinrad (sometimes), Lucius Shepard (maybe), and even A. E. van Vogt (a Second Wave genius ahead of his time, and inadvertently). Sheer novelty, or even quality, are insufficient to qualify as postmodernists such writers as Brian W. Aldiss, early Thomas M. Disch, Gene Wolfe, and the early Roger Zelazny—exemplary sf modernists all, but not postmodernists. (Disch's late lacerating fiction was clearly postmodern, especially his playful, scathing text *The Word of God*

[2008] where he ludically presented himself as a, or even the, deity.) More recent distinctively postmodern writers include Kathy Acker, Kage Baker, Pat Cadigan, Paul Di Filippo, William Gibson, John Kessel, Kelly Link, China Miéville, James Morrow, Lance Olsen, Justina Robson, Rudy Rucker, Neal Stephenson, Bruce Sterling, Jeff VanderMeer, and several writers at the margins of the sf mode such as Michael Chabon and Jonathan Lethem.

Such catalogues, however, may miss a deeper point. Brian McHale, in *Postmodernist Fiction* (1987), saw postmodernism as defined by its focus, as *ontological* rather than *epistemological*. While modernism focuses upon "knowing" and its limits, including what we know about others and ourselves as subjects, postmodernism by contrast asks about "being," the worlds the subject inhabits; it is about objects rather than subjects. This shift reflects a realization that the world of human experience is multiple and open-ended. The postmodern condition perhaps has an analogy in quantum theory, where phenomena are modeled by abstract waves in many superposed states, decohering to a single value or "reality" only in the act of measurement.

Contemporary sf undoubtedly intersects the postmodernism of mainstream literature, especially when it follows the kinds of strategy pioneered by Delany in such self-reflexive texts as, perhaps, *Dhalgren* (1975) and, definitely, *Triton* (1976). For McHale, sf is "perhaps the ontological genre par excellence. We can think of science fiction as postmodernism's noncanonized or 'low art' double, its sister-genre in the same sense that the popular detective thriller is Modernism's sister-genre." Sf is, of all the genres, the one that constructs "realities" as a matter of course.

Perhaps the most influential critical account is the Marxist critical theorist Fredric Jameson's. In "Postmodernism, or the Cultural Logic of Late Capitalism" (July/August, 1984, *New Left Review*), he itemized its stigmata. He found "a flatness or depthlessness" to be "perhaps the supreme formal feature of all the postmodernisms," and also a waning of feeling linked to an alleged loss of people's sense of themselves as individuals, and the consequent replacement of "affect" (especially alienated angst) with "a peculiar kind of euphoria"; the end of personal style and a sense of history (and memory) and their replacement by pastiche (not parody, but the transcoding of modernist styles into jargon, badges and other decorations) and nostalgia; a schizophrenic fragmentation of artistic texts, marked especially by collage; and, most of all, the "hysterical sublime," in which the alien or "other" surpasses our power to represent it and pitches us into a sort of Gothic rapture.

All of these qualities often characterize not only the arguably postmodern environment in which we live but also sf in particular, which Jameson himself recognized in his many essays on sf topics in *Science Fiction Studies,* consolidated in his important book *Archaeologies of the Future* (2005). (His early theorizing was borrowed explicitly and persuasively for sf by Vivian Sobchack in the last chapter of her *Screening Space: The American Science Fiction Film* [1987], which projected a "postfuturism".) Jameson suggested specifically that today's information networks "afford us some glimpse into a post-modern or technological sublime," which is perhaps what we find in the virtual realities of the cyberpunk writers, where simulation and reality dissolve into one another. Indeed, Jameson claimed in *Postmodernism* (1991) that cyberpunk was "the supreme literary expression if not of postmodernism, then of late capitalism itself."

Innovative sf writers have adopted several of the expansive possibilities of metafiction, magic realism and poststructuralist fabulation in general. More specific both to sf and other postmodernisms is a comparable adoption of the language of scientific discourse, rather than that of traditional literature, and this too tends to the abolition of modernism's subjectivity—a common feature in cyberpunk, as in Bruce Sterling's *Schismatrix* (1985) and "Kiosk" (2008), and Michael Swanwick's *Vacuum Flowers* (1987) and *Stations of the Tide* (1991). In their emphasis on the technological surround, on the dense new lexicons bursting up especially from the consumer-oriented market productivity of postindustrial science, both sf and postmodernism give a privileged position to outward context, code and world rather than to a poetic inward "message", although not always to the detriment of heart. They stress object over subject, ways of being over ways of knowing. The universe itself—and better yet, the multiverse—becomes a text, open to endless interpretation and rewriting.

* * * * * * *

Transrealism, as we saw in the opening chapter, is the Conceptoid coined in 1983 by mathematician, computer scientist and novelist Rudy Rucker (Rudolf von Bitter Rucker [1946-]) to describe *fantastic* fiction that draws much of its power and density from closely observed reality, especially the biographical experience of the writer. Equally, the term conveys an enlivening approach to *realistic* fiction that enhances the vividness of its characters and events by imbuing them with elements drawn from fantastical imagination.

"The Transrealist," declared Rucker, "writes about immediate perception in a fantastic way." The specific goal was an enrichment of generic writing: "There will always be a place for the escape-literature of genre SF. But there is no reason to let this severely limited and reactionary mode condition all our writing. Transrealism is the path to a truly artistic SF" (see the online text of Rucker's "Transrealist Manifesto"). So a transrealist writes about the fantastic, the invented, the inverted, the dementedly shocking, via well-known literary techniques developed to capture and notate the world of immediate perception.

Transrealism is less a way of reading fiction, and more a recommendation to writers who intend to create fantastic worlds, or who wish to intensify narratives generally grounded in ordinary life. "The tools of fantasy and SF," to recall Rucker's dictum, "offer a means to thicken and intensify realistic fiction." Yet "a valid work of art should deal with the world the way it actually is." In consequence, "Transrealism tries to treat not only immediate reality, but also the higher reality in which life is embedded" (Rucker, 1991, 435). The "trans-" part indicates aspects of the text that are transgressive, transformational, transmutational, and transcendental. Rucker coined the term "after seeing the phrase 'transcendental autobiography' in a blurb on the cover of Philip K. Dick's *A Scanner Darkly*" (1991, 529).

Parallel to transrealism, adjacent modes have emerged or been discerned and named: *slipstream* (Bruce Sterling: "a contemporary kind of writing which has set its face against consensus reality...fantastic, surreal sometimes, speculative on occasion...simply makes you feel very strange....We could call this kind of fiction Novels of Postmodern Sensibility"), *interstitial* (Delia Sherman: "breaks the rules...lurk[s] near or on the borders of two, three, or more genres, owing allegiance to no single genre or set of conventions"), *postmodern sf* (texts with fluid reality boundaries, exemplified by Gibson's *Neuromancer*) and the *New Weird* (China Miéville: "Something is happening in the literature of the fantastic. A slippage. A freeing-up. The quality is astounding. Notions are sputtering and bleeding across internal and external boundaries").

All share a tendency to repudiate the restrictions and often the tropes—the standard symbols, icons, plots, shortcuts, etc—of genre sf and fantasy, emphasizing instead more complex psychological development, stylistic sophistication, and what might be called social embeddedness, and sometimes political engagement of a distinctly personal coloration. Meanwhile, *magical realism* found its way out of Latin America, inserting impossible or fantastical elements into rich descriptions of life. All these methods share the interesting technical device of using metaphors and other figures of speech *mimetically,* that is, as if they referred directly to the real world. For example, if a child flies into the sky in company with a talking dog, this is to be taken literally; it is not a Freudian dream image, nor a fanciful way of conveying the child's inward loneliness and aspiration. It might well do that also, and more, but the events are to be taken as part of the realistic record of events imagined by the writer, not the characters.

To date, there has been little analysis of a transrealist contribution to the cinema, photography, drama, music, or other media. Any fantasticated work with a palpable autobiographical coloring might benefit from transrealist analysis. Some of the surrealistic and whimsically playful movies of Woody Allen seem transrealist (*e.g., Purple Rose of Cairo,* 1985), as does *Field of Dreams*, 1989 (dir. Phil Alden Robinson; writing credits W. P. Kinsella and Robinson), *Big Fish,* 2003 (dir. Tim Burton; writing credits Daniel Wallace and John August), and indeed the wilder flights of many stand-up comedians who readily refer to spouses, work mates, friends, the detritus of their daily lives, pushed into a heightened and fantastic narrative. Pop music, from the Beatles through Kiss and Michael Jackson to rap, often creates a fantasticated *mélange* of the glamorous or grungy real lives of the musicians and a romanticized or degraded representation of those lives.

* * * * * * *

The need for a transrealist approach to fantastic fiction arose from those frequently debased and stereotyped characters and plot events of consumer science fiction and fantasy which comprise the bulk of the genre. Indeed, when the rotoscoped movie adapted from Dick's *A Scanner Darkly* was released in 2006, its director, Richard Linklater, commented: "What appealed to me about [the novel] is that it's not really about 'the future.' It's about Joe Everyman and his pals, worrying about money and sex and being frustrated. A lot of sci-fi deals with these amazing futuristic worlds where humans have suddenly lost all their humor and become emotionless automatons" (2006).

Is this charge justified? Dick was clearly unusual in this regard, compared to most science fiction writers of the 1950s and 1960s, but it would be misleading to read the fictional characters of Isaac Asimov (1920-1992) and Sir Arthur C. Clarke (1917-2008) as emotionless automatons—except for Asimov's stoic robots. It is true that stories and characters of the period, and still today, tend to be driven by curiosity or wonder rather than, say, passionate romantic love or world-weary angst. James Blish's (1921-75) characters, often regarded as "cold," seethe nevertheless with ferocious intellectual energy. Robert A. Heinlein's (1907-1988) fiction is full of emotion and humor, of a kind reminiscent of an updated Mark Twain (1835-1910), and the figures in Ursula K. Le Guin (1929-), Joanna Russ (1937-), and Samuel R. Delany (1942-) are very far from stereotyped or impassive.

On the other hand, sf critic Gary Westfahl has suggested that the "geeky" cast of much sf and fantasy is due to its specialized appeal to writers and readers sharing some measure of Asperger's Syndrome: "a persistent failure to establish eye contact, visible discomfort in most social situations, obsessive interests in a few subjects, a tendency to fall into routines...and a tangible aura of emotional detachment, even in extreme situations." For an Asperger's teenager in the 1930s (or even today), "a story about an astronaut encountering aliens on Mars might have had an air of comforting familiarity, in contrast to stories set in the bizarre, inexplicable, and thoroughly socialized worlds of Andy Hardy and the Bobbsey Twins" (Westfahl, 2006).

More generally, the tropes of fantastic fiction in the West were adopted or invented mainly by adventure storytellers writing hurriedly for the barely educated mass readership of inexpensive pulp magazines. Consequently, since much of today's fantastic fiction evolved from that pulp history, it often remains decidedly generic and formulaic in the ways it is constructed and read. The tired narrative conventions it frequently embodies, far from challenging us as "the extreme narrative of difference" (Broderick, 2004, 10), are designed as comforting, minimally-confronting mind candy. Stock characters and settings are templates put into creaking, predictable action. The craft of reliable genre writing is to disguise or superficially refresh this tired pattern of narrative action.

In part, this use of instantly recognizable stereotypes is understandable, since the figures and behavior of fantastical fiction are always, to some large extent, allegorical. Each represents or dramatizes only a handful of aspects of individual psychology or cultural dynamics. Genre characters are not intended as rounded portraits of humans in a richly known world. They tend toward the archetypal, the schematic, the iconic. One way to defeat or surpass such generic temptations and limits is to draw upon the internalized understanding—the cognitive and emotional models within one's head and heart—of the endlessly surprising people one knows best:

In real life, the people you meet almost never say what you want or expect them to. From long and bruising contact, you carry simulations of your acquaintances around in your head. These simulations *are imposed on you from without;* they do not react to imagined situations as you might desire. By letting these simulations run your characters, you can avoid turning out mechanical wish-fulfillments. It is essential that the characters be in some sense out of control, as are real people—for what can anyone ever learn by reading about made-up people? ("Manifesto").

* * * * * * *

Because transrealism is not a school of writing (although Rucker's own acknowledged influences suggest that it can be seen as a very belated revival of Beat poetics), but rather a suggested method for enriching all kinds of imaginative writing, it is difficult to identify any particular trends, beyond the observation that the best fantastical fiction seems increasingly steeped in the experiences of the real world. For example, a thriller/mystery novel of telepathy, Spider Robinson's *Very Bad Deaths* (2004, discussed below), effectively reuses the author's own harrowing medical and other problems, which both restricts his narrator's capacity to act heroically and provides him with strengths of endurance that allows him a sort of muffled victory. Without this added texture, the book would have been slighter and less involving. By contrast, most bestsellers in the fantastical genres continue to recycle long-established idioms—starship captains, male or female, and their brave crews of loyal humans, aliens and androids boldly going to very much the same places they have been for the last 40 years, sexy werewolves and vampires, mediaeval landscapes of magic and struggle against Dark Lords. The best of these traditional tales do enrich their time honored plots and casts of characters with imaginative density—Lois McMaster Bujold's Vorkosigan sequence and her more recent fantasies, for example—evincing a serious confrontation with the complexities of the real world. The commercial success of smooth familiarity, however, tends to ensure that any transrealist element, with its unexpected turns and potential for offensive shock, is minimal.

If there is any single theme recurring in transrealist writing, aside from the simple decision to throw much of the plot and representation of characters over to the machineries of the unconscious, it is an implicit interest in *epistemology* and *ontology*. The first, as noted above, asks how we know what we think we know about self, others and world, while the second investigates the very nature of that world, that reality. During the twentieth century, it seemed increasingly obvious that our intuitive understanding of how things work is absurdly naive and often misleading. What we see as solid is more deeply a quantum haze of probabilities. The sky just overhead extends for billions of light years. The apparent unified mind looking at the deceptive world is itself an eerie composite, and its partitioned workings can be viewed in subtle brain scanners or modified by subtle pharmaceuticals. Questions of epistemology can tend, therefore, to whirl into gulfs and voids of ontological terror. To the extent that our knowledge of the world is constructed rather than simply given, do we have any certainty or security of that world's persistence, of its reliability, or indeed even of our own selves? These rather abstract concerns drove Dick's enjoyably crazy and sometimes incoherent plots, and they surface repeatedly in Rudy Rucker's work as well. Meanwhile, the same issues have been identified by Fredric Jameson as the very hallmarks of postmodern textuality (see Jameson 1991, Broderick 1995), and in the best science fiction (*Archaeologies of the Future,* Jameson 2005). Let us consider Jameson's contribution in a little more detail.

* * * * * * *

To put the necessary warning in place at the outset: *Archaeologies of the Future* is a difficult book, a seriously difficult book. As academic Erica Sheen says of Jameson (1934-), William A. Lane Professor of Comparative Literature and Romance Studies at Duke University and before that Professor of Literature and History of Consciousness at UC Santa Cruz, "his sentences do their utmost not to finish." It is also a book that cannot possibly stand by itself, cannot be understood simply within its own covers—a lucid brief introduction to his thought is:

http://prelectur.stanford.edu/lecturers/jameson/

Yet it was one of the most important and long-awaited theoretical works about science fiction, and to a lesser extent fantasy, of the last

thirty years, by one of the world's most significant cultural critic/
theorists.

Begin with the difficulty. The opening of one of Jameson's
books won a parodic Bad Writing Contest, but that should not be
allowed to put off the serious reader. Sheen, a British Shakespeare
and cinema specialist, wrote with refreshing candor in *Film-
Philosophy* (Vol. 3, No. 29, 1999):

> I always look forward to reading Jameson, with a
> strong expectation of illumination. I always look
> back at having read him with a sense of captivated
> enrichment. What happens in between, however, is
> more of a problem. The word-by-word process...is
> extremely, almost physically, painful, and I have to
> force myself over and over again to concentrate, to
> keep reading, and to finish—which, notwithstanding,
> I do...Jameson makes me feel so bad that I read him
> in a state sensitized to the extent of my own failure,
> and finishing him is one of the few things I can do to
> atone.

Decades ago, Fredric Jameson defended such difficult dialectical discourse thus: "...density is itself a conduct of intransigence: the
bristling mass of abstractions and cross-references is precisely intended to be read in situation, against the cheap facility of what sur-
rounds it, as a warning to the reader of the price he has to pay for
genuine thinking." I should disclose a personal interest. A large part
of my doctoral dissertation staged a kind of running dialogue with
Jameson's elaborate cultural theory mechanisms. (That somewhat
ungainly verb "staged" is itself typical of such lumpy poststructural
vernacular.) Yet, while I'm one of the few people in the world particularly prepared to read him sympathetically and in context, I understand exactly Sheen's intellectual bulimia, the sense of exhausted
delight and illumination when the gorging and its aftermath are
done.

A second hurdle is far more daunting. For more than half a century, his brilliant and far-ranging mind has gulped down and organized into an astonishing jerrybuilt Rube Goldberg device of analytic
and synthetic machinery everything from Plato and Aristotle,
through theologians Jewish and Christian of the high Middle Ages,
and on to the central traditions of European thought from Kant,
Hegel and Feuerbach to Marx (especially), Heidegger, Sartre, Al-
thusser, Lacan, Derrida, Deleuze, a dozen more recent philosophers

such as Slavoj Žižek, not to mention modernist and postmodern literature, music, architecture, film. In fact, the very concept (or signifier) "postmodern" hinges on Jameson's early articulation of the mode. His quotations, although these days usually translated for the English-only reader, spring readily from his pen in French, German and Russian. Discussing *Pattern Recognition,* he notes that William Gibson's late style is "a kind of hype-up name-dropping...the names being dropped are brandnames." A similar dazing, disconcerting exoticism attends Jameson's encyclopedic and multilingual and multicultural citations. In short, we are dealing here with the very model of a modern (and postmodern) major generalist.

Familiarity with this immense corpus is impossible, of course, so you can only get a sense of this gigantic machinery, or at least its shadow, by working through Jameson's most important works: *Marxism and Form, The Prison-House of Language, The Political Unconscious, Ideologies of Theory,* and the last decade's cascade of volumes, often fix-ups of polymathic articles written (like *Archaeologies*) across a span of thirty years or more. Here's a thumbnail sketch: Culture is above all the expression of *history* and its class struggles, its bouts of false consciousness and thwarted or poisoned revolutions, coded into what we might nowadays call memes. Jameson identifies these "ideologemes" and "mythemes," and with great ingenuity examines the degree to which each epoch characterizes itself unconsciously by these cultural elements and their contraries (which are mutually exclusive, like life and death) and their contradictions (embattled inconsistencies or lapses). When used dexterously to explore the nuances of a text by Philip K. Dick or Ursula K. Le Guin, no less than with Joseph Conrad, the device proves curiously informative.

For a science fiction reader, the first simple excitement is just in seeing these sf greats, and quite a few not so greats, treated with deep and rewarding seriousness by a world-class scholar. What's more, and refreshingly, Jameson makes no concessions to his largely high-toned and snooty academic audience. His quotations from sf texts are seldom buffered by a comforting and condescending plot outline; characters are named and quoted, and it is assumed that if we wish to follow the cultural argument we just have to go out and read the damned paperbacks.

Even more unusual, something I find especially praiseworthy, is Jameson's enduring insistence upon history as a project of (non-stultifying) utopian potential, driven by unyielding hope and fortitude. Utopia is, of course, by definition a no-place, one that does not exist—at least not yet. Traditionally, its evocation has been seen as escapism, a fanciful recipe for extreme alternative ways of living. Jameson insists that "it is rather simply the imperative to imagine them," a task for which science fiction is especially apt. This can be derided as a kind of sublimated religious or idealist zeal, or perhaps its reductive, materialist cartoon, but I certainly do not see it that way; rather the opposite. Jameson was born ten years too soon to be a Boomer, but his work seems always driven by the kind of redemptive, communal spirit of the 1960s at its best. By today's jaded standards that might be off-putting, but even to the sympathetic of other persuasions his early and continuing embrace of bogosities like Marxism and Lacanian psychoanalysis makes it hard to transcode his fluent but doctrinal analysis and synthesis into more recent terms (for example, neuroscience-influenced cognitive narratology). It seems distinctly strange, uncomfortable, to find offered as guides to the perplexed such discarded thinkers as Herbert Marcuse, the Hegelian Marxist Freudian denouncer of one-dimensional capitalist man, or indeed the existential Mao fancier, Jean-Paul Sartre.

For all his immense learning and early appreciation of Gibson's cyberpunk, Jameson also invokes without embarrassment such superannuated terms as "cybernetics," "transistorized" and "automation" as if these still figured capitalism's and Utopia's futuristic agendas, exemplifying the difficulty of keeping pace with both fashion and real accelerating change. Nanotechnology and singularity-grade AI, even as a distant prospect let alone imminent, seem to stand beyond the horizon of his own socialist utopian estimate—oddly, since he has read Kim Stanley Robinson's great *Mars* trilogy with considerable respect and enthusiasm. It is significant, I think, that so thorny, dialectically complex and hyper-theorized a reader of sf and fantasy as Fred Jameson should be driven to confess: "I am probably not alone in finding the latest hard sf based on informational processes (even by so estimable a writer as Greg Egan) relatively unreadable." The elaborate decentered artificial life-worlds of later Egan novels such as *Diaspora, Schild's Ladder*, and *Incandescence* are probably simply too remote from today's urgencies to achieve utopic relevance. Yet Egan's anarchist Stateless, in *Distress*, a significant, though doomed, near-future Utopia, is worth Jameson's attention, as is Neal Stephenson's pivotal *Diamond Age*.

So, while a large part of *Archaeologies* is devoted to a scrutiny of science fiction texts, it is in the service of the first part of his faintly self-mocking subtitle. History and its always problematic, always receding horizon of utopian hope is inscribed as the approach of choice to sf. But not as blueprint or program, paradoxically: "at best Utopia can serve the negative purpose of making us more aware of our mental and ideological imprisonment...therefore the best Utopias are those that fail the most comprehensively." Still, Jameson is explicit in declaring his "decision to limit my engagement with sf to its Utopian functions." That is a perfectly reasonable restriction, equivalent to the choice by other critics to focus on science fiction's portrayal of space travel, or mutation, or transcendence, or gender relations. But Jameson mounts a stronger case, repudiating "the standard aim of traditionalist aesthetics...in the case of sf, to differentiate its narrative sentences and their content, not only from realism, but also from the literary fantastic," and adds:

> This is not in the long run a very interesting or productive line of inquiry, although it can certainly throw off many useful or striking insights in the process. Indeed, the sterility of the approach documents the structural limits of aesthetic philosophy as such and confirms its obsolescence. (18)

Only the historical conjuncture or utopian impulse, he asserts, can salvage from these aesthetic swamps the correct approach to sf as a mode. But surely sf as a mode can hardly be restricted to so partisan and agenda-driven a policy of investigation.

For all that, Jameson's own readings of Thomas More, Edward Bellamy and William Morris (the Utopians proper) and Olaf Stapledon, Huxley, Orwell, Aldiss, Le Guin, Lem, the Strugatskys, Vonda McIntyre, Delany, Gibson, van Vogt, Philip K. Dick especially, and finally Robinson, while diagnostic in tenor, do indeed throw off many useful and striking insights in the process. (If you had trouble holding on to that sentence, don't even *think* of reading Jameson.) Most of these latter meditations arrive somewhat piecemeal in the second half of the book ("As Far As Thought Can Reach"), and comprise a gathering of key essays from 1973 to 2003. The first half ("The Desire Called Utopia"), which stages an elaborate hearing into the status and prospect of Utopia and its literary figurations, draws, often brilliantly, upon some of these writers, but I suspect that an sf reader unfamiliar with Jameson's methods might be best advised to begin with the second chapter of Part Two and later loop back to the opening. I can only hope that at some point Jameson will offer us readings of important, powerful and often beautiful utopian/dystopian sf by Cordwainer Smith (The Instrumentality), Damon Knight (*A for Anything*), Jack Vance (*To Live Forever*), John Varley (his loose Eight Worlds sequence), Iain M. Banks (The Culture), among many others.

Has Jameson anything special to teach us as science fiction readers and writers? A great deal, I think, as is proved by the intellectual debt paid to his approach by Kim Stanley Robinson in his masterful and developing oeuvre. Robinson did his Ph.D., on Philip K. Dick's novels, under the supervision of Jameson, who may perhaps be figured (with some suitable measure of irony) as his Aristotle to Robinson's Alexander. I believe that Robinson's work will be regarded in decades to come as an imaginative equivalent of Tolstoy's; no teacher of fantastic literature had a better student, and perhaps no student a more unsettling and provocative supervisor. If occasionally Jameson's splendid final essay on the Mars trilogy lapses into a faintly comic historicist reductionism, translating one of Robinson's magnificently detailed poems of alien place and adapted life into an allegory of political stress, still, he knows the good stuff when he sees it, and he helps us see it anew. If his difficult theorizing also helps save the future from a rapacious globalism of greed, so much the better.

* * * * * * *

Transrealism's approach to imaginative fiction, by contrast, might be mistaken for the banal advice: "Write what you know." It also runs the risk of inviting the reader to commit the Intentional Fallacy, the error of supposing that the *meaning* of a text is identical to the author's *intention*. Rudy Rucker might tell us that he is basing his characters on himself and his friends, but we cannot be sure that this is so; transrealist fictions are not *Romans à clef*. Nor should we really care which life experiences are infiltrated into the text. Still, some writers in and out of science fiction have fruitfully combined wild ideas with their own experience, creating a realistic thickening of the supposedly airy fantastic. "Geeky" writers soaking their culture's fantasies in the broth of their own idiosyncratic ways of construing the world will create work likely to unsettle and reward readers at large.

Here is a rudimentary example of how the process can work, from Rucker's extensive notes on his novel *Mathematicians in Love* (2006). Writing a scene, he was visualizing his characters as *The X-Files'* Fox Mulder and Dana Scully, but found the result "flat and dull. And I remembered the [transrealist] injunction that I've often given to beginning writers: 'Model your characters and situations on life, not on movies and TV shows!' ...I thought of familiar human models for the agents, Michele G. and my college friend Dick S. and the agents got human and came alive" (Rucker, 2005). Unless we happen to be close friends of these particular people, it cannot help us to know this. But it does illuminate the process of an enriched, fantastical, transrealist creation.

Interpenetration of novelistic realism and the fantastical imagination has not been to everyone's taste. Thomas M. Disch's novel *On Wings of Song* (1979) drew significantly upon his oppressive youth in mid-twentieth century heartland America. Discussing the novel, *New York Times* reviewer Gerald Jonas noted that "except for an occasional *tour de force*, there is no room in science fiction and fantasy for the traditional novel of character. A science fiction author may create characters to demonstrate how a change in technology or social organization alters the human condition; or he may invent entire exotic worlds to show how certain human traits—such as passion or greed—take different forms under different circumstances. But the focus is typically on the forces that shape character, rather than on the character development itself." It was precisely Disch's attention to character that dismayed Jonas: "Mr. Disch's primary interest is in delineating character. In a science fiction context this is at first startling, but as a narrative strategy it is finally self-defeating." Perhaps, Jonas suggested, Disch chose the wrong model of realism. "Science fiction and fantasy have more in common with experimental fiction than with the novel of character."

It is certainly true that Rucker's transrealist work is very much closer to Beat experiment than to the traditional novel of manners. While only the last of Dick's books approach experimental fiction (*VALIS* [1981] in particular), his blend of headlong delivery and down-to-earth characters, many of them blue-collar or frankly mad rather than bland starship admirals or galactic game players, was rare in the genre. Only one of Dick's mainstream novels of character was published during his life (*Confessions of a Crap-Artist*, 1975). Revealingly, they have seldom been deemed successful. It is interesting that while these novels seem even more directly based on the author's life and obsessions, it is the absence of the fantastical, the whimsical and terrifyingly ontological that reduce their value and impact. It is arguable that Dick's realist novels are insufficiently *trans*realist.

In Dick's non-sf novels—*Confessions*, *In Milton Lumpky Territory* (1985), *The Broken Bubble* (1989), etc—all action springs from character, rather than from externalized menace (precognitive doom, robotic simulacra, slime molds from outer space, the crushing pressure of entropy itself). Yet that choice compromises the peculiar power of Dick's imagination, derived from his own odd, well-documented relationship to reality. Perhaps this is why transrealism is not the narrative tool for all writers. A certain dislocation from consensus reality in the originating experience is needed, a detachment and even a somewhat delirious reworking that cannot be willed but needs to be known autonomously, from within the writer.

* * * * * * *

Since a considerable amount of "Golden Age" science fiction (roughly 1938-50) was written by engineers or working scientists, often about characters solving engineering or scientific problems, it might seem that transrealism ought to have made an early appearance in such magazines as *Astounding Science Fiction*. Actually, the representation of such professions, concerns, and lifestyles in sf was significantly restricted by its adventure story formats, or their comic parodies of life at the workbench under the tedious thumb of oppressive bureaucracies. In fact, it was not until Thomas Pynchon's zany madcaps devastated these tropes that transrealist methods began to influence fictions written in the shadow of the technological age (*Gravity's Rainbow*, 1973), although there were predecessors such as G. C. Edmondson's (1922-75) charming *F&SF* series in 1959-64, which reported on the exploits of his "Mad Friend," employed at the Saucer Works (a version of Lockheed's "Skunk Works"). Subsequently, novels indebted to Pynchon, such as Robert Grossbach's *A Shortage of Engineers* (2001), brought the touch of transreal absurdity to the literary depiction of an absurd social order—in this case, a military-spec aerospace company on the order of Lockheed or Boeing. From an entirely different quarter, the supernatural fictions of Nobel laureate Isaac Bashevis Singer (1902-91), written in Yiddish, were frequently drawn from his own life and circumstances. "The world is entirely an imaginary world," says his Gimpel the Fool (1957), "but it is only once removed from the true world." This somewhat transrealist perspective informs the more uncanny fiction of Marge Piercy, Joyce Carol Oates, Margaret Atwood and many other non-genre writers.

There has always been an anarchic but somewhat autobiographical aspect to science fiction, portrayed as part of the background of *Rocket to the Morgue* (1942) by mystery and science fiction writer Anthony Boucher (1911-68), which features lightly disguised versions of Heinlein, Jack Williamson, L. Ron Hubbard, and other pulp writers, but this should not be mistaken for transrealism. In the 1950s, Wilson Tucker, a notable writer for science fiction fanzines, used the names and physical descriptions of his friends and foes in such novels as *Wild Talent* (1954), a gambit now known as "tuckerization." More anarchic and genuinely transrealist, a quarter of a century later, was the Greenwich Village Trilogy (*The Butterfly Kid*, 1968, by Chester Anderson; *The Unicorn Girl*, 1969, by Michael Kurland, and *The Probability Pad*, 1970, by T. A. Waters), in which stoned hippies save the world from Blue Lobsters and other amusing aliens; the characters and their setting very faithfully represent the authors and their circle. It is a trope that Rucker would revive with a vengeance and a mathematical spin a further decade later in such books as *Spacetime Donuts* (1980) and *The Sex Sphere* (1983). The lyrical and snapping shaggy dog surrealism of R. A. Lafferty (1914-2002) startled genre readers, but is perhaps not quite transrealist; his drug of choice was alcohol.

The psychic and social upheavals of the 1950s and 1960s, often fueled by amphetamines and other mind- and mood-altering drugs, had their impact on Dick, especially in such books as *Time Out of Joint* (1960), *Martian Time-Slip* (1964), *Three Stigmata of Palmer Eldritch* (1964), *Now Wait for Last Year* (1968), *A Scanner Darkly* (1977) and especially *VALIS* (1981), where he appears as Horselover Fat. Dick played a central role in exemplifying and provoking the transrealist program, although Rucker's "Transrealist Manifesto" was not published until a year after Dick's death in 1982. Highly intelligent and self-taught, Dick built an explanatory system from the philosophy of Immanuel Kant, Gnosticism, existential psychoanalysis and a mix of acid culture theories of mind and reality. These concerns pre-date the 1960s: *The Cosmic Puppets* (1953) stages a small-town conflict between embodied Zoroastrian divinities Ahriman and Ormazd, who transform daily reality into symbol. In *Eye in the Sky* (1955), a nuclear accident disrupts the local reality of eight characters whose shared world fluxes as they struggle for dominance. Alternatively, as a Dickian protagonist's personal construct of the world decays, the true essence of the world is revealed, often dreadfully. The transrealism in Dick's work reveals the fantastical transformations of his daily, if unusually eccentric, life-world. He was a writer drenched in sf imagery, where even in his bleakest and most intensely lyrical moments he found the perfect correlative to his inner states. His sometimes bleak, much-married life is echoed in the refrains of his life's work: doppelgangers, simulacra, apparent humans who turn out to be "electric ants," programmed constructs. Arguably it was exactly his mastery of transreality that spared him the final banal temptation of guruhood. Our world, Dick assured himself, was already a collage, a superposition, of all possible worlds.

The feminist fiction of James Tiptree, Jr. (Alice Sheldon, 1915-87), beneath its male disguise, is often powerfully transreal, transforming the appalling confrontations of her life into unyielding science fiction. Sheldon was the daughter of widely traveled anthropologists, and worked in military intelligence. "Young Alice saw the genital mutilation of Kikuyu women, babies dying in the streets of Calcutta, a riot in Shanghai that was the start of the Chinese Revolution. She heard the screams of a man being killed for the cannibal pot. She even saw a crucifixion: 'The men had been stripped, tortured, tied to posts, and left to perish in the sun....Auschwitz—My Lai—etc...did not *surprise* me one bit, later on.'" (Scholz, 2006). John Clute notes: "Tiptree/Sheldon's life very deeply shaped what superficially might have looked like simply another competent set of iterations of familiar sf tropes. What was miraculous was how professionally she was able to fit her interior intensities and drives into the mold of those seeming conventional story types, ruthlessly infusing every great story she wrote with those extraordinary intensities, which cannot be copied." The same might be said of black novelist Octavia Butler (1947-2006), whose sf fables transduce the tragedies of poverty and slavery. That dislocation need not be uniquely strange, though. Russ achieved a quite terrifying intensity in *The Female Man* (1975), her important feminist utopia, by contrasting several invented alternative worlds to her own stifling middle-class experience growing up in the 1950s. Joe Haldeman's own history, the bruising and morally conflicted experience of an American soldier badly wounded in Vietnam, made *The Forever War* (1974) stand out even in a period of striking technical advances by science fiction writers such as Roger Zelazny (1937-95) and Disch. On the other hand, two metafictional works that describe the anguished disintegration of science fiction hack writers—Barry N. Malzberg's *Gather in the Hall of the Planets* (as K. M. O'Donnell, 1971) and *Herovit's World* (1973)—are perhaps not transrealist so much as satirical or parodic, however revelatory.

Delany's early fiction from the 1960s, while less immediately identifiable as realistic let alone autobiographical, is vividly coded with his experience as a black, gay man in America. In his early masterpiece, *Dhalgren* (1975), his genius flowered fully in a transrealist work set in a deconstructed cityscape where history is fallible, Sun and Moon(s) are unreliable, and the central figure is a possibly deranged amnesiac and dyslectic poet. Not until his non-science fictional *The Mad Man* (1996) would this confronting blend of scrupulously observed and somewhat biographical realism and highly disturbing perverse fantasy gel completely. Ray Davis notes: "In Delany's earlier porn, appalling acts are executed by dehumanized monsters. In *The Mad Man*, perversion, like other violations of taboo, is instead a profoundly humanizing act of courage" (in Sallis, 1996). So too is the candid, lacerating and funny soul-baring of a failing writer in Jamil Nasir's *Distance Haze*, in which the direct mystical experience of the divine is first simulated/stimulated and then obliterated by neurological engineering.

It might seem that transrealist work must be excessive in some degree—that since transgression is part of its definition, it must be offensive, even indecent, as well. By the standards of reigning power and convention, this might seem to be so. Jack Kerouac (1922-69) and William Burroughs (1914-97), whose work altered the course of mid-century US fiction as radically as that of Ernest Hemingway (1899-1961) a generation earlier, spoke truth not so much to power as to the illusion of a safely domestic self simulating shocking adventures from the comfort of an armchair. Yet the shocking devices of one period are the commonplaces of another. The endless road peeling away in front of Kerouac's windscreen was replicated in the scroll of paper nearly thirty-five meters long upon which he typed *On the Road* (1958); Rucker emulated that method a generation later when writing *All the Visions* (1991). Today, by contrast, almost all writers do just that, without any shock of release, on the infinite virtual page of the word processor screen. What was also unpeeled in this kind of radically autobiographical writing was the experiencing self, harried away from comfort by ruthless self-examination and crazy bursts of invention and lyricism. In a similar line of descent is Hunter S. Thompson (1937-2005), whose hysterical and bitingly insightful prose (notably, *Fear and Loathing in Las Vegas*, 1971) is better understood as transreal rather than satirical or simply mannered, unlike the New Journalism of the 1960s and 1970s in general.

Thompson names himself explicitly as his protagonist, and this is one explicit marker of transrealism. *Crash* (1974) by J. G. Ballard (1930-2009) is narrated by James Ballard, and in *The Empire of the Sun* (1984) his child-self surrogate is Jim. Rucker sometimes calls his central character "Rudy Rucker," as in *Saucer Wisdom* (1999), presenting itself mockingly as the true story of his mad friend Frank Shook, and Shook's adventures with saucer-borne multidimensional time travelers. In *Gaudeamus* (2004), John Barnes, former Assistant Professor of Theater and Communication in a small Colorado college, narrates very much in his own person a tale reported to him in a number of broken-off cliff-hanger segments by his mad friend Travis Bismark, another traveler in a flying saucer.

But is this narrator, who has the same job and the same former wife as Barnes, a fully rounded representation of the author? Probably not, but it does not matter, because the weariness, the venom, the ambition, the bleak humor of the narrator are plainly motivated by reality, and speak to us for that reason more urgently than many of Barnes's more perfunctory entertainments.

Yet the transrealist prescription or diagnosis does not require excess. Justina Robson's *Silver Screen* (2005) is packed with detail and naturalistic rendering of character that evades sf's expectations of melodrama and spectacular setting or event. For all their exotic idiosyncrasy and special gifts, Robson's super-smart characters are flattened into a sort of desperate ordinariness. A proponent of slip-stream, she suggests that it "strives to duplicate the complexities of actual experiences by allowing experience to be paramount and letting everything else serve a purpose." The parallels with transrealism are clear. Her narrator seems at least in part transrealist, drawn to an unusual degree from the daily grind, irritations, opacities of her author's ordinary experience, fantasy enriched in its artful and persuasive rendering by the miseries and rewards of life here and now. Certainly this is true of the transrealist fiction of Jeffery Ford, one of the most talented current fantasy writers. In "Botch Town" (2006), for example, a coming of age novella blending autobiography and an uncanny mix of fantasy and horror, a facsimile town of plywood and clay in the narrator's basement echoes and then manipulates events in the already shadowy exterior suburban world. Thus, reality enriches and activates the fantastic imagination, *and vice versa*, of the transrealist artist.

Nor is transrealism necessarily marketed as genre. As noted in the first chapter, a best-selling romance, Audrey Niffenegger's (1963-) *The Time Traveler's Wife* (2003), is an elaborate time-twisting invention, a realist novel grounded in a fantastical Vonne-gutian premise—that some people can come unstuck in time—a fantasy enriched by copious detail drawn from the real world of the author. Jonathan Lethem's *The Fortress of Solitude* (2003) can also fruitfully be read as transrealist, a supernaturally heightened autobiographical tale of growing up Jewish and white—with magic gifts of flight and invisibility—in a black part of Brooklyn in 1972. Philip Roth's *The Breast* (1972) and *Our Gang* (1971) are satirical surrealism, but his blend of autobiography, invention, and an alternative history of a near-Nazi America in the 1950s, *The Plot Against America* (2004), is a transreal transformation. Roth, however, might disagree, and it is cautionary to recall his remarks from 1960, reprinted in *Reading Myself and Others* (1975):

the American writer in the middle of the twentieth century has his hands full in trying to understand, describe, and then make credible much of American reality. It stupefies, it sickens, it infuriates, and finally it is even a kind of embarrassment to one's media imagination. The actuality is continually outdoing our talents, and the culture tosses up figures almost daily that are the envy of any novelist. (121)

Still, Paul Di Filippo, in a buoyant appreciation of Rucker, captured the key moves of transrealism: "as a unique individual, each of us must report back as faithfully as we can, sharing our insights in whatever artistic modes best suit us...." Whenever he got stuck while writing, he "just 'twinked' Rudy (...a coinage...meaning 'to run a mental simulation of an individual on your personal wetware') and instantly all roadblocks vanished. I even tried to follow Rudy's scheme of 'transreally' incorporating bits and pieces of my autobiography into *Fuzzy Dice*. Transrealism being, in Rudy's memorable phrase, 'writing just like yourself, only more so'."

Transrealist writing is founded, finally, in an insistence that empathy, or a suffering awareness of its absence, must suffuse the fantastic, supplanting rote blueprint or egotistic wish-fulfillment. It goes beyond stipulating cozy formulae about our world (traditional naturalist realism), or even asking how it is we know that world (the modernist, epistemological project). Situated in the complexity, the psychic and social density, of observed life, transrealism takes an extra step into systematic, exploratory doubt—the step intrinsic to postmodern science—and confronts the experiential varieties of all possible worlds: the liberating project of radically *ontological* fiction.

Has twenty-first-century science fiction lived up to this possible expansion and deepening of its mode? Yes, the best of it has done so, I think, and if the best is (as always) just a thin layer of rich cream atop a cracked jug of thin porridge, still it is worth examining some samples of the goods on display to see how far today's sf ventures from its roots in coarse but ideatively exciting adventure romance.

CHAPTER FOUR

SCIENCE FICTION OF THE TWENTY-FIRST CENTURY: A CASE OF SAMPLES

M. JOHN HARRISON: *LIGHT*

Half a century ago, sf satirists parodied a brainless future where people handed over tedious choices to machines but failed to rue their decision because the marrow was leached from their lives. Ironic, then, that the same fate encroaches upon sf itself. Shelves are crammed with what we might call Stepford Sci-Fi. That mightn't matter—people have a right to their denatured comfort food—if publishing conglomerates' accountancy programs leave enough *lebensraum* for challenging books, the rich meat, texts that don't give up their meaning in a single glazed pass. True, such books have not yet all gone, but they struggle, at least in the USA, against strangling odds.

That numbing grip can be seen in the slowed or blocked passage into American editions of many fine novels from the UK. Charles Stross, currently a darling of reviewers, took years to get his novels into print. Iain M. Banks, Ken MacLeod, Mary Gentle, M. John Harrison, Steph Swainston, others—you had to wonder if the British specificity of their locales (even their galactic locales), their independent accents, made such work abominable to readers who mistook their own backyards for the cosmos.

So we had the extraordinary sight of Harrison's Tiptree Award-winning novel from 2002, only arriving in a (handsome) Bantam trade paperback in 2004, although without the nifty chapter-head flourishes of the Gollancz edition. The Tiptree judges (whose remit is to find the year's premier work exploring gender issues in sf and fantasy) declared it "rich, horrible, sad, and absurd," a novel that "says a lot about how the body and sex inform one's humanity. It will reward rereading." Indeed, it almost demands rereading. I suspect many readers recoiled in revulsion, or at the demands it imposes.

Worse yet, the redeeming feature for some will be Harrison's consummately wrought space battles, fought in infinitesimal fractions of a second by a brutally truncated woman starship captain wedded to her ancient sentient K-ship *White Cat*. These scenes are genuinely prodigious, intense genre textuality at full throttle yet shaped with a pre-Raphaelite tenderness. But Harrison is deconstructing exactly the visceral, stoned excitement we gain from such scenes; he is showing us the bitter emptiness at the core of K-captain Seria Mau Genlicher as she slaughters people out of the leached yearning of her own void:

> Out in the flat gray void beyond, a huge actinic flare erupted. In an attempt to protect its client hardware, the *White Cat*'s massive array shut down for a nanosecond and a half. By this time, the ordnance had already cooked off at the higher wavelengths. X-rays briefly raised the temperature in local space to 25,000 degrees Kelvin, while the other particles blinded every kind of sensor, and temporary sub-spaces boiled away from the weapons-grade singularity as fractal dimensions. Shockwaves sang through the dynaflow medium like the voices of angels, the way the first music resonated through the viscous substrate of the early universe before proton and electron recombined. (95)

In the epoch of the blog, we have access to Harrison's own mordant, rich commentary on his intentions in creating this lapidary work of art. It is not especially surprising that a working draft title was *Empty Space*. What fills the novel to flooding is the paradoxical fullness and emptiness of space: the foamed, invisible dazzle of quantum virtual particles rushing in and out of reality, sustaining our apparent solidity. At the core of the narrative is the Kefahuchi Tract, fecund waste land boundary of the black hole seething in its infinitely dense vacancy at the heart of the galaxy. On its shores, its Beach, are the derelict traces of extinct species drawn to its transfinite, transgressive promise: whole abandoned star-plying planets, great enigmatic machines.

Everywhere in this cosmic absence and emptiness is always *more,* and then, as Harrison insists, always *more after that.* His serial killer mathemagician, the obsessed and terror-haunted Michael Kearney, plunged dizzyingly as a child into the fractal endlessness of the sea's edge, an aperture of insight that finally gives humanity faster than light travel. Ed Chianese, the book's third chief player, is client and then tormenter and cuckolder of a mock human New Man named, absurdly, Tig Vesicle. "Chinese Ed" retreats from the intoxicating confusion and fertility of his and Seria's twenty-fifth-century interstellar world (pursued by the standover Cray Sisters, a British joke perhaps opaque to outsiders) into a VR cartoon of *noir* mean streets. Ed the twink, as usual in such picaresques, is being educated: like some zany in a Philip Dick Ace double, he is being programmed as a medium, a precog, a shaman of the Tract.

But in the cauldron of this simmering bouillabaisse of broken people, other fishies mingle, flesh peeling from their hearts, perhaps curing their egregious and haunted lovers. Kearney's waif wife Anna, in her abiding sexual solicitude, her regaining of her self, is not a character one would find in Stepford Sci-Fi. Nor is the great-limbed Annie, Ed's simple-minded rickshaw girl saint. (I'm less sure about W. Anker, Seria's bully boy thrill-seeker and victim.) It would be easy to read this casting of characters as mean-spirited, even misogynist; that would miss the point utterly, as the Tiptree judges understood. But so, too, would the temptation to see *Light* as just a recuperation for the twenty-first century of, say, Alfred Bester's *The Stars My Destination,* for all that Kearney cries out like synesthetic Gully Foyle, in the moment of his apotheosis:

> "Too bright," he said.... The light roared in on
> him unconfined: he felt it on his skin, he heard it as a
> sound.... The vacuum around him smelled of lemons.
> It looked like roses. (287-88)

And the Shrander, the awful horse-skull entity in its maroon wool winter coat haunting his blighted trajectory to heaven, explains: "Everywhere you look it unpacks to infinity. What you look for, you find." It is like that with Harrison's marvelous novel, indeed his entire *oeuvre*, which constitutes a reproach to the McSci-Fi racks and a healing proof that the form of science fiction is not exhausted after all. More, and then always more after that.

ADAM ROBERTS: *SWIFTLY: STORIES THAT NEVER WERE AND MIGHT NOT BE*

If you're moderately familiar with the eighteenth-century classics, you'll swiftly notice that "Swiftly," the novella opening Adam Robert's first US collection, and "Eleanor," which closes it, are spins on Jonathan Swift's *Gulliver's Travels*. In Roberts' parallel reality, that book was a simple history of Lemuel Gulliver's explorations. In the century and a half after his first shipwreck on the island of Lilliput, the British Empire and their French rivals swept through all the places Gulliver visited, subduing and bearing back to Europe as slaves the small, dexterous craftsfolk of both Lilliput and their mortal foes from nearby Blefuscu, giants from Brobdingnag, wise talking horses or Houyhnhnms. Physicists puzzle over the antigravity mysteries of Laputa's flying island while building clockwork dragonflies to carry urgent mail. But what's this? Are the French using Babbage's Analytical Engine, with its myriad of miniaturized gears built by tiny fingers, to calculate the course of invincible battle plans? As London burns, we are told that these Victorians themselves surely shall be judged to be little people, moral pygmies, by a more liberated history. If that seems merely politically correct, the glibness is offset by the pungent realization of Roberts' settings and the vivid pastiche of his mid-nineteenth century cast, and by the disturbing sense that its likely outcome has brutal parallels with our own history.

Adam Roberts is something of a latecomer in the recent British sf revival, with its immensely confident, sardonic and enthralling space operas and its invention of the New Weird, a blend of revisionist fantasy, ferociously exact writing, and leftish disdain for scientistic or pastoral triumphalism. His predecessors include, as well, notable American fantasists like Michael Swanwick (especially with his sulfurously murky and piercing *The Iron Dragon's Daughter* and *Jack Faust)*, and Lucius Shepard's "The Man Who Painted the Dragon Griaule" and other consummate tales). Still, at thirty-six he had already published in Britain the novels *Salt, On, Stone*, and *Polystom*, two comic parodies, a book-length study of sf, and numerous short pieces, mostly marked by the degree to which they differ from each other in subject, tone and manner.

Consequently, *Swiftly* served as a first case of samples for this talented writer in the country where sf thrived best, as a commercial art form, after it was invented in Britain and France. His ambitions are larger than those of many mind-candy writers who sell well by not offending their contented readers with novelty, once the hallmark of sf. That said, it has to be admitted that Roberts is not best served by this particular collection. Its twelve stories are mostly idea variants on classic sf tropes, played in an unfamiliar key. "The Siege of Fadiman" is Freudian sword and sorcery, where a warrior's genitals shrivel as his blade swells into a mighty killing sword. Again, though, Roberts arrives at a grim end that owes less to Norman Spinrad's *The Iron Dream* (pulp sword and sorcery purportedly written by Adolf Hitler) and more to the bleak honor of a Poul Anderson yeoman. "Dantesque" follows a man via a long climb through less salubrious zones to Heaven, where he find the denizens taking bracing holidays in the infernal regions due (yawn) to the boredom, because "pain is more info-rich" (39). This is froth, but amusing enough, as are the rest: "Tour de Lune" (biking to the Moon), "The Time Telephone" (calling past or future), "New Model Computer" (the mandatory VR story, with a real reality twist), "The Question of [Query Term]" (which leaves me asking "why?") and the one real dud, "Stationary Acceleration" (another allegory, perhaps on bipolar disorder, perhaps on, you know, life, that depends on an idea so silly not even a famous scientist would consider it).

Bizarrely, the third major piece, "Jupiter Magnified," appears in a bowdlerized, significantly shortened version; it is a dreamlike allegory of perception and a ruined marriage projected mysteriously into the outer world as an immense Jovian eye, belly, *presence* in the sky. This eerie novella appeared in Britain in 2003 from Peter Crowther's innovative small press PS; the narrative in *Swiftly* was there accompanied by poems by its Swedish woman narrator, and an introduction. Roberts has said, illuminatingly, that the total composition not only includes poetry and explores the state of mind of a poet, but also shows how poetic meaning "evades precision of definition," the poetic symbol focusing and articulating "without holding, delimiting or murderously dissecting" (Introduction). That is exactly what the poet Keats accused science of doing. In this case, the American edition dissected away part of the story, which is ironic anyway. But there is a deeper problem with this tale and some of the others in the book regarded *as sf rather than as allegory.*

In "Blindness and Invisibility," a ravishing gay spy is turned transparent, and thus blind (his retinas don't work), but guided about his business by infrared camera and feedback from his sighted controller. Meanwhile, allegorically, the story deals with the tortured love of his protective companion, a plain fellow who usually would be invisible to such a god, and still is. This is effective in a rather easy figurative way, but the sf reader might be left gnawing at that

IR detector. Would it work if transparent? Could it be miniaturized and remain opaque but not be seen bobbing along—could the lens aperture be large enough? Such quibbles seem absurd, since the story *is* an allegory, not an *Analog* tale. But note how the sf's special reading protocol interferes with the reception of a parable. One can't help fidgeting and prodding at the details as presented, exactly because figurative language becomes reified and has to operate flawlessly within sf's literal frame of reference as well, or even *especially* within that frame. In "Jupiter Magnified," a rationalized explanation is finally provided; if Arthur C. Clarke had written it that would be the unnerving Ramaesque payoff. But Roberts is after a quarry lurking in *inner* space, as they used to say during the 1960s' New Wave somewhat revived in such Fourth Wave tales. It doesn't matter that the orbital dynamics of the Jovian effect seem haywire, not when we're feeling their pain. Or does it? Adam Roberts brings a fresh turn of the spade to sf's humus. Let's see what grows there.

IAIN M. BANKS: *THE ALGEBRAIST*

Bloat is the enemy of promise. Sadly, like supersized servings of greasy fast food, bloat sells. It is part of the comfort food formula. But not all thick-waisted novels and trilogies and multi-volume chronicles are lard-laden. Some have a pleasant amplitude, a relaxed and bountiful attitude to their vast but shapely tale and its setting. Richly decorated, generously stuffed with captivating characters, they make you grin with anticipation as you tuck in for the long haul from soup and salad all the lingering way to dessert, brandy and coffee.

Iain Banks began with short, brutally compressed and cruelly brilliant novels hailed by mainstream critics, and used this acclaim to shoehorn his long, elaborate, wandering and equally brilliant sf into print. The Culture, his dementedly funny and ferocious space opera setting of a post-scarcity, super-AI-supported communist utopia, allowed reworked early non-Culture novels like *Against a Dark Background,* and the richly vernacular, mature *Feersum Endjinn,* to find a market against all odds. But with this non-Culture world-immersion novel, Banks seemed to be tilting heavily toward bloat, and that's a crying shame.

The Algebraist was promoted in Britain as "the most eagerly awaited sf novel of the decade," which might be the problem. Banks has the gift of the gab, a wonderful fluency and range that outdistances almost all the field, but under pressure I suspect he starts babbling, flinging gauds and baubles, dancing as fast as he can on the spot, vamping at the console. Here is the start of a broody meditation by our hero Fassin, a Slow Seer of Sept Bantrabal of the moon 'glantine, who has been breathing blue oxygenated gel inside an instrumented sardine can for rather a long time:

> The waves came booming in like blindness, like stubbornness bundled and given liquid form, an unending slow laughing against the ragged fringe of massively sprawled rocks, each long, low rough ridge of water heaving heavily up to tumble like some ponderously incompetent somersaulter, rolling up and falling forward, hopeful and hopeless at once

and so on for twenty-eight lines of naked epiphany (380-01). Poul Anderson, another sf poet, would have done it like this: "Waves boomed."

Worse still, Banks's new bad guy, ludicrously named the Archimandrite Luseferous, warrior priest of the Starveling Cult and Executive High Admiral of the Shroud Wing Squadron of the Four-Hundred-and-Sixty-Eight Ambient Fleet (Det.) and former Hariolator, is a comic-opera version of comic-book Darth Vader, complete with transparent diamond teeth, re-engineered genitals, red eyes, and a way of offering himself jejune commentary on his psychopathic approach to life: "...one last throw, one final chance to find what they'd come for.... The Archimandrite knew he was at his best when he was under pressure, when the odds were against him and victory far from certain.... Forget playing it calm and quiet, fuck diplomacy, abandon all thought of being reasonable and hoping people would be reasonable in turn. Just fucking do it" (482). There are a lot of naughty words in Banks which oddly enough, these days, lends the book a somewhat juvenile air.

Luseferous is in pursuit of a McGuffin, as is gel-breathing Fassin Taak, through an immensely detailed galaxy two millennia hence, after Earth's humans discover the wormhole transit system linking many worlds and many species, most notably the jovial child-killing Dwellers of Jovian gas-giant worlds who built the first access system not long after the Big Bang and tend to live forever, unless they die in formal battles run by sporting clubs. In fact they talk like absent minded chaps in a jolly old club story, which is hard to believe of people billions of years old (who, one fancies, would be as unintelligible as a burning bush).

The arteria portal system is vulnerable, however. Wormholes need to be carried sub-light to the next port of call, positioned in flat space far from gravitational disruption, and hence can be destroyed if a foe slams past in a starship accelerated nearly to the speed of light—because relativistic effects, see, increase the warcraft's mass so greatly that it is like dropping a planet into a bathtub (84). Poof! goes the disturbed wormhole, and you're back to isolation for a few hundred years until a new arteria is fetched from afar, as happened to our hero's system, making them easy pickings for local predators.

The trouble with this skiffy explanation is that relativistic mass doesn't work like that. Really fast spaceships *don't* become as massive as planets in the sense that they deform spacetime with acquired gravity. Poul Anderson probably wouldn't have made that mistake. A similar problem arises when the McGuffin (a secret, ancient Dweller system of wormholes linking the whole galaxy) is tracked to its apparently clever, and artfully prefigured, lair. Alas, you can't get it from here to there, because the rules forbid it. Does that matter? In a fat fantasy, it might not. In a fat New Space Opera, it's as annoying as finding (to borrow a tired joke) that you can land safely on the Sun as long as you do it at night.

But this *is* Banks, and so it is tasty despite the bloat and the curate's-egg bad portions that in principle spoil the whole effect. If there were passages where my eyes glazed over (but war game fanciers might thrill with excitement), there were also pleasingly silly decorative set pieces that reminded me of delicious sf comics of the 1950s (a globular mansion set atop an artificial geyser of water) and fun twin-wheeled aliens of a Keith Laumerish sort but portrayed without xenophobia, and surprise betrayals, and adapted humans who'd been transported long ago from Earth to seed other worlds (as in Poul Anderson's *The High Crusade)*, although they don't play any obvious role; presumably Banks is building up his new playground for sequels.

The universe he has populated is hugely fractal, in a David Brinish way but far better written, and any story-ruining technological singularity has been averted via ancient wars against pesky fast Machine minds (anathematics) and the proscription of horrific nanotechnology. It is fascinating to see how many sf writers nowadays make that a key establishing move, allowing old fashioned narrative to continue with only modest changes in the human condition. If there are posthumans, they have been seen off, or hidden themselves. It is technology made safe for science fiction, but the temptation remains powerful to sneak those new narrative demons back into the plot, so it is not entirely startling when Banks does rescind some of these stipulations toward the close of the novel. The trouble is that once you do that, the whole fabric of the tale tends to unravel backwards. If *this*, now, why not *that*, then? But we are not meant to worry our heads about such quibbles, I suppose. This is sf, the literature of imaginative fun, not futurist solemnity. And *The Algebraist*, like the ancient eponymous lost text that Major Fassin and his pals and enemies pursue across the starscape and within the wonderfully described gas giant world Nasqueron, is "all about mathematics, navigation as a metaphor, duty, love, longing, honor, long voyages home...all that stuff" (166). Somehow that also reminds me of Poul Anderson. But Poul's dialogue was terrible, wooden, and forced, and Banks make the words tumble and soar. There are worse crimes than bloat, I guess.

JOHN BARNES: *GAUDEAMUS*

A different way to have fun with words, as we saw in chapters 2 and 3, is transrealism. At its most direct, this technique places the author slap in the middle of the narrative, as a character. John Barnes, prolific writer of sf ambitious and less so, although never run of the mill, was until recently Assistant Professor of Theater and Communication at party-school Western State College in Gunniston, Colorado (Smallville with ice, snow and spectacular scenery). *Gaudeamus,* set in just such a locale, tells the tale reported to him in a number of broken-off cliff-hanger segments by his mad friend Travis Bismark, a traveler in a non-Gray flying saucer. This one is built by Uncle Sam (it is an Air Force Boeing SR-8) and powered by a "Gaudeamus device" that yields unlimited zero point free energy, moves stuff instantly in space and time, "and for that matter it allows you to always hang wallpaper correctly on the first try" (212). So it is not just a McGuffin; the Gaudeamus is a cornucopia machine and a sly joke at the expense of traditional sf tropes, readers, and the ghost of John W. Campbell.

For Barnes, like his All-Father Robert A. Heinlein, almost nothing is sacred and beyond mockery. Unlike Heinlein, that includes himself, although he generously spares his ex-wife Kara Dalkey, who appears a few times in the novel. Is his self-portrait just? It probably doesn't matter, but I suspect that he lay it on a bit thick: somewhat cowardly, fat and in pain, aging badly as he approached 50 (Barnes was born in 1957), marooned in the middle of nowhere at a distinctly undistinguished school, vise-gripped by Calvinist guilt, churning out scenes of "adding sulfur to thermite [to make it] spatter molten metal around, and the molten metal carries the sulfur right through flesh to give deep disfiguring horrible burns, and I was already bored" (14). I assume that Bismark is not just a redemptive alter ego having heaps of wild fun but also some true part of his self-estimate.

In any event, this spoof rollicks along and if many of its scenes leave a slightly bitter after-taste that's forgivable in a tale that seems to dice so nearly with the complex truth. Barnes opens with that compulsively watchable net 'toon of the late 1990s, *Gaudeamus,* now "at least as forgotten as Apollo 2000, Pugwash, *My Name is Not Bitch*" (19), and other allohistorical blends of reality and fiction. Soon all kinds of cool or at least enviably obscure fads are turning up with versions of the same name, not least the expensive designer drug "goddies," which proves to create a leaky telepathic bond between people who have had radiantly great sex with it (a boon to spies). "It felt like—oh, I don't know—like having porn-style sex while you're in a Vulcan mind-meld. Like having a whole human heart, body and soul, all perfectly responsive, that you could use as a soft rag to beat off with, a whole human being just as responsive as your own hand" (97). It is a weirdly adolescent image of True Romance.

The machine itself is one of those devices that appear like rail-roads when it's steam engine time. Folks all over seem to stumble upon its design, cobble one together, and find themselves connected to one of the 89,000 civilizations in the galaxy, each of which seems eager to buy the Earth outright in exchange for gluts of jewels, endless life, the usual fairytale bad bargain temptations. The downside is that whichever of these greedy aliens wins the prize is likely to strip the planet down for parts, ablating the humans off it, or turn it into a green sanctuary also human-free. It is a very silly idea; the question is whether it is silly enough, and I think it probably is.

Travis keeps turning up at John Barnes' doorstep, in trouble, pursued by superscience killers or the like, or madly besotted by some fatally attractive dubious woman, keeping himself awake with heroic quantities of lethal black coffee and Scheherazade episodes of his soapy space opera detective life, then on the run again, interspersed by Barnes' own prosaic life as a theater prof, driving across Kansas with his class to a performance contest, wishing he could avoid a previous commitment to an sf convention. Barnes (or "Barnes") is unrelenting in his scathing assessment of sf fans, although Travis chides him for his uncharity. "Like being caught in a mass police roundup of geeks and your lawyer's out of town for the weekend...Most sf writers complain about them. I'm just one of the few who actually avoid them" (47, 159).

The trouble with sf fans, Barnes explains, is that they are weird, but not weird enough. "Most of them have completely reactionary tastes in everything, haven't caught up with the paintings of 1910 or the poetry of 1930, and many of them lead very circumscribed lives, like any suburbanite that belongs to a strange little church or anyone in a dead-end job who puts most of their attention into some all-consuming hobby" (160). He hastens to add that he *likes* the *really* weird ones. And there are a few of them in the novel. It is hard to know if the other kind will like it. But hey, man, it's *the transreal thing.*

LIZ WILLIAMS: *THE BANQUET OF THE LORDS OF NIGHT AND OTHER STORIES*

Liz Williams, a Cambridge Ph.D. in epistemology much traveled in the East, daughter of a Gothic novelist and a conjuror, isn't one of the sf reactionaries John Barnes or "John Barnes" rails against. Here is her position statement, from a 2002 *SF Site* interview with Nick Gevers: "I am a prose junkie. I would much rather read something that is beautifully written than a well-plotted story in clunking prose (though I don't see why you can't have both, of course). [Such] writing, to me, brings back the sense of magic for which I'm constantly searching."

In her first collection of short fiction, ranging from her first sale to *Interzone* ("A Child of the Dead," 1997) to "Loosestrife," from 2004, a sinuous and agile voice creates and recreates small windows into large worlds. Her poise and variety are startling in a fairly new writer, although she hadn't yet quite attained the formal perfection she clearly hungered after. The high-toned flow of some of her consciously prose-poetic effects can have a sedative effect: "Smiling, Ainé gazed up at the faint shadows of the towers as they rose around her. At their height, their windows caught the last of the sun and as Ainé watched they flared as the light was gone. She could taste the summer twilight like a mist in her mouth" (52). Well, yes, all right.

But Williams also has a wicked sense of fun. In several delightful pieces, she invents (or maybe appropriates) a Chinese myth structure to tell tales of skewed detection or exorcism set in prosaic near-worlds infested with demons, chi, the Tao. Detective Inspector Chen, in the opening story ("Adventures in the Ghost Trade," *Interzone*, 2000), fights a demon with a flailing coal-hot rosary and the Fourteen Unnameable Pronouncements, beating his opponent by a single syllable. "The smoke crystallized into dust motes and fell to the floor, where it turned into a swarm of tiny red locusts that raced down the cracks of the floorboards." Next morning, Chen's swollen demon-seized ankle aches, "lined with a ring of puncture marks; fortunately, his inoculations were up to date...He went to the precinct early and spent time cross-checking the franchise death register" (7). his easy acceptance of an amusingly uncanny world, where death is final but taxes must be paid even beyond its doors, shows a comic talent one might not have expected from some of the more traditionally Faustian stories and quasi-fantasies.

In "A Quantum Anthropologist," a naive observer is systematically ignored by the mutant or adapted objects of his investigation, and finds himself, rather absurdly, fading away. This is less Schrödinger than *Back to the Future*, but conducted, disconcertingly, with the gravity of a Le Guin fable. That, in turn, though, is a sort of mask; I guess that Williams is snorting gleefully behind it. She is uncompromisingly serious, though, in stories such as "Sharecropper" (*Interzone*, 2002), which luminously tracks a young Muslim and his father in an Uzbekistan reduced to a gruesomely Western global capitalist future of genetically engineered tasteless terminator crop abundance, as he seeks the seeds to a sturdy strain that will grow from its own grain. "The bare earth waited, like a grave" (87).

In "Loosestrife," a retarded young woman seeks to support her apparently autistic infant in a future Britain where environmental ruin is sterilizing most women. The nature of her child will not surprise most sf readers, but the elegant unpreachy sorrow of the tale's narrative arc is moving. Perhaps less assured is one of the most formally exact stories, "Nightside" (*The Third Alternative*, 1999), where dandyish Mauve decade exquisites of a medically advanced future loiter palely in a becoming consumptive sheen. Serena awaits her new illness fix, but when it arrives she had been disconcerted by rude Nola, who is actually dying of untreatable Sumari fever, her body blistered with fatal ulcers. In the final fall of the story, Serena opens her Christmas present of disease phials and throws them in the fire (95). A more limpid ending—Williams' own seems more appropriate for some *Just Say No* advertisement—would have her shooting up as usual. Better yet, Serena might take the phials out and distribute them, Lady Bountiful, to the rudely healthy poor.

Tragically, Williams' partner Charles died in 2002 of a brain tumor. In the Tao of transrealism, many of these excellent and promising tales, although written earlier, seem shadowed by illness and that bleak loss. The collection has eighteen stories, nearly as many voices, although there are recurrent dark images: blindness, cold, and yet finally a kind of recovery through and beyond despair.

CHARLES STROSS
THE FAMILY TRADE: BOOK ONE OF THE MERCHANT PRINCES
THE HIDDEN FAMILY: BOOK TWO OF THE MERCHANT PRINCES
ACCELERANDO

Like Greg Egan a decade earlier, Charles Stross seemed to come from nowhere and leap immediately to the top rank of science fiction and fantasy writers. This is an illusion in both cases, but especially so for Stross, who for years pounded on many dozing publishers' doors with several exciting book manuscripts before *Festival of Fools* was eventually bought by Ace, released as *Singularity Sky*, and went straight on to the Hugo ballot for best novel of the year. As did his audacious post-singularity novelette "Nightfall" (poking its tongue out at Asimov's most famous title). Neither won, but it was a remarkable debut.

Here is the sort of thing posthuman beings say to each other in "Nightfall":

> "We-us use the DMZ to establish informational value of migrant entities, sapient currency units and the like. We-us banked you upon arrival against future options trades in human species futures.... There is a runaway semiotic excursion underway in the zone. We-us believe only you can fix it. If you agree to do so we will exchange value, pay, reward cooperation, expedite remuneration, manumit, repatriate."
>
> Amber...raises an eyebrow at the ghost. "This looks like the start of an abusive relationship."

But a writer has to live, and that can mean appealing to the largest available audience. These days, relentlessly clever and enticing science fiction at the bursting edge of technology wins wows and near-awards from the cognoscenti, but risks alienating regular sf consumers seeking less confrontational or demanding reading material. The mode *du jour* is, of course, domesticated medieval fantasy with spells, Dark Lords, schoolboy wizards and battles waged by sword and magic spell. It is hard to imagine a writer as good and interesting as Charlie Stross buckling up his magic sword and churning out a lucrative fat fantasy trilogy of many parts. Luckily he hasn't. Like Sean McMullen, but more inventively, Stross is trying the bold experiment of offering a user-friendly confection that *re-*

sembles fantasy (I prefer "science fantasy") but actually is a kind of sly sf enabled by aspects of the quantum cosmos that mimic magic, like a working cell phone in the hand of a real medieval peasant. Stross set his Merchant Princes adventures in a multiverse of alternative Earths mapped in classic sf terms by H. Beam Piper, back in *Astounding* and *Analog* of the 1950s and '60s, candidly acknowledging Piper's influence, along with a tip of his hat to Zelazny.

It is rather as if an Isaac Asimov in a parallel universe had set out to write the *Foundation and Magic* trilogy. Asimov, too, invoked Merchant Princes, and soon found historical forces pressing his scholars and traders into battle against the conservative inertia of an ancient imperial past. Unusually, brain usually beat brawn, except when the brain in question was skewed into a strange psychic brawny power over other minds.

The jacket cover to the opening volume, *The Family Trade*, informs us that it is a "bold fantasy in the tradition of Roger Zelazny's *Chronicles of Amber.*" Actually it is a bold pretend-fantasy in the tradition of management guru Peter Drucker. And what a relief it is, in this age of endless orcs, enchanted swords, unicorns and dragons, to find a sensible laptop-packing journalist girl caught up in lethal problems of interdimensional best practice accounting and sophisticated business restructuring.

On the face of it, that is much the same lateral device powering the more wildly exotic narrative of "Nightfall," an engaging blend of Egan and Philip Dick:

> The rogue corporation rears up slightly and bunches into a fatter lump; its skin blushes red in patches. "Must think about this. Is your mandatory accounting time-cycle fixed or variable term? Are self-owned corporate entities able to enter contracts?"

That's funny, and fun, as well as knowing. *Family Trade*, too, is a tale of process, of the industrious and sometimes inspired application of competence, as were many of Robert A. Heinlein's. Story arc, the fated fall of plot, is not the key aspect to consider in seeking the pleasure of this text. Nor is character, in the traditional sense. Granted, the background of computer reporter and failed medico Miriam Beckstein and her adoptive parents is interesting, but we quickly learn that it is of less moment than where she is headed and how she will get there. A tough-minded foundling, Miriam finds that she is a dweller in two worlds. And as *My Fair Lady*'s Zoltan Karparthy, the oily linguist from Budapest, revealed gloatingly, but mistakenly: "Not only *Hungarian*...but of *royal blood!*" Miriam's genes have a stranger provenance than Hungary, but her lineage (inevitably, for a mock-fantasy) is almost as royal as it gets in the other world. She is the scion of a criminal family of awesome pre-democratic clout, although not actually of royal blood, since the nobility of her otherworld homeland lack the inherited power to slip from their Earth to ours.

The family trade of these snooty and elegant ruffians is the carriage of parcels, not usually regarded as a very glamorous job. What *would* you transport across world lines for immoral purposes (the most lucrative kind)? Weapons? Antibiotics? Drugs? Technological insights? Gold and jewels? Great paintings? Fat fantasy novels as yet unwritten in the other world? When the only way to cross between worlds is by giving yourself a splitting headache staring at a twisty Celtic knot—a sort of semiotic excursion, to borrow from another Stross universe—there's a limit to how much mischief or good a lone individual can manage. In the deviating worlds of Piper and Keith Laumer, you got there and back by machine; Miriam's lost family can't. Their method is more akin to L. Sprague de Camp and Fletcher Pratt's "syllogismobile," from the celebrated *Incompleat Enchanter* tales from the 1940s, except that here only two worlds can be accessed by those with the lucky inbred genes. Or might other breeding lines, or other lost world-sliders, find different paths, taking them to histories even more deviant?

There's lashings of hugger-mugger, lavish frocks (Miriam detests them), beguiling and artful conversation, cross-world culture shock (back and forth alike), danger, romance and a fair swag of management theory. The *Merchant Princes* is a series of considerable range, more muted than Stross's hi-tech and Lovecraftian gonzo escapades—for example, *Accelerando, Saturn's Children, The Atrocity Archives, The Jennifer Morgue*—but nicely thought out and confident in its delivery. (I will deal here only with the first two volumes.)

Stross's intensely sensible thirty-something hero Miriam Beckstein proves to be the grand-daughter of a crusty old hochsprache-speaking duchess, her own true name the Countess Helge voh Thorold d'Hjorth. (Well, of course.) Apparently her mother died on our Earth, fleeing from enemies unknown but presumed to be political rivals from World Two, leaving baby Helge abandoned, with the magic locket tucked away thoughtfully for her to find in maturity. Luckily, the infant was adopted by a pair of take-no-bullshit class warriors perhaps not entirely unlike Charles Stross himself, and now her adopted mother (or is she?) buzzes about in a wheelchair dispensing mysterious and canny advice. Anything is conceivable in such an open-ended tale, and shocks, surprises, reversals and elaborations keep tumbling from Stross's nimble fingers. These books are immensely enjoyable, a sort of twenty-first century version of the solid, thought-out costume sword-and-spaceship fiction that provided the enduring spine of science fiction entertainment.

In the opening salvo, we learn that only some members of the family can travel to our world and back, yet long ago a single member of the family disappeared or was driven away during a typical bloody Jacobean squabble. Might he have found another portal device, retreated to a third world, or become exiled there until recently? Miriam is under attack on all sides. Perhaps some of her foes are scions of the lost ancestor. This would require a new knot-icon, and luckily one is to hand. Miriam's journeys to the third world offer her a useful bolt hole from her known enemies, and a beachhead where a resourceful young woman might use her brains and gumption to build a fortune and gain security. It also strikes her as a lot of fun, and increasingly as a moral duty as well. But it is not all plain sailing in the anti-popish, totalitarian, steam-powered Boston of world three, because they, too, do not much like uppity women, let alone the sort who smuggle in gold ingots and fence them to known Leveler radicals. Matters become fraught as she introduces and patents appropriate technologies, starting with brake liners—not the most obvious choice, but nicely justified.

A satisfying aspect is that Miriam/Helge does not do it all on her own. Of course, sidekicks are handy to give your protagonist someone to talk to. In the movie *Castaway*, even solitary marooned Tom Hanks needed a volleyball as a conversational partner. Luckily, Miriam's friends on all three sides of the magic loophole are brave, quick on the uptake, and engagingly committed, even if they sometimes verge on the pert or plucky. Nor is Stross afraid to expend some of his cannon fodder; at least one important character comes to tragic grief, possibly leaving tender readers dabbing at their eyes. Stross knows how to make this damp hanky-panky work, and to keep an increasingly recomplicated plot on the boil. The narrative arc of the series is completed in the sixth volume, *The Trade of Queens*, published in 2010.

* * * * * * *

With *Accelerando*, the long-awaited compilation of his sequence of nine astonishing stories from *Asimov's,* begun in 2001 with "Lobsters," Charles Stross was sealed as the new Poet Laureate of the Vingean technological singularity.

The project's five years of development (it is tempting to apply this sort of corporate language to Stross's dense techno-speak art-artifact) yielded an early twenty-first-century counterpart to John Brunner's compressed future shock Hugo-winner of the 1960s, *Stand on Zanzibar,* complete with rich idiomatic sidebars or side loads of Baedeker guidance to the non-native. Some will decry this as infodumping of the most blatant kind. Yet it seems unavoidable when a torrential cascade of novelty is the very topic of a work of art. Approached with an appreciative generosity of response, these are tight, compressed, inventive, brilliantly illuminated gems, or perhaps genomes (or memomes) that will unfold in a prepared mind into wondrous ecologies of image and idea:

> Welcome to the moment of maximum change.
>
> About ten billion humans are alive in the solar system, each mind surrounded by an exocortex of distributed agents, threads of personality spun right out of their heads to run on the clouds of utility fog—infinitely flexible computing resources as thin as aerogel—in which they live. The foggy depths are alive with high-bandwidth sparkles; most of Earth's biosphere has been wrapped in cotton wool and pre-served for future examination. For every living hu-man, a thousand million software agents carry infor-mation into the farthest corners of the consciousness address space.
>
> The sun, for so long an unremarkable mildly variable G2 dwarf, has vanished within a gray cloud that englobes it except for a narrow belt around the plane of the ecliptic....
>
> The ten billion inhabitants of this radically changed star system remember being human; almost half of them predate the millennium. Some of them still *are* human....They cower in gated communities and hill forts, mumbling prayers and cursing the un-godly meddlers with the natural order of things. But eight out of every ten living humans are included in the phase-change. It's the most inclusive revolution in the human condition since the discovery of speech.

Of course, since this is genre science fiction and not Stapledonian futurism, such crystalline chunks are not representative of the unfolding comic-horrific family drama Stross uses to anchor his narrative in the experience of humans and weakly posthumans passing through the twenty-first century singularity.

Versions of the singularity trope threaded their way out of Vernor Vinge's mind into novels and stories by Greg Egan, Iain M. Banks, Ken MacLeod, Bruce Sterling, Wil McCarthy, John Barnes, Sean Williams and Shane Dix, Robert Metzger, Robert Wilson (and me, for that matter). Early hints can be traced to Sturgeon, Clarke, even J. G. Ballard. Mostly, though, the utterly transformative impact of the Singularity or Spike or Sublime or Acceleration is glimpsed largely offstage in sf. The changes implied by such headlong acceleration are by definition too immense, too subtle, to be portrayed or perhaps even imagined. Stross has the audacity and, luckily for us, the imagination to come close to pulling it off.

Manfred Macx is a venture altruist ("Manfred's on the road again, making strangers rich")—Stross is not afraid to have us smile even as he jolts our preconceptions—a decade or so hence, encrusted with computer wearables and the latest WiFi connectivity, affianced until recently to Pamela, a dominatrix headhunter for the IRS who tries to persuade global megacorps to cough up the tax they owe. Their venomous bond is manipulated sardonically by their robot cat, Aineko, which is being hacked and upgraded on the sly by Pamela. This nicely observed android animal—"It sits on the hand woven rug in the middle of the hardwood floor with one hind leg sticking out at an odd angle, as if it's forgotten about it"—might be the secret narrator of the novel. Its augmentation and expansion toward the condition of a low-level demiurge mirrors the transitions of humankind and our posthuman Vile Offspring.

In a bondage scene of hilarious erotic vividness, Pamela gets herself pregnant with their daughter Amber, who will carry much of the long arc of the story to the singularity and beyond, as human minds export themselves increasingly outside the skull into machine substrate exocortices. In turn, Amber's son Sirhan (well, son of one of her many instantiations) takes the generational saga to the destructive *Childhood's End*-style Transcension of the solar system into a Matrioshka Brain (energy-hungry Dyson shells of computronium hosting untold trillions of superminds), the return from death of an extremely augmented Manfred, and a blind plunge beyond the provincial Milky Way to a realm where a galactic superintelligence seems to be mounting a "timing channel attack on the virtual machine that's running the universe, perhaps, or an embedded simulation of an entirely different universe."

It is typical of Stross's full-on method that he declines to define "timing channel attack": a sneaky method of undermining encryption by observing how long it takes to complete various aspects of the coding or decoding process. That does not matter, nor should there be any problem in the book's inundation of references from a dozen or a hundred different disciplines, not least Internet lore, mined by his jackdaw and inventive mind. This is how high bandwidth science fiction works. If some item baffles you, rush on and rejoice in the confusion; or, if you are an obsessive, Google on it.

Stross's text points in both those directions simultaneously. As the decades pass, as the rate of change accelerates, his characters *become* Googlized, so to speak. And yet even with their inbuilt channels of information and communication, they are lost like us in the hydrant gush of available knowledge. (For example, "Accelerando," the music term for a quickening pace, is pronounced approximately ARCHER-luh-RAND-oh, but I suppose everyone will default to Ack-SELLER-rando.) All around them, intellectual tools are mutating into predatory life forms, feral tax auditing software roams the solar system, entire economic systems convulse in ecological firestorms of contest. And then there are the aliens...which, of course, are just as likely to be autonomous spam attacks as anything we would recognize as people.

It is a *Fantasia*-bright cavalcade of borrowed and adapted landscapes—the Atomium globe from the 1950 World's Fair, the deck of the *Titanic* emulated in a virtualization stack, a phony debased Islamic heaven—transplanted to Saturn's icy atmosphere or a virtual reality world inside a soda can starwhisp or an alien router network. Plus pleasantly arcane jokes: Rousseau's universal robots.

Does it work? *Can* it work? It is an impressive attempt upon the impossible. For all its Catherine-wheel sparkle and intellectual bravura, there is evidence that the impossible must remain always out of reach (but kudos to the brave writer who attempts it!). "History is a foreign country," Stross observes, "and the old are unwilling emigrants, tired out by the constant travel." The novel's genesis in nine separately published stories remains evident. One grows frustrated at the nth run-through of information we already knew from fifty pages back, a hundred pages back, 150 pages back. Probably Stross felt it necessary to remind some readers with repeated cues, but the book would have gained from more work with the razor. This small irritation is, though, doubtless a matter of individual taste and familiarity with the tropes. Certainly his work has proved enormously popular, and justly so. "Elector," the penultimate chapter, was on the 2005 Hugo shortlist for best novella, which made a total of four Hugo nominations, one Nebula nomination, two Sturgeons, one BSFA, and a Seiun shortlisting before the novel was published; it won the 2006 Locus award for year's best novel. By the middle of the first decade of this century, Charles Stross was no longer just the sf writer to watch—he had well and truly arrived. In 2009, he became the first author to have a novel on the Hugo shortlist in six consecutive years. The only troubling question is whether, given his astonishing output in several variants of sf/fantasy and horror modes, he risks burning himself out. It is a fate that might literally have killed Philip K. Dick.

SPIDER ROBINSON: *VERY BAD DEATHS*

If Stross's quasi-fantasy *Merchant Princes* series drew upon the writer's own experiences as a pharmacist and computer journalist, Spider Robinson's *Very Bad Deaths* is a poster candidate for transrealism. All sf writers, of course, unleash the strange in the familiar from the standpoint of their own richly personalized reality, but the autobiographical aspect of the performance is mostly conducted at arm's length, or even across the width of the galaxy or into the depths of the future. Spider Robinson's *noir* novel *Very Bad Deaths* fairly rings out with transrealism, which is perhaps a little surprising. After all, many of Robinson's tales, right from the start of his career, centered on a Heinleinian hippie whorehouse where all the men and women are golden-hearted, psychically gifted, and way above average, like the folks of Lake Wobegone but raunchier: *Cheers* for sexy, caring, sharing mutants.

You will have little doubt, though, that Russell Walker, blues singer, doper and columnist for the Toronto *Globe & Mail* (Robinson lost a *G&M* column after some years of saying what he thought; he notes in a jaundiced Afterword to a collection of non-fiction occasional pieces, *The Crazy Years*, "In 2004, the *Globe & Mail*'s Comments editor abruptly stopped buying my columns. I could not say why, because he also stopped answering my e-mails and voice messages"). Walker is married to a Buddhist dancer (like Robinson's wife Jeanne), is Spider himself lightly transformed, in a story of telepathy, unspeakably cruel murders, thwarted detection, soppy and heart-warming love, and crucifying quantities of pain. It is the last that rings truest. The simple plot, while comprising the meat of this crime mystery-cum-sf novel, hangs upon a vivid recounting of physical suffering that actually *is* drawn directly from Spider's experiences as a victim of recurrent pneumothorax. That is where your lung collapses, and a fist of steel crushes half your chest and you breathe in small terrified sips while trying to reach the hospital. This is so remorselessly described I wondered if it might be autobiography or whether, fiction being made up, after all, he had asked his named medical advisors for the most aptly agonizing, debilitating disorder they could think of, and placed it artistically in a tale hinging on maximal psychic and physical pain. If based on his direct experience, that would make *Very Bad Deaths* a prime instance of transrealism. Or was I falling into the oldest, most vulgar critical fallacy, mistaking the narrator or protagonist for the author?

In this case, no mistake. Spider Robinson had his first spontaneous pneumothorax at fourteen. Recovery from a thoracotomy to correct the disorder—after ten percent chance of death on the table—is rated the most painful survivable operation. I am assured that what he writes about lung collapse and repair is literal truth: "I have a scar from my right nipple to my spine." This is more genuinely frightening than most invented horror stories, and Robinson wrings from it pathos and laughter as well as squicked misery.

In 1967, Russell's sophomore year at a Marianite college, he finds himself lumbered with a ghastly roomie: Zandor Zudenigo, campus legend for his brilliance, ugliness, apparent autism, but above all his overpowering stench. "Smelly" proves a fastidious gentleman as a room mate, an aficionado of the right kind of jazz, but a drug abstainer.

In "flashforwards" to 2003, many years later, Smelly seeks out Russell, who is mourning the death of the love of his life, in retreat on an island strikingly similar to Spider Robinson's Bowen Island. Smelly has caught the scent of the world's worst serial killer, a sadistic monster whose life is dedicated to the extreme sport of inflicting extreme agony. This beast is a millionaire computer specialist who plans to entrap and mutilate to death a nice family of four as they munch on their pizzas, inflicting unendurable agony indefinitely prolonged. The descriptions of his past cruelties provoke cold sweats and repeated projectile vomiting in Russell, but left me fairly unmoved; you probably had to be there. The task is to track down this vile madman, knowing only that his name is Allen and that he will be driving a certain hair-raising coastal road on his diabolical mission.

Spider plays fair in this quest; in some scenes he is reporting, with bitter anger, precisely the treatment he got from Vancouver police while researching his plot. There is some gruesomely entertaining stuff about the laziness, stupidity, malignity and corruption of police forces in general and particular. It is hard to know what Heinlein would have made of it. On the one hand, these are civil "servants" gorging at the public trough; on the other, they are the brave band of blue standing between us and lawless ruin. (Spider Robinson has been acclaimed for decades now as Heinlein's natural son, so to speak, his voice and attitudes catching many echoes from the master's, but always with a sixties' skew. Heinlein, one gathers, remained the ramrod military man in private life, while his heir is a laidback dude with a taste for the mild natural chemicals of merriment. It is hard to imagine Heinlein with hair halfway down his back working in a hippie commune and singing r&b while strumming his guitar. Still, if the hands are the hands of an adopted Canadian, the voice is often the voice of Annapolis and the man who sold the moon. But there's nothing slavish about Robinson's *hommages*, his candid appropriations.) Luckily, Russell runs into a cop with the right stuff, although Constable Nika Mandiç is narrow, rigid, and career-stranded in the contemptible Police Community Services Trailer detail. Together, and with Smelly Zudie's cellphone-mediated help (he cannot bear to get close to people), they find themselves trapped by the madman, and...

...Spider Robinson does his good deed for all the scrawny or obese or half-blind or physically inept readers of fantastical crime fiction (I am one, too): he has Russell solve his way free without having to be John D. MacDonald's Travis McGee, or Robert B. Parker's highly physical Spenser and Hawk. It is a geek's treat of wit and thwarted super powers against weapons, cunning and evil genius. Most of us enjoy this sort of imaginary comeuppance, and all the tooth-grinding frustration leading to it; we'd be fools not to.

GEOFF RYMAN: *AIR (OR, HAVE NOT HAVE)*

Some twenty years ago, Geoff Ryman published his sublime novel of genetic engineering, *The Child Garden*, winner of the 1990 Arthur C. Clarke and John W. Campbell Memorial Awards. Milena, amnesiac refugee to British purgatory from Eastern European hell, halfway through her truncated life, was a prim, sour Tenniel Alice climbing toward Paradise. Her story was a *Bildungsroman*, taking Milena from cramped repression to insight, redemption, indeed sainthood. It was funny while genuinely moving, teemingly fecund, baroque yet cleanly and beautifully written. That novel came very close to being the long-awaited work successfully bonding the force and aspirations of both literature and sf. *Air* belongs to the same shortlist of candidates.

The grittily realist, soaringly fantastical story of Mrs. Mae Chung, a robust middle-aged woman and mother of grown children in the imaginary nation of Karzistan, bordering China and Kazakhstan, inverts almost every aspect of *The Child Garden*. If Milena's frame was her Dantean ascent through the Divine Comedy, this novel moves in a pavane amid the balanced forces of the *I Ching* and other divinatory manifestations of the four ancient elements: air, fire, water and earth. *Air* manifests an abundance of memory, still more teemingly fecund. Kizuldah, the Happy Province of rural peasants, is saturated in its own past, even as the flood of a belated today and then an instantaneous tomorrow crams memory into ruinous mud while its insistent presence invades poor Mae's mind like a plague of memetic computer viruses.

Air is the next technology after the Internet, 2020's mercantile version of what sf has long postulated: access to a group or gestalt mind. It is Google in the head, without need of chips, display, data gloves or keyboard, Theodore Sturgeon's gestalt connectivity for the age of quantum superspace and petaflop computation. It is the all-at-once of Theory of Everything's timeless unity of space and change, accessed via a Format burned into the brain that—in trial runs in Karzistan, Tokyo and Singapore—uses an under-construction UN software template. Unluckily, the Format test suggests that it is liable to disrupt and even madden unprepared brains exposed even briefly to Air's 11-dimensional ubiquity. The rival, slower Gates Format struggles for preferment, seizing eagerly on the UN test's collateral damage. From the big centers of power among the Western Haves, these global contests cascade in surprising ways over the ill-equipped but richly complex social arrangements of the Have Nots—who, naturally enough, bitterly resent being labeled as such by their patronizing benefactors.

Local fashion-advice specialist (and dirt-grubbing farmer) Mrs. Chung is perhaps the most extreme victim of these side-effects. In the moment of formatting, her elderly, blind, sweet-natured neighbor dies in her arms, so their minds are entangled. With typical comic bravura, Ryman explains that this is because they share an email address in the timeless realm of Air. Due to this industrial accident, Mae Chung's personality is infused with the dead woman's yearnings, and with Mrs. Tung's now forever-unchangeable history, like one infested by a dybbuk or demon. Bad luck. Then again, a second effect of her unique immersion in Air is enhanced creativity. Mae gains access to the world's plenty, learning to use the old-fashioned Web via a classy digital TV to contact markets for her fashion business, which soon goes global. This clever, illiterate woman's faltering but growing competence is delightful to watch. Her naivety allows her to promote her wares with flyers teaching a women's circle of fellow villagers

HOW TO MAKE BIG BUCKS FROM INFO

for this is the last corner of the world not yet awash in spam (304).

In a delightful on-line interview with Kit Reed, Ryman stressed that the setting is wholly invented, although it owes something to his experience of Turkey. The village of sinewy Karz peasants and tolerated, beautiful but delicate Eloi is richly evoked, utterly believable. But this really *is* a construct. Eloi? The Wellsian reference is impossible to ignore, yet hard to make sense of. Are the Eloi a kind of Sheep, or vulnerable angels? Pitched against them, are the Karz Morlocks? Or perhaps those are other citizens now deracinated and brutalized by urban life? Perhaps this is exactly the sort of thing that shouldn't be probed for fear of rupturing the delicate fabric of allusion. (Besides, Geoff Ryman tells me it is simply a tribute to his favorite sf novel, *The Time Machine*, of no deeper significance.) But then I can't help wondering about Mr. Ken, Mae's newly widowed neighbor and, behind her rather stupid husband's back, her scandalous post-Air lover, cause of her downfall in the prudish village. Given a Mr. Ken, a Western reader can't help seeing a Mrs. or Ms. Barbie behind every bush, mistakenly in this case.

Because *Air* is authentic literature, not paraliterature, Mae's emotional involvements, her love affairs, her friendships and their subtle or brutal ebbs and flows, form the tense focus of the narrative. Still, to a degree no mundane novel could permit, the fanciful element of Air plays an equally compelling and impelling role. (There is irony, therefore, in Ryman's recent championing of a splinter group among sf writers who dub themselves the Mundanes, devoted to eschewing space opera theatrics and preposterous physics in favor of dense near-future realizations, more Dostoyevsky than Doc Smith.)

Echoing the tidal disruption that Air's full implementation threatens, the very snows of the high places cupping the village hang at the edge of melting and flood, a threat only Mae and her memorious but increasingly spiteful ghost can see. Because this is an sf novel and not a Booker candidate, Mae fails to wring her hands and draw a despairing existential moral from this threat; she knuckles down, learns meteorological Arcana and bullies her way to the expensive software needed to interpret the local weather data she and her charge laboriously gather. As water rushes finally across earth, the fire of her unstoppable will snatches many of her mocking fellows to a redemptive safety only a bodhisattva could have managed.

Against this hard-headed peasant empiricism, Mae's immersion in Air reveals reality's mutability under desire. She rips asunder a wire fence by a sort of quantum magic: "The fence was mere fiction. So she tore it" (214). By the same means, an absurd, even grotesque, miracle brings Mae a pregnancy like nothing seen since the age of myth and legend. Perhaps I reveal too much even in mentioning this bizarre invention, but it seems indisputable that Mae is a sort of paradoxical Virgin Mother figure, and her joyous *hibakushi* son (I am thinking of the burned survivors of Hiroshima and Nagasaki), scalded and blind like Mrs. Tung but awash in Air's music and light, is a sort of Redeemed New Human/Buddha/Christ, conceived in a loving, sinful Eucharistic feast.

Yet the novel itself rejects interpretation:

> Everything has always been and has always happened at once. Which means nothing causes anything else. Which means stories only happen in this poor balloon-world of ours. Stories have no meaning. Nothing can be interpreted. Everything just is, without meaning...It is all just one big smiling Now. (310)

This resembles nothing so much as the dicta of Kilgore Trout, Vonnegut's crackpot sf genius, or perhaps one of the New Age gurus who flog their mystified versions of quantum theory in the self-help shelves. Don't tell a critic to stop looking for meaning. Don't tell any reader. Don't tell that to *any* human! Arguably, *only* fiction can create meaning, or elicit one's constructed perception of it. (We must include, of course, the handy, testable, simplifying fictions of science). The wondrous art wrought in Ryman's *Air* shows some of its meaning plainly, calling forth grins, astonishment and tears. More of its meaning is tucked away inside, like the seven hidden curled-up dimensions of spacetime, like the final pages of the third book of Dante, beyond words or imagining high and low. Treasure this book.

ALBERT E. COWDREY: *CRUX*

The purpose of power, Orwell chillingly informed us, is power. That is a cynical opinion, not always borne out by our daily experience, despite power's nuanced or ruthless exercise in every corner of our lives. At the fine grain, it is not much more use than learning that everything we do, everything we are, ultimately derives from mindless genes and memes, the buzz of quarks and electrons. So what? In any case, fiction (at its best) is a lens for projecting those hues of our lives not easily reduced to the elemental spectra of raw power.

You wouldn't know it from Albert Cowdrey's first novel, a fix-up or mosaic of three long novellas first published in *F&SF*, plus an unpublished coda of more than eighty pages which loops this time travel picaresque into sf's usual leap to undetermined freedom. So the purpose of power, abundantly and coldly demonstrated throughout the jerky, jolting toboggan ride of the narrative, suddenly mellows into a Tao of liberation.

Formerly Chief of the Special History Branch of the U.S. Army (an unnervingly Orwellian title itself, perhaps), Mr. Cowdrey is a notable military historian turning to sf in retirement. He made his mark swiftly: a World Fantasy Award in 2002 for "Queen for a Day"; the year before, "Crux," opening story of this volume, was a selection in Gardner Dozois's *Year's Best SF*. Military expertise lends a certain gristle to the cruelly sordid and depopulated global culture clinging savagely to power 300 years after the Time of Troubles in 2091-3—when twelve billion people perished—like some gaudier echo of Stalinism. (Tsar Stalin the Good is a saint, Genghis Khan the Great Unifier.) Civilization has clawed back in despised barren places, especially Siberia, where Ulanor is the new Worldcity and everyone speaks Alspeke, a Creole blend of Russian, Chinese and English. Fragments of this language add a certain color; Cowdrey helpfully tells us that *svini* means "swine," and, more usefully, that *shosho* is "torture" and *mosh* is "power". The purpose of *mosh*, we find again and again, really *is* power, although this universal prize and solvent can be diverted now and then, corruptly if humanly, to save a kidnapped child, fetch a beautiful woman from the fire storm of the twenty-first century holocaust, renovate or restore history.

It is an unhappy coincidence, for Cowdrey, that his orientalized future arrived at the same time as Ryman's, for alongside the subtle realism and gentle invention of *Air*, the world creation of *Crux* (praised by Dozois as "richly layered and fascinating") is coarse, hostile, arbitrary and clichéd. The surprise ending of section One was old half a century ago, yet we are meant to be startled when an operative who seeks to change the future brings it into being. This is sound four-dimensional causality, but dull story-telling in a genre where every variation has been rung on time paradox. Besides, it is quickly forsaken as the book proceeds. If you go back and encounter yourself in the past, it turns out, the earlier version...*evaporates.* You can watch it happen. *Back to the Future* has a lot to answer for.

Cowdrey's principal narrative device, which he uses with thudding enthusiasm, is to follow one reckless, driven character after another and wipe each of them out, *blam,* just when something interesting is about to happen. This can create an agreeable whiplash, but it gets old fast. The justification, I suppose, is that in such a polity *that's just how life is.* It is like living under the kind of insane autocracy of Caligula or Nobunaga, but with better medicine and surveillance devices for those at the top of the heap. It gives the setting a fevered air of living for today since tomorrow....Sorry, too late, no tomorrow. Maybe I'm too complacent, but it seems a tad adolescent as a driving motif. Die young, and leave a brutalized, feculent corpse.

Because so many of the active characters keep getting bumped off, it is hard to speak of a plot. In essence, this impoverished world—which just happens, even so, to have faster than light starships and weaponry, antigravity in its bumpy old crates, three Alien wars behind it but only a bunch of stinking Chewbacca mercenaries on hand to prove it—invents the wormholer, a time portal. The inventors are slain, naturally. An attempt to prevent the Troubles brings about that very disaster, as noted, and we spend the rest of the book lurching along through the connivances of cold Confucian bureaucrats, some with a soft spot for their wives and kids, a mad geriatric Controller or de facto queen, and the brave but confessedly dim-witted timesurfer Hastings Maks. His search for love and perhaps liberty clunks along, while his enemies cry in the heat of battle, to encourage their troops: "Universal power or universal ruin!" Well, maybe. Then there are the duplicitous whores and the whorehouses of the Clouds and Rain District, and that sort of richly layered and fascinating detail work. Teenaged readers unfamiliar with sf's back story might warm to it.

Lisa Tuttle: *The Mysteries*

The call of the wild, these days, for most of us, is the whir of a can-opener slicing aluminum, our lilting lifted voice: "Here, kitty! Puss, puss...." Or perhaps the true remnant call of the wild is its antiphon: "Mrrowww," and the quick padding of soft paws across tiles or carpet. We are domesticated, most of us, we sf and fantasy devotees. If we hear the call of the Big Hunger, Walter M. Miller's classic urgent cry summoning us to deep space and adventure among the stars, or a summons to roam with the King of Elfland's daughter, it is usually with a TV remote firmly in one hand. So it takes a bold writer to squeak open a door in the fourth wall and summon us, eyes open, into the country of legend and fairytale without benefit of runes, swords, cozy magical empires or incomprehensible super-science.

Lisa Tuttle, once of Texas, now living in Scotland with her British husband and child, gives it a good shot. Whether it works is up to each reader's capacity to hold one eye fixed firmly on domestic reality and the other on Faerie. We grow accustomed to suspending disbelief, or more exactly to emulating belief, but only while the book covers remain open or the film frames run. It is an interesting paradox that we find it easier to get caught up in a wholly contrived world than in a familiar one at the very margins of the workaday ordinary. That narrow terminator is known to scholars of the fantastic as the *uncanny*. It borders sf on one side and full-blown fantasy on the other, with allegory and utopia somewhere sideways in the Venn diagram of genre. Henry James's uncanny *The Turn of the Screw* is the classic case: are the children haunted or vicious? Is the governess wicked or mad or psychically gifted? The whole point is our suspension in uncertainty. That is where creepiness lurks, *frisson* and gooseflesh.

Tuttle starts her nicely written novel in that landscape of ambiguity, setting us up with uncanny tales swiftly dissolved into ordinary sad realities, only to switch the bait of the quotidian and lure us back into fright and hints of antique British magic older than the Matter of Britain, than grail-hunting knights and sly sorceresses. The mythoi she draws upon are the ancient Celtic belief in a Secret Commonwealth of fauns and fairies dancing in the gaps and hesitations of our mortal world, the Welsh Tylwyth Teg, the Greek legends of Cupid and Psyche, abducted Persephone and her grieving mother Demeter, the disappeared and the recovered. It is territory familiar enough in today's recycled fantasies, more commonly in embroidered versions of Tam Lin, or Thomas the Rhymer, where a young man is enticed by the Fair Folk and held in a sort of narcotized half-life unless rescued at some cost by mortal love. Jane Yolen has told it, and Ellen Kushner, but here Tuttle revises the tale into something that Colin Wilson might have written when he was at his peak (and I hope Ms. Tuttle will not be offended by the comparison).

Ian Kennedy, her curiously limp American detective in London, has been obsessed by mysterious vanishments since his father wandered into a Milwaukee field and winked out of existence, witnessed by nine-year-old Ian and a passerby. The novel's first agreeable shock is that this supernatural event is a mask memory for a more routine runner by a man obviously driven to his wit's end by Ian's mother, free spirit and artsy hippie. In maturity, Ian falls in love with a woman who, to his anguished bafflement, does a midnight flit in her turn. We readers see all too clearly that Jenny, like Ian's father, was siren-summoned by the call of, well, the *anti*-wild, the suburban, the domestic. It is a nicely subdued irony, because Ian is a rather dithery fellow, less Jack London than a gawky Ralph Fiennes playing Charles van Doren in *Quiz Show*.

Ian's self-taught specialty is finding the lost, funded by an inheritance and plainly not paying terribly well but driven by an obsession reflected in the many classic anecdotes of mysterious disappearance sprinkled between chapters. His first case unfolds in flashbacks also woven through the book, in parallel with his current search for Peri, the vanished beautiful daughter of Laura Lensky, a Texan New Yorker in London and disturbingly reminiscent of his lost Jenny. Peri's abandoned film-maker boyfriend Hugh (to be played, I imagine, by Colin Firth, not Hugh Grant), helps and hinders the search in London and the highlands of Scotland. Has golden Peri been spirited away by unspeakably handsome Mider, of the *Sidhe*? Both cases have their increasingly eerie aspect, seeming to enact the legendary seductions and fairy bargaining of those old tales where an immortal jousts sneakily with a human for the release of an englamored lover. The book moves through a carefully elaborated and folded pattern of disclosure, or what TV might dub *reveals*.

The novel's opening demystification and its attention to daily detail seeks to seduce us into supposing that all this palaver is a fanciful cover story for more conventional escapades, drug overdoses, sex murders. But of course we know in advance that we read a fantasy, so genre expectations drain away that very ambiguity the narrative seeks to impart. If A. S. Byatt's name were on the jacket, or Iris Murdoch's, we might remain suspended in the uncanny until the end. But Tuttle's book is marketed as fantasy and to that extent the clanking mechanisms of legend made all too concrete clamp down through the artful mists and heather to throttle the very mood it wishes to sustain.

Or so it struck this reader. Others might manage the imaginative suspension more readily, maintaining a dual grip on the real and the rather silly in the way that can make immersion in Gene Wolfe and John Crowley so intensely pleasurable. (Although, to their cost, plenty of readers find it impossible to get past the whimsical names and the fairies of Crowley's superb *Little, Big*.) Faerie's supersaturated beauty and timeless amoral bliss, its habit of replacing stolen lives with fake things that die swiftly, its shape-shifter games and bargains—all these do seem somehow to strike a resonating note from our dreaming selves. Perhaps the edge of sleep is the right mood for their enjoyment, which might be why the detailed wide-awake recounting of hairy driving on the wrong side of the road, eating hearty breakfasts, checking the internet for clues, all the scratchy *ordinariness* of Tuttle's background tale puts us in the wrong frame of mind to take seriously dolls who speak, hefty guardian animals emerging from shoulder bags, characters who buzz about like flies. Or maybe that might just tickle your fancy. Tuttle is brave in attempting something very difficult to carry off, perhaps opening pathways to a renewal of urban fantasy superior to rote medieval trilogies.

JUSTINA ROBSON: *SILVER SCREEN* AND *NATURAL HISTORY*

Lou Anders, publisher of Prometheus Books' sf offshoot Pyr, made what is presumably an economical as well as slightly risky decision by buying a number of well-received UK and other novels nobody else in the USA had picked up, as well as republishing some classics—such as George Zebrowski's *Macrolife*—that were allowed to fall out of print. So his list includes Australian Sean Williams' 1998 *The Resurrection Man*, John Meaney's ambitious if finally dire space opera trilogy (discussed below), and several Justina Robson novels. It might make an intriguing if not especially joyous dinner party game to try to come up with plausible reasons why the major New York publishers allowed these books to slip through their fingers, as for some years it seemed they were going to do with the best-selling fantasies of Australian Sara Douglass.

One reason might be that some of these books are quite conspicuously set in locales other than the United States, and peopled by characters speaking in vernaculars unfamiliar to Americans. You might suppose that this restriction would be less oppressive in a genre like science fiction, where all of space and time is allegedly the *mise en scène*. Still, in the same way that most movies are focused on exceptionally beautiful and winsome actors, candy fantasy does best when it comforts readers with familiarity in the midst of domesticated and recognizable variations on strangeness. British Justina Robson, trained in philosophy, had already made her mark with *Silver Screen* and *Mappa Mundi*, both short listed for the Arthur C. Clarke award. One of the appeals of *Silver Screen* to British and more generally European readers might be precisely for such elements of local place and voice.

Narrator Anjuli O'Connell is the overweight, self-hating daughter of a Pakistani mother and an Irish father, absentee parents selfishly concerned only with their own lives and professions, or so she sees it. Anjuli is also a genius, or at any rate extremely differently abled: she is possessed (perhaps almost in the diabolical sense) of eidetic memory, perfect recall that permits spectacular achievement in IQ tests and examinations for which she has been prepared. Part of her self-detestation springs from a sense that she has lived a lie since childhood, when she was selected by the Massey Foundation, "an organization funded by large corporates and used specifically for the hot housing of children who were exceptionally gifted in one of the foundation's areas of interest"—principally, technology and science. Some 500 children of "all races and many subdivisions" live with their teachers in an idyllic setting, cramming their astonishing minds before proceeding swiftly to university. A social isolate, like many brilliant children, Anjuli falls in with the even weirder and far more brilliant Roy and Jane Croft, genius kids psychologically maimed by their father, the crazed fundamentalist abbot of a post-New Age cult and representative of what Roy calls the "Hippyshit Shift" (he means "Hippie-shit," but maybe that is Jules' weight issues talking) from Green nature spiritualism to postmodern mechaphilia. If pugnacious, fearless Jane is Roy's early protector, she delegates this role to Anjuli and boyfriend Augustine when they enter university, and so matters stand five years later as they work on the orbital station Netplatform, creating one botched artificial intelligence or "biomechanoid" after another for the monstrous Corporation OptiNet.

It might seem that Robson is setting up a sort of Frankenstein hybrid of Wilmar H. Shiras's classic 1940s' "In Hiding" (and the other stories of super-intelligent youngsters collected as *Children of the Atom*), Gibson's cyberpunk cosmos, and maybe "Flowers for Algernon," all of it rendered in the accents of British discontents. In fact, the novel meanders in these territories for nearly 250 pages before taking a brutal and captivating turn into Iain M. Banks landscape, perhaps literally. Her absent lover Augustine proves to be heavily wired and infiltrated by an interface network designed to make him part of a military cyborg, if and when he dares to dress in a suit of fatally powerful and mission-driven AI armor. I was reminded of an early Banks story of creepy attachment where an augmented spacesuit absorbs the dying human it encases, or perhaps of John C. Wright's *Golden Age* with its almost miraculously powerful adamantium suit (except, of course, that Robson's book was published before Wright's), in a tour de force battle scene as effective as Heinlein's first-person account of capture by an alien puppet master. Soon the register of the tale shifts yet again: Anjuli is obliged, Fair Witness-like, to depose in Strasbourg at a historic hearing into the legal status of her friend and manipulator 901, an advanced AI. Is she to betray this immensely complex machine consciousness, or her vicious employer? (Apparently something strange befell an earlier iteration of the AI, 899—has it been deleted, or escaped?) Betrayal haunts her; it seems the leitmotif of the novel, but perhaps that is only her guilty conscience speaking, her sense of herself as fraudulent.

Meanwhile, after discovering and encrypting the Source, the basic divine algorithmic Secret of Creation, Life and Mind (or something along those lines), Roy is dead, apparently by his own hand. We learn of his death at the start of chapter two, and very quickly see hints that Roy is not really gone, but simply downloaded into an immense furtive artificial intelligence structure known as the Shoal. Meanwhile, also, her chunky best friend and fellow cineaste Lula is apparently an augment—"there was distinctly something odd about her" (134)—but Jules is hardly the best judge of such matters. "This entire drama swings around two poles," she tells the Shoal. "The values of humanity and the continual theme of false witness" (234). Maybe so.

Anjuli is not precisely autistic nor even Aspergerish, but it is clear that she negotiates the world of her fellow humans and the emerging AIs with a defective "theory of mind," as if her memory makes her a kind of living instance of philosopher John Searle's celebrated Chinese Room thought experiment. In that imaginary experiment, someone ignorant of Mandarin sits inside a vast library of Chinese words together with an immense guide, in English, to appropriate syntax, and must provide a sort of upmarket Turing test reply in Mandarin when a message is displayed in that language. That is, an appropriate response is to be generated just by following the rules and the lookup tables, with no comprehension of its meaning. As numerous specialists have pointed out, this is a bogus analogy for the way the mind works, but it does convey something of poor Anjuli's sense of dispossession. Partly to cobble together a non-intuitive understanding of how other humans work, she is trained as a psychologist, as well as a twenty-first-century version of an Asimovian robopsychologist. The world of other people presents itself to her as if it were an image on a screen, and indeed at every key moment in her voyage of discovery and transgression she finds herself viewing some allegorical twentieth century movie, preferably a black-and-white classic such as *The Maltese Falcon* with its misleading Grail quest. The world as silver screen. Not so much Searle's Chinese room as Grauman's Chinese Theatre.

The novel is packed with detail and a kind of naturalistic rendering of character that some readers have found two-dimensional, banal. I think that is because science fiction arouses expectations of melodramatic character as well as spectacular setting and event, while Robson's characters are, if anything, flattened into a sort of desperate ordinariness, for all their exotic idiosyncrasy and special gifts. Around the time she was publishing this first novel in England, Justina Robson was a proponent of slipstream, planning an anthology of such stories. She told me that "slipstream strives to duplicate the complexities of actual experiences by allowing experience to be paramount and letting everything else serve a purpose." It is tempting, though impertinent, to wonder if the character of Anjuli is at least in part transrealist, drawn to an unusual degree from the daily grind, irritations, opacities of her author's ordinary experience (although she has a degree in philosophy and linguistics, and is a yoga teacher, presumably in better trim than Jules), fantasy enriched by the miseries and rewards of life here and now. Perhaps that is just another way of praising the novel for its artful and persuasive rendering. It is very far from perfect, Robson has meanwhile grown as a writer, but Pyr did their American readers a service by retrieving this ambitious book from its disheartening transatlantic isolation.

* * * * * * *

Robson's *Natural History* was runner-up for 2004's Campbell Memorial award, a distinguished feat attained previously by such luminaries as Kurt Vonnegut, Ursula K. Le Guin, Ian Watson, John Crowley, Michael Bishop, Lucius Shepard, Kim Stanley Robinson, Neal Stephenson (and Greg Bear three times). She suggests the main question raised in this space opera of Forged (modified and augmented human stock) and Unevolved (same old earthly us) is whether you are locked into a specified identity "because of your physical form. Whether you can still possess a human identity if you are some sort of radically different gigantic cyborg type of creature that lives among the stars" (Interview with Cheryl Morgan, 2003).

Voyager Lonestar Isol is just such a cyborg or MekTek, adapted for deep space and heading for Barnard's Star when she slams into exploded alien detritus that pits her savagely and leaves her doomed until she awakens in the debris that an advanced M-Theory engine-thing made of silicon Stuff. In a trice, the Stuff whips her, 11-dimensionally, to an enigmatic world near the galactic hub, and then home. Ironhorse Timespan Tatresi, a kilometer-long solar system bulk carrier, takes her to feathered Corvax, formerly a Roc, Handslicer class, for investigation, on behalf of a burgeoning insurgency of Forged against Monkeys or Hanumaforms (us again, their creators).

The Forged are not slaves, not exactly. Their own consoling ideology poses them as sole custodians of meaning and true freedom (their Form and Function, designed teleologically into them) that the Old Monkeys lack, dull creatures of Darwinian happenstance that we are. All that holds them back from decamping to a home world of their own, a seemingly abandoned earthlike planet found by Isol, is the regard in which they hold their mythic Forged Citizen "father-mothers." Even this is a simplification, as Aurora quickly explains to Zephyr: "Clinging to Function is a puritan ideal...Form is likewise irrelevant; only what you can contribute to the lives of others should be a measure of a soul's value" (71). Here is a striking echo of to-day's conflicted ideologies over, say, reproductive, gay, and trans-gender rights to choice, and a foreshadowing of the shape these tussles will likely take in any early transhuman or posthuman future.

More generally, Robson's political setting, which at first resembles black slaves against white masters, or Third World against First, or workers against capitalists, strikes the habituated sf reader as an echo of that enormous mythic future sketched so hauntingly by Cordwainer Smith, Underpeople ranged against the Lords of the Instrumentality. Those modified animal people struggled for redemption and self-determination against the true and augmented humans of Old Earth, Norstrilia and the rest of Smith's unfinished crypto-Christian universe. Here, Tom Corvax is an aging, damaged bird-man tech and VR bootlegger, dreaming a banned virtual human life. Soon we find a Jamaican cultural archaeologist, Zephyr Duquesne, taking her swift if squeamish flight inside the flesh and metal body of an immense Passenger Pigeon person, Ironhorse AnimaMekTek Aurora. Impossible not to recall the E'telekeli eagle-man messiah from Smith's long rebellion; just as impossible, grinning, not to recall "Blackie" Duquesne, E. E. Doc Smith's anti-hero from the *Skylark* books. So what's up with this surfeit of Smiths and Forged? A nod to the megatext, that immense repository of sf iconography, whimsy, heartbreak, tools shaped for getting us into the inconceivable and back? No; in fact, it is either an accident or a convergence of memoryless sf with very old images from folklore. Robson told me: "I have never read any Cordwainer Smith. Ever. I never read any Al Reynolds until this week. I never read any Bruce Sterling. Or

Doc Smith. For many of my teenage years when I was doing my formative reading I didn't dare actually read SF, so I used to imagine it off the covers and blurbs" (personal communication, November, 2004).

For all its conceptual underpinnings of problematic identity and struggles for independence or existential meaning, Robson's novel is no improving homily but a New Space Opera ripping yarn. If her reinvention of numerous wheels does cause some grinding of the axles, some bald infodumping, it adds a certain freshly spun aroma to her saga of machined folks seeking Paradise Regained and finding...well, as usual, epiphany and transcendence, of a sort. Dispatched with Isol via Hypertube to the mystery planet's surface for eight days of study, Zephyr is warned that while the tube forms a continuous surface with our four familiar dimensions, "it is only a single Planck length in extent" (95). Crossing it, therefore, takes only ten to the minus forty-three seconds—to get anywhere. "Everything in transit, for that instant, no matter its size in our universe," becomes superposed, jammed together—the secret, perhaps, of Stuff. "Nice, nice, very nice," as Kurt Vonnegut chanted in *Cat's Cradle:* "So many different people, In the same device." That's an entanglement you could drive a mystical insight through, and Robson does, along with her complex tale of self-making and self-transcending in spaces outer and inner. Quite nice.

STEPH SWAINSTON: *THE YEAR OF OUR WAR*

And speaking of birdmen, a first novel by British writer, archaeologist and information scientist Steph Swainston won swift acclaim for her own reimagining of science fantasy. *The Year of Our War* is first of a sequence, followed by *No Present Like Time* and *The Modern World*, arguably in the vein of the New Weird, certainly with hints of M. John Harrison's mythic city Viriconium and other classic and recent loci of UK phantasmagoria. Her winged narrator Comet, or Jant Shira, is an hallucinogen-addicted Messenger for the immortal Emperor San of the island Fourlands in a war millennia old against human-sized malign Insects that ravage the land. War is confounded by internecine fury among rival immortals or wannabes, and by an alternative and somewhat comic surreality, the Shift or Epsilon, accessed by the drug cat. In Swainston's world, a sort of feudal-with-benefits Great War endlessly protracted, many of god's chillun got wings, some humans without and some, the Awians, winged but flightless. His mother from the disfavored Rhydanne clan, father Awian, Comet alone can fly, painfully, exultantly. Insects have built an immense Wall of fire-resistant "paper," slimed garbage and dead bodies stretching from one sea to the other; they pour forth from its protection like mindless lethal vermin. The familiar is suitably estranged, therefore, and the strange not just unleashed but made commonplace, part of the fun with sf and fantasy.

Can Comet be trusted to tell the truth? He holds guilty secrets. On behalf of the Castle of the fifty deathless Eszai he advises or perhaps commands mortal King Dunlin Rachiswater and his effete brother Staniel, helps protect the mortal Zascai from the Insects, carries the Emperor's diktat from the Castle, engages in the machinations personal and political that comprise so large a part of such novels. The year is 2015 (a blood-drenched Passendale-like battle was 90 years ago), and they use pounds as currency; the vile Insects therefore arrived around the time of Christianity, when in Fourlands history god died or went on retreat. Hmm. Quickly, one suspects that this is another holodeck world of virtual Tiers, an intensely vivid Matrix-like simulation that leaks at the edges when Comet shoots up his drug. That would be tedious, a hi-tech version of the most primitive narrative cop-out: "I woke up, and it had all been a dream." (John Clute had the same suspicion.)

Comet rapidly makes himself a regicide, although with the best of intentions. Having saved the King in a fit of mad bravery, while convinced of his own cowardice, he kills the agonizingly wounded and terminal human with an overdose of cat, his own gate-opening drug. Transported thus to the counter-city of Epsilon, with its dual suns, via the Shift, King Dunlin pursues a vigorous afterlife warring there against the Insects, whose home this pun-riddled realm seems to be. Perhaps the sleep of reason breeds monsters. Soon they are pouring through even faster into Fourlands, and threaten to plague worlds not yet infected. Oops. It certainly makes things tough for Comet and his associates in the remainder of this elegant, bloody, perversely sexy book, but he has his compensations:

> She trailed a moon shadow rapidly over the tiles of the Inner Ward; muscled, bone-thin and athletic...there's something essential in her, an animal's constant hunger. Genya is sex on a stick to me, just the stick to everyone else. (64)

On its British release in 2004, commentators noted at once that in tone and logic it is remarkably structured backwards, with shambly divagations and amusing or piquant asides. For all this knotted disarray, Swainston's is a powerfully compelling and expert vision, lifting with muscular grace into the airy blue, feathering its vanes for the long flight.

ROBERT CHARLES WILSON: *SPIN*

For some years, ambitious but quiet sf novels by American-Canadian Robert Charles Wilson have established him as one of the finest writers in the genre, his books at once as beautifully written and moving as many a mainstream work, yet impelled by well conceived sf speculations. Increasingly, these have taken a powerfully audacious cosmogonic turn, especially in his Aurora award-winning *Darwinia,* with its dizzying conceptual breakthroughs, *The Chronoliths* (Campbell Memorial Award in 2002), and *Spin* and its sequel *Axis,* with a third to come. As always with truly fine sf, we tussle with a disconnect between the small intimate scale of human lives, motives, joys and agonies, and the immensity of cosmos and deep time. Perhaps the wisest technical solution for an sf writer is to display the latter's grandeur and sublimity through the confusions and evasions of ordinary people faced with shocking insight and life changes.

A year or two from now, the sky goes utterly black. A dark shell has enclosed the entire globe, blotting out stars, Moon, infalling meteorites and luckless astronauts in orbit. Satellites fall from the sky in shreds. Yet the Sun also rises in its accustomed celestial clockwork. Or does it? The sunspots are gone. This solar disk, or rather its emulation, radiates like a dream of pre-Galilean Plato. Yet the tides sway in the lost Moon's embrace. Someone up there likes us enough to keep the planet's ecology ticking over. For what reason? Who are these Hypotheticals? The first glimmerings are not gained for several years. The gateway in the sky is permeable, it turns out, but the universe beyond is running faster than our daily round. A hundred million times faster. Or rather, the world's time has slowed, and the shield protects life from the storm of blue-shifted radiation outside.

It is as if the entire world were trapped in orbit at the event horizon of a black hole, its appalling gravity braking the planet's time in a demonic demonstration of relativity theory. But this terrifying anomaly is the tool of a science beyond anything we know. The media start calling it the Spin; everything customary, it seems, is spinning out of control (172). Beyond its opaque shroud, the entire universe spins like a crazy playground carousel. Cosmic time sleets through its hourglass. Within decades, by shroud time, the Sun is doomed to boom into red giant expansion, presumably obliterating the world. The galaxy itself will age and wane even as children like youthful Tyler, Jason and Diane (we meet them first in budding adolescence, as the stars go into hiding) grow up, fall in and out of love and power, human lifespan matched finally to the aging of the cosmos, or our corner of it.

It is a conceit that echoes Greg Egan's first sf novel *Quarantine*, but while Egan's was a dazzling noir exercise in quantum prestidigitation, Wilson's moves with a lovely melancholy through three decades of terror, accommodation, power ructions, Faustian ambition (Mars is seeded with life, which flourishes as we watch), dreadful insight, contained apotheosis. And all of this history is wrought small—or rather, at a meaningful, intuitive human scale—in the reflecting life of a handful of people, most of whom are neither the rulers of the world nor sf's frequent secret mutants destined to rule the sevagram (although Jason verges on both conditions).

Perhaps Canada's literary ambiance, poised as it is between a languid Commonwealth tradition and the hegemonic impact of its great boisterous southern neighbor, and perhaps by the curious flavorings from its Francophone regions, holds onto forms of writing, even in popular genres, that in the US have been replaced by a more headlong melodramatic brutality. It struck me that there was a sort of Evelyn Waugh or Anthony Powell elegiac quality suffusing *Spin*. That is not only found in Commonwealth writing, of course; there is also more than a touch of F. Scott Fitzgerald's *Gatsby* here. Tyler Dupree, a physician of modest gifts, writes much of this book in a graphomanic surge, driven by a healing virus that is making him more than human, in, predictably, a modest way.

Tyler's voice is placid, resigned, displaced from center yet with a deepening assurance of his own. He opens with words borrowed from his brilliant friend, the Odd Johnish Jason Lawton: "Everybody falls, and we all land somewhere" (9). This is more Maugham or the Waugh of *Brideshead Revisited* than, say, Kevin J. Anderson, David Brin or (that other Canadian sf success) Robert Sawyer. Indeed, during his harrowing, Tyler finds a batch of "swayback Somerset Maugham novels more tempting" (183) than a biography of his famous friend, with a measly five references to himself in the index. "We're as ephemeral as raindrops," Jason tells him, in a posthumous letter (344). When stoical, good-hearted, perhaps faintly Aspergerish Tyler falls, he picks himself up and trudges on to the end of the world, driven perhaps by his dogged, doggish, heart-breaking devotion to Jason's gifted sister Diane. She traps herself in despairing commitment to just the sort of mad fundamentalist dogma people fall into when the world seems to fail their heartfelt longings. We see it today in murderously militant Islam, and in the crusader resurgence of elements of Christianity that have echoed, in power and in powerlessness alike, its grieving bluster.

We guess at the outset that time will be the hero of this novel, for the opening chapter is headed "4×10^9 A.D.," four billion years hence—as far into the future, very nearly, as we are now from the accretion of our planet. How Tyler fetches up there with Diane, racked as he is with an alien disease in a drastically changed social order, comprises the curve of the tale, like an arch across the heavens, which alternates between this deep future where the sky is clear again, and the back story beginning in the second chapter titled, suitably, "The Big House." Tyler's mother is house-keeper to wealthy Carol and E. D. Lawton; E.D. is a ruthlessly Campbellian competent man whose aerostat company forges vastly profitable global communications links once GPS and commsats have been smashed by the Spin. Tyler's late father Marcus was once E. D.'s partner, but now the orphaned boy watches the world of his lost heritage from across the lawns to the Big House. Just so, of course, humankind watches the cosmos, small fry at the edge of an expanse crowded with godlike Hypotheticals who gradually come into some sort of numinous focus, perhaps more Gregory Benford than Arthur C. Clarke, as the entwined narrative threads strive toward maturation and completion.

Tyler, perhaps inevitably for this kind of role, seems a bit of a sap much of the time, tending his hopeless lifelong crush on Diane, duped (for the greatest good, naturally) by Lawton *père* and *fils* alike, witness to great doings, and even, amanuensis and handy factor to some of those pushing the levers of world historical change, playing his obliterated part. At the end, he has earned hope, and perhaps finds it. Wilson writes like an autumnal, melancholy angel. *Spin* was a finalist for the Campbell Memorial Award, and deservedly won a Hugo award in 2006.

CHRIS ROBERSON: *HERE, THERE, & EVERYWHERE*

In 2002, Texas writer and small press publisher Chris Roberson released a short novel, *Any Time at All*, through Clockwork Storybook, a writers' collective. That year, it seemed that Print on Demand technology was about to revolutionize genre publishing, making it feasible for unusual new work to find readers via the Internet and the mail, bypassing the lumbering dinosaurs in New York and the big bookselling chains with their ever-more restrictive policies and bestseller myopia. Bad luck. As Roberson notes, his small book was handsomely received by reviewers at *Asimov's* ("a blithe and giddy romp across the multiverse") and the online *Infinity Plus* ("highly enjoyable"), but managed only "extremely tepid sales."

Not content to let the book subside and die, Roberson expanded it by one-third and tried the mainstream publishers again. No luck. It was rejected, he tells us in an interesting endnote, as "not commercial" and "too smart." Luckily, Lou Anders liked the revision (by now called *Here, There, & Everywhere* and not just because that's where it had been), and it was one of the imprint's early offerings, Pyr's first "original" novel.

That is a frustrating history, and probably more common than we know; I have some intensely frustrating stories I could tell. Well, just one. Some years ago Penguin Books liked one of my novels quite well, but an editor suggested some improvements. These suggestions were extremely astute and welcome, so the book was rewritten and sent back. Six months of silence followed its enthusiastic reception. Where is the contract? Silence. That editor had long since moved on. Come on, people, isn't it about time I saw a contract? Oh, sorry—we've had a rethink. We don't do science fiction anymore. Bye now, and don't let the door hit you in the ass as you leave. That sort of thing is appallingly common. I suspect many interesting but quirky novels never have the good fortune to be saved by a newly empowered editorial director. Taking the PoD or e-download route, however, seems not yet to have attained escape velocity. (This might change as Kindle and similar hand-held e-reader technology improves and unit prices fall.) So one question we have to ask at once is whether the major traditional sf publishers *were* blindly wrong in rejecting Roberson's "giddy" and "enjoyable" novel? Frankly, I'm not sure.

As a fractious and alienated eleven year old, Roxanne Bonaventure receives from a dying old woman a bracelet allowing her passage back and forth along her own unique worldline, and sideways into any alternative history of the Myriad. That this is a closed circle tale—"By Her Bootstraps," so to speak—is never really in question, and the metaphysical nature of that closure does provide a transcendental, if by now routine, sf climax. Along the way to her death and beyond, Roxanne has more than her fair share of ripping good adventures, and of heartbreak and hard-won insight.

But *is* it hard-won? She is effortlessly competent, with martial arts skills we never see her acquire. Nothing even seems at stake, at the level of threat and action anyway, because her Sofia device shunts her away from hazard in slippery knight's moves. Roberson deploys a narrative device that makes it hard to take Roxanne's story seriously even during immersion in her tale. The very structure of the book tries to make us read it as a jest or *jeu d'esprit*: it is a faux fix-up or mosaic, a pretended gathering of stories independently published in magazines (as van Vogt's *The Voyage of the Space Beagle* actually was, half a century ago). This is an odd conceit—somewhat subverted by the fact that several segments in fact have been e-published separately, in Opi8.com and elsewhere—but it has the virtue of allowing Roberson to switch register now and then, from young adult to nineteenth century pulp mystery, from early Wellsian to adventures with Egyptologists and Nazis in the desert, from Beatles fancier tracking the lads through all the variant worlds to Kuttner-like confrontations at the end of time. Good trick, especially in these cross-genre days. But the conceit makes it hard to treat the book as a novel rather than a collection of novelty items.

Roberson *has* thought hard about the implication of travel in time and across the multiverse or Myriad. Surprisingly, given the number of writers who have explored this trope ahead of him, he comes up with some notions that seemed to me plausible and new. Whether they would convince a physicist is irrelevant; they are contributions to the long and entertaining conversation within the genre.

I was rather disheartened, though, by a sort of narrow tough-minded conservatism in his chart of the future. As Roxanne's father lies dying sometime soon, she goes ahead a decade or so, a century, two centuries, trying one medical cure after another. But you can't cheat death; he ups and dies each time, no matter how advanced the treatment. This might seem a satisfying moral to many readers, but really it is about as likely as learning that a time traveler treating septicemia with antibiotics in the tenth century is doomed to fail. The only sense one can make of this death-embracing fatalism is that some deliberate instrumentality, as in Cordwainer Smith's tales or Asimov's *The End of Eternity*, must be paralyzing change in the future, halting science in its tracks. This, though, is not Roberson's point. No, it seems that people in the future *just don't care*, rather as we today have not bothered going back to the Moon (214). It seems an oddly resigned and blinkered view, at a time when a small robot spacecraft has sent us data from the surface of Titan, as genomic research homes in on cures for what maims and kills us.

Perhaps this is to treat Roberson's light-hearted book too pompously. It is a frolic, after all. But it yearns to be more than that. I was reminded of the 1990s' BBC television series *Goodnight, Sweetheart*, about a bamboozled man shuffling back and forth between the present day and the Second World War. That comedy had a bitter-sweet edge that enriched and layered the jokes. Roxanne's tangled history gets there now and then. Yet her moral—"in the end, technology was simply a tool to allow people more easily to live the lives they would have led regardless"—seems highly doubtful, pretty much exactly the opposite of what such time-leaping abilities would truly demonstrate.

CORY DOCTOROW: *SOMEONE LEAVES TOWN, SOMEONE COMES TO TOWN*

Cory Doctorow's third novel (parts of it had been on-line for some years) blends ordinary technology, nerd tech, myth, horror, sheer astonishing silliness, and the Aspergerish quest of the outsider, into a demented nonstop juggling act that struck me as the 1950-ish Absurdism of Eugene Ionesco and Boris Vian melted into the heart-touching whimsy of Jonathan Carroll and Jonathan Lethem, steeped in the crazed fractured realities of the Goon Show. Perhaps US readers are unfamiliar with the Goons, a BBC series from the 1950s (Spike Milligan, Peter Sellers) that crunched its way through genres and grotesque voices the way *Monty Python* tried to do a decade later.

Sometimes it works, sometimes it doesn't. When it works it is laugh-out-loud funny, or engagingly affecting. When it doesn't, it is irritating as hell.

Alan comes to town to become a human, to find out how these creatures work, and finds himself compelled to help out, offer advice, butt in. He might have no navel, but he is a highly sympathetic invention. Less appealing is Doctorow's trick of changing his name, and those of his brothers, to alphabetical variants: Albert, Andy, Adam, Andrew. He has one nature but many names, as do his brothers (Billy, Benny, Brent, George, Greg, the polynomic rest). One of these is an island, in the water. Three more comprise a Russian doll, concentric brothers literally fitted together, "fat as housecats, with the same sense of grace and inertia in their swinging bellies and wobbling chins":

> Ed was working on his suspenders, then unbuttoning his shirt and dropping his pants, so that he stood in grimy jockeys with his slick, tight, hairy belly before Alan. He tipped himself over, and then Alan was face-to-face with Freddy, who was wearing a T-shirt and a pair of boxer shorts.... Freddy tipped

to one side and there was George, short and delicately formed and pale as a frozen french fry. (201)

Fans of hard sf might have some trouble swallowing this, but hey, lighten up. The boys' parents, after all, are a mountain (an actual green geographical rocky mountain) with a pool of crystal water at his heart, while their mother is a working washing machine mysteriously located in a cave. Golems made of mud provide the kids with rough country nourishment and later with flakes of gold that set them up for their lives in town. Alan's adventures as a small schoolboy, given this unusual childhood, are detailed and engaging. When his brother Danny comes on the scene, feral, sly, cruel—psychopathic, in a word—things start to get strange, especially after the others kill the monstrous pest and his decayed corpse sets out to avenge his death.

This history emerges slowly and with never a wink or smirk. Alan is an oddball, but his reality is established with novelistic expertise. Doctorow's writing chops are never in doubt, except for some info dumps about setting up a town-girdling WiFi network, and really there is no easy way to convey this stuff outside of pasting in an URL to boingboing.net. Dumpster diving for discarded electronics has rarely seemed so interesting. Negotiating with the local store owners and managers for placement access of their wireless boxen makes for a surprisingly gripping read. More: Alan's initiation into these geek activities anchors the insane fizzy fantasy of his Gothic background deep into urban reality, however far from Main Street that reality seems to most of us (although it will be meat and potatoes to plenty of Doctorow's blogger readers).

I invoked Jonathan Carroll in my list of predecessors, and his work comes closest in its blend of the gratifyingly annotated and the preposterous. Maybe Peter Straub's conscientious and literate horror is a close second. It is probably too early for Doctorow to have a voice so distinctive that such comparisons are unwarranted, but the particular blend of knowingness and wild absurd surrealism is surely his alone. *Down and Out in the Magic Kingdom* struck me as interesting for its promise, but a tad precious, and way too self-satisfied. This latest confection seems altogether more settled, if not without its jagged edges.

Alan's burgeoning relationship with a young woman next door, who starts trapped in a nasty dependency with a vicious, bigoted representative of *Homo sap.*, does unfold some genuinely new erotic feathering. "Mimi" (we never learn her real name, as we never stop learning his) is no less isolated than Alan, perhaps born somehow of electronics, at any rate singular, from childhood, in her possession of wings that her vile lover hacks off every three months with a knife. Here is Alan's sensuous encounter with these very female yet oddly phallic wings:

> They were leathery...covered in a downy fur that glowed where it was kissed by the few shafts of light piercing the gap in the drapes. He reached for the questing, almost prehensile tip.... It was muscular, like a strong finger, curling against his palm like a Masonic handshake.... They were as he imagined them, these wings, strong and primal and dark and spicy-smelling like an armpit after sex. (173)

So what kind of fiction is this, anyway? It is observant, following Alan through six exhaustive and sensuous months of sanding and repairing an old house then stocking it with old books and toys. The poignancy is never simply pointed: Alan and his brothers, children of a washing machine, never owned these sorts of timebinding possessions as they grew up attended by clay monsters. It is instructive, after the Tom Wolfe mode, taking us inside varieties of geek culture high and low. It is absurd in the existential mode, like *Catch-22*. But is it symbolic? Is it allegorical? How are we to read a child born of a mountain and a domestic appliance? As a Greek or Roman legend updated? As a displaced way of coming to terms with alienation, repressed creativity, the fear of corruption, the insolence of office? This might be an unavoidable temptation, but everything in the specialized training and apprenticeship of an sf and fantasy reader says: No! What's hidden inside the Russian doll is just another brother, smelling meaty and musty perhaps, but not a sermon.

We know how to deal with ordinary ghost stories, frighteners about rotting avengers from beyond the grave. Although most of us no longer *believe* in such nightmarish threats, we allow ourselves to sink into a deliciously creepy pretence of belief. You can't do that when Mom's a washing machine inseminated via her water inlet tube, worn out by endless cycles. You just have to gulp and clap your hands. I'm happy to applaud, anyway. But let us hope the market doesn't twist too far in this direction, or the new New Weird will become the New Kitsch quicker than you can say New Kitchen Sink.

MARY GENTLE: *A SUNDIAL IN A GRAVE: 1610*

When this wonderful novel came out from Gollancz in Britain in 2003, its title was *1610: A Sundial in a Grave*. I have no idea what this reversal signifies, unless it is a terror of names and dates among young Americans ill-schooled in history and mathematics. Both of these frightening topics are at the heart of Gentle's astonishing alternative history-that-isn't. By that year 1610, King James I, a Scot, had been placed on the throne of England following the death of childless Elizabeth. Protestant England faced down Catholic France and Spain. Decades of horrific religious warfare would shortly tear Europe to pieces. Prince Henry, James's adolescent heir, chafed. Empirical science was just starting to boil, often in the alembics of astrologers and alchemists.

One such, Robert Fludd, a propagandist for the perhaps non-existent order of the Rosy Cross, has learned from the martyred Giordano Bruno a mathematical Arcanum permitting indefinitely accurate forecasts of individuals and nations alike. (He can even calculate his way safely through a ferocious bout with the narrator, a premier swordsman.) In the tradition of Nostradamus, Fludd learns of planetary doom half a millennium hence—that is, perhaps a century from now—when an impacting comet will raze life from the Earth. To forestall this disaster, Fludd must rearrange the currents of time and fate to ensure the rise of a global scientific civilization competent to meet the threat. The cost will be nuclear devastation in many lands, not least Japan, the likely global imperium in Fludd's future, but at least the world will be spared. It is an awful predicament, an appalling moral choice. Fludd and his associates are pitiless in their efforts to shift the fulcrum and levers of power. Their key move is the assassination in 1610 of James, and his replacement by headstrong Henry.

In our history, James lived for another fifteen years, while young Henry died of typhoid, was replaced by his brother Charles, whose autocratic rule ended with his head chopped off, and the path to revolution in many nations laid down. If Gentle's novel were a typical alternative history romp, Fludd's plan would succeed, history would veer wildly, and Charles Dickens would be a starship captain. The impressive balancing act in this delightful tale maintains the path to our history, which, while hideous enough, turns out to be the least horrible vector into a survivable future.

But while *1610* begins with extracts from the ciphered journal of Dr. Fludd, the bulk of the book is drawn from the (allegedly) recently discovered and computer-enhanced fire-damaged pages of the memoir of a French spy, disgraced noble and adventurer, Valentin de Rochefort, the Duc de Sully's man and accidental killer of French King Henri IV. He and a goading associate, on the lam from Fludd and others, rescue a samurai in the service of a drowned ambassador from Nihon to the court of King James, and eventually find themselves in Japan unintentionally manipulating the Shogunate into withdrawing from all contact with the West. His unreliable memoir is (purportedly) rendered into idiomatic and fluent English by Ms. Gentle, who has a pair of relevant Master's degrees and is a swordsperson to boot. Previous attempts upon Rochefort's Memoir have been bowdlerized, she tells us, and famously filmed as *The Son of Sword and Hazard* by Richard Lester and others before him; versions starred Fritz Leiber, Sr., and Leo de Caprio, and Russell Crowe's, with Angelina Jolie, is due any day. The mention of Jolie's imaginary role in Gentle's "Translator's Foreword" is perhaps justification enough for a huge spoiler, but I'll restrain myself, although reviewers of the original UK edition declined to do so. (The US edition has been significantly rewritten by Gentle, clarifying some plot points and shortening an extract from a mock-Jacobean play.)

As this sword-and-astrology narrative arc began to emerge, I found myself musing—fully aware that the author might regard this cheesy summary as too glib and unfair for a thumbnail—that I was reading *The Three Musketeers Meets Shogun, plus Hari Seldon.* Then I found a five-year-old SF Site interview where Gentle herself described the plot as "*Shogun* meets *The Three Musketeers*—with some weird shit involved," and had to smile. I mentioned my conjecture to her; she commented: "I wouldn't have picked Hari Seldon, but of course you're right. Just another one of those SF things I read so long ago that the shape of it is embedded somewhere in the hindbrain. (And I absolutely will not speculate on whether there's a Second Foundation knocking around in the *1610* history somewhere...because that way Sequel lies...)" (personal communication, March, 2005)

If we regard Fludd's astrologically guided interventions as something like Asimov's psychohistory, we might expect to see his applecart upset by the emergence of a truly random, utterly unpredictable factor. To nobody's surprise but his and Rochefort's, just such a Mule soon arrives on the scene, a louche teenaged Billy the Kid aristo whose sword is mightier than erotically unsettled Rochefort's, and whose whims seem capable of disrupting Seldonish Fludd's terrifying but conditional accuracy. Behind and beyond the Mule, as readers of the Foundation sequence will recall, there is indeed a hermetic order of psychic manipulators: Asimov's Second

Foundation. So, too, here, no sequel required, although in Gentle's version it might be argued that these secret manipulators are simply the First Foundation conducted by other means. It is not altogether startling to find that Cardinal Richelieu, eventually secret master of France and King Louis XIII, is a player in this multi-generational conspiracy.

Entirely unlike Asimov's bland, cerebral adventures in imperial restoration, Gentle's is perversely erotic, playing with gender and desire in ways that should have excited the judges of the James Tiptree award. Rochefort is a large powerful man, whose quirk is an appetite for humiliation and punishment, and by a stroke of luck, almost like a relationship in a Samuel R. Delany novel, he finds himself tormented through 600 pages by his opposite number. It would be too coarse to describe this relationship as sadomasochistic; naughty games between tops and bottoms have been quite fashionable for some decades now. I suppose it could be argued that this is the armature of Fritz Leiber's Mouser-Fafhrd duo, which has its echo here. At any rate, even for those of us who lack this bent, Gentle's long drawn-out teasing of poor Rochefort and the ambiguous object of his desire makes its occasional electrifying spark.

Describing in detail the plot, characters, or historical setting of this charming, affecting escapade would be pointless at best, and at worst would ruin the reader's pleasure in watching the inevitable unfold inevitably and, inevitably, fall apart in inevitably unexpected ways that mimic the tormented interplay between chaos and necessity.

IAN R. MACLEOD: *THE HOUSE OF STORMS*

Here's Alice, in front of her mirror, about to enter Looking Glass land—yet she's also the Wicked Queen, asking her mirror who's the fairest of them all, ready to stamp her foot in rage and crush any upstart. Here's England divided down the middle, financial and judicial sophisticates to the right, rural and maritime toilers and thrusters to the left, Tweedledum and Tweedledee, eager to plunge into ruinous civil war. Here's the hothouse city boy, fatally ill, falling in love with the unschooled seashore girl, buoyantly healthy. Here's the great rotten trunk of authority mirrored by its own burgeoning but stifled seedlings. Here's the fruit falling not far from the tree, into the same loam that fed the tree, yet growing a-slant from heredity and nurture both. Or is it? Is the seed in the fruit determined by, and determining, all the long history of the tree and its blood-soaked soil?

These are archetypal oppositions, dichotomies, puzzles, reversals, storybook clichés meeting themselves like faces in a crazed mirror, unexpected yet inevitable, predictable as legend. The mood, of course, is melancholy. The telling is drawn-out, somber, steeped in long-shadowed afternoon light.

Ian MacLeod is a fine British writer of large ambition and copious talent. He has twice won the World Fantasy Award, two Asimov's polls, as well as the Sideways Award (twice), a Locus Poll award, and in 2009 the Arthur C. Clarke award. When Nick Gevers reviewed the British release of *The House of Storms* in 2005, he called it (justly) "unfailingly elegant, full of brilliantly realized English landscapes, deftly sensitive characterizations, luminously reworked fairy tales, and poetic elegies to lives and opportunities lost. ...*The House of Storms* is that uncommon thing, a sequel to be treasured as much as its precursor." That precursor was *The Light Ages* (2003), MacLeod's first venture into an elaborately realized alternative history separated from our own in the seventeenth-century with the discovery of "aether," a quasi-magical substance/ force/ quintessence that powers a botched industrial revolution as dreadful as our own, sustains cheap and shoddy workmanship (it puts lead, so to speak, or more exactly a kind of fairy gold, in your craftsman's pencil), permits localized control of the weather, useful for a sea-going culture—and damages its luckless handlers as if it were a diabolical blend of radioactivity and chemical mutagens.

Aether is at once a science fictional device—not unlike Walter Jon Williams' *plasm* or J. Gregory Keyes' Newtonian alchemy in the *Age of Unreason* sequence—and a ferocious figuration of the industrial process and its often inhuman side-consequences, its astonishing wealth, beauty, temptations, corrosive power. So this is not fantasy at all; it is not science, but it is assuredly science fiction. Probably the publishers don't want anybody to know this, given fantasy's current dominance in the marketplace. But I'm not sure how many habitual science fiction readers will be enthralled by the slow pace, *glacé* and glacial, of MacLeod's telling. "Darling," one character tells another two-thirds of the way through the book, "I can't wait for this to end" (283). Despite the abundant praise MacLeod's supple and inventive prose has won from critics, some readers might find themselves echoing that sentiment.

In the earlier book, a poor Northern boy narrates his rise through a Dickensian world of squalor, horror and unbreakable hierarchy. A century later, this quasi-sequel tells from several viewpoints the aching and rather too fairytale-like generational saga of the collapse of aether and the rise of electricity, the very force that in our world catalyzed versions of democracy and industrial totalitarianism alike, and the final triumph of mass consumerist culture. So *The House of Storms* is not Dickensian, but perhaps Wellsian, not Victorian so much as Edwardian, with all the nasty poverty, pollution, bigotry, suppressed class hatred that would burn through into the First World War, here enacting in small—rather as the Vietnam war performed its surrogate theatre between the US and the Soviet Union—a conflict between the great European powers, as a second English Civil War purportedly waged by the East against the West to end slavery in an underexploited Thule, our America. Inevitably, we read undertones of both the American War of Independence and its internecine War Between the States; inevitably, too, alas, perhaps a Monty Python tenor cannot be evaded. We have seen too much real horror on too large a scale to be greatly moved by a sort of backyard trench warfare, especially one where ignited dragons are pounded by artillery.

More troubling is the compressed allegorical weight borne by the principal characters. Great-grandmistress Alice Meynell is a beautiful wicked witch from the land of Grimms' fairytales, a sort of Mrs. Coulter (in Philip Pullman's *His Dark Materials* trilogy): conscienceless, ambitious, murderous, yet strangely devoted to her ailing son Ralph (whose name, I expect, is pronounced "Rafe"). Alice comes by ill fortune from the wrong side of the money mirror. Born Alice Bowdly-Smart to a wealthy couple, she is plunged after their perhaps accidental deaths into poverty, makes her way as a sort of upmarket whore to London, ruins a grandee of the powerful Guild of Electricians and marries another, connives, kills, steals; in short, she is a sort of Becky Sharp (in Thackeray's *Vanity Fair*) who never comes a cropper. Ralph is her weakness. She takes him west to the Guild's seaside mansion Invercombe, not far from the Bristol seaport, close, as well, to Einfell, where changelings huddle, poor detritus smashed by the touch of aether. Alice herself is addicted to the stuff, using its corrupting power to retain an unearthly beauty, learning an employment of the aether-entangled telephone mirrors that link the nation like magical wormholes and permit her access to a kind of cyberspace or psychic netherworld into which the spirit might be uploaded even as the body grows transparent as glass. Is this, then, another essay in steampunk, a version of Gibson's and Sterling's remarkable *Difference Engine?* (There are punch card "reckoning engines" here, too.) Not quite; at almost every point in his narrative arc, or beautifully wrought longeur-filled meander, MacLeod squibs it, ducks away, ducks his head, looks somewhere else. Yes, he is deliberately avoiding the vulgarly obvious, and thank heavens for that. But I cannot help thinking that the price is considerable.

In place of more conventional huggermugger, he gives us a diorama of Great Men and Women from the nineteenth and turn of the twentieth century. It is tempting to identify Ralph with a nascent Darwin, intent on finding in the Canaries (here, the Fortunate Isles) his own Galapagos. Together with the shoregirl Marion Price, with whom he falls radiantly in love, Ralph develops the theory of Habitual Adaptation. (Their bastard child, Klade, raised by uncanny changelings, is a sort of Caliban whose name, in our world, suggests a group of organisms with a single ancestor, as well as a new Adam made from clay.) While there are aspects of natural selection in the hypothesis, the term suggests more than little of Lamarck. What is clear is that Ralph's vile mother is the very embodiment of Social Darwinism, acting out a brutalized and simplified version of Darwin: nature red in tooth and claw.

This much is excellent; where the story seems to me to topple into unintended farce, ever so slowly and beautifully and elegiacally, is in Ralph's abrupt repositioning, after magical recovery perhaps induced by aether, as a soldier, and not just a soldier but a general, and not just any general but *the* general, once again coughing his bloody guts out at the front. Meanwhile Marion grows up to be not only a sort of Florence Nightingale (stop grinning, this is serious), but also an unwilling Joan of Arc. Neither of them paints the Sistine Chapel or invents the perfect soufflé, but there is a fatal taint of skiffy superman overkill in all this, perfectly appropriate in van Vogtian mythopaeia but absurd in fiction that aspires to the condition of Thomas Hardy or Cowper Powys or even John Fowles.

And yet...and yet...there are so many moments of powerful evocation of place and mood in *The House of Storms*, so much justified ferocity against the way things are, the way we live now. Forgive the overwrought aspects of the thing, and read it for the remarkable experience it manages to convey despite its worst angels. MacLeod has a large future, and we are lucky to have him here, on this side of the mirror.

VERNOR VINGE: *RAINBOWS END*

In 1899, when H. G. Wells sent his Sleeper into cataleptic trance for two centuries, he saw one advantage:

> "[C]ompound interest has a way of mounting up."

"It has," said Warming. "And now the gold supplies are running short there is a tendency towards... appreciation."

"I've felt that," said Isbister with a grimace. "But it makes it better for him."

"If he wakes." (*When the Sleeper Wakes,* 15)

When he does, he is owner of the world. It is a curious coincidence that one of the Sleeper's guardians is named "Warming." Aside from Wells's own time machine, cryonic suspension to temperatures very much colder than freezing would replace catalepsy as imagination's favored method (and Conceptoid) for carrying an observer of our time conveniently into the future, thus providing a handy point of view for scrutinizing tomorrow's shocking possibilities. In Fred Pohl's *The Age of the Pussyfoot* (1969), a contemporary is frozen for more than half a millennium, warmed, revived, healed of cancer, and paid his accumulated insurance policy: a quarter of a million dollars. "'I'm rich!' he yelled. 'And alive!'"

Of course, forty years later, that doesn't sound like such a windfall. Inflation gobbles up most of the benefits of modest compound interest, as Pohl pointed out sardonically. Besides, catalepsy and cryonics no longer seem especially vivid fictional devices. Vernor Vinge, in his extended sequel to the Hugo winning novella "Fast Times at Fairmont High," brilliantly solves the narrative problem, instead, by curing oldsters from our own time who have been lost for years or decades in the ruinous amnesia of Alzheimer's.

Robert Gu, aged Nobel laureate in literature and prize sadistic son of a bitch, returns rejuvenated from a condition nearly as lost as Wells' Sleeper, painfully reconstructing his soul in a San Diego of 2025 that is at once a wild science fictional jamboree and an extraordinarily detailed futurist extrapolation grounded in today's tech. Far from gloating over illusory wealth, Gu is forced to return to school, literally, while living as a snarling supplicant in the household of a son and daughter-in-law who despise him, getting up to speed in an accelerating future that seems well on the way to Vinge's great genre-warping postulate, the technological singularity. (The eeriest dislocation from our own world is that no one in 2025 seems to have heard of the imminent singularity, not even to dismiss it as twentieth century apocalypticism.)

Selecting an unlikable person as a key viewpoint character is a considerable risk, and asserting his sublime gifts as a poet only adds to the difficulty unless you are a genuinely brilliant writer yourself. Vinge is remarkable in many ways, but his *Analog*-honed style rarely rises above satisfactory competence. He skirts these problems and turns them to advantage by making Robert Gu's neurological recovery only partial. His poetry is lost, along with the piercing insight into human frailties that once powered and focused both verse and sadism. So we have some sympathy for him in his estrangement and his loss, and await his redemption through fire, which Vinge does not deny us.

But Gu *père* is not alone at the center of the novel. His son Bob, a Lieutenant Colonel in a frighteningly post-911 America, together with Bob's formidable intelligence operative wife Alice, and Bob's chubby mid-teen "Chinese ninja" daughter Miri, function fluently in this familiar yet alien sped-up world two decades hence. We participate in their daily activities, learning the vernacular and the technology without much authorial handholding. Robert Sr., now a retread in a school for the slow, bumbles his way into competence and then conspiracy in the company of other old farts and youthful differently-abled learners who are augmented up the wazoo, Googled and hotwired to a fare-thee-well, and hence each equivalent to genius by today's standards. This does not deter them from stupidities, adolescent insecurities, rebelliousness, cheating—but it makes such time-honored quirks fresh and illuminating. Lena, Robert's estranged and bitter wife, whom he supposes to have died, lives in nearby Rainbows End, an upmarket retirement village without an apostrophe, e-lurking upon his every dubious move.

Meanwhile, framing these domestic dramas and woven through them, mysterious and potentially appalling schemes are woven, manifested, detected, countered, redoubled. The globe in 2025 might seem to us a genuine utopia, yet it is, as one plotter muses, "a Red Queen's Race with extinction." There has not been a city lost in five years, but we have finally reached the stage where "Grand Terror technology was so cheap that cults and small criminal gangs could acquire it....There were a dozen research trends that could ultimately put world-killer weapons into the hands of anyone having a bad hair day." The European Union's Intelligence Board, drawing upon extravagant computational facilities perhaps a million times more powerful than we yet possess, detect the trial run of a monstrous weapon intended as "effective YGBM technology"—You-Gotta-Believe-Me, or mind control. (Akin, presumably, to the totalitarian mimetic plagues in sf novels by John Barnes, Ken MacLeod and Raphael Carter.) Among their number is a dogooding traitor whose scheme this is, and a mysterious third-party presenting as a sort of holographic Bugs Bunny cartoon, Mr. Rabbit. Is Rabbit a representative of China? Of some covert American agency? Of a criminal gang? Is he perhaps an emergent artificial intelligence, prelude to a Vingean singularity? Or something stranger still, a hive mind of up-lifted lab animals? This innovative and amusing entity is the thread running through the center of a novel of tension, apprehension and dissension, but I am bound to say, to my chagrin and perhaps to my shame, that his identity never became clear to me. Maybe the thread of tension will be drawn through into a sequel. (I asked Dr. Vinge, but he was not giving anything away.)

Probably it doesn't matter. This ambiguous and desperately un-stable—or rather, metastable—utopia is displayed in a bravura blend of the everyday, homework, household stresses and all, and the melodramatic, deployed with rigorous attention to detail and ex-travagant set pieces. It is arguable that this is the most impressively conceived and mounted invention of the future that science fiction has yet seen, the most densely realized, a kind of early twenty-first century version of Hal Clement's *Mission of Gravity*. That 1953 *Astounding Science Fiction* serial is often regarded as the representa-tional high water mark of a profoundly alien but lived-in world and its inhabitants. Half a century later, Vinge brings the same scrupu-lous attention to our own planet, less than a generation hence but as remote from our time as we are from the Victorian era. Consider this show-and-tell event arranged for the assembled parents, staff and fellow students at Fairmont High by a couple of the less gifted stu-dents:

> They had some kind of wacky suspension bridge...that put down steel caissons on each side of the bleachers, and then climbed higher and higher into the north-east until it broke into the departing daylight. Seconds passed—and the construction re-appeared out of the *southwest*, their 19th-century masterpiece making a virtual orbit of the Earth. The climax was the roaring passage of vast, steam-powered trains across the sky. The bleachers shook with the apparent power of the locomotives. (335)

It is a three-dimensional collage of VR imagery piped directly into the onlookers' augmented senses plus manipulation of "intelli-gent" buildings responsive to tectonic shocks (the old UCSD cam-pus having suffered devastating earthquake damage in our own near future). Yet the A grade student mark does not go to such flamboy-ant showiness, but to a subtle and lucrative piece of practical water-filtration engineering. Meanwhile, the UCSD Geisel Library holdings have been brutally shredded and digitized, on the model of shotgun genomics, provoking lurid demonstrations, the 1960s' campus revolt revisited as Super Mario Brothers.

Above and beyond, or beneath and everywhere, 2025's world is multiple, overlapping, interpenetrated by filiations derived from today's and yesterday's board and computer games. Very little is truly as it seems. Landscape is cloaked by beautified or grandiose *faux* structures and gardens (a notion foreshadowed in Delany's *Stars in my Pocket Like Grains of Sand* [1984] and my own *The White Abacus*). People and machines are reconfigured as animals and gaming figures, all of them engaged with each another—parallel to their humdrum lives—in vast contests, some proprietary to Spielberg-Rowling, or Pratchett, others apparently open source. It is a plausible extension of today's massively multiplayer online role-playing, Wi-fi-melded with CGI and more intimate simulation platforms. Vinge projects a world of *Homo ludens*, surprisingly believable but disturbing even for habitués of Niven, Iain M. Banks, Tad Williams, or Rowling and Pratchett themselves.

Despite everything I have revealed about some of the characters and their settings, this discussion has steered clear of the plot dynamics driving the story (although I must note, recalling *Marooned in Realtime*, that Vinge does like to immerse his characters in lava). Charles Brown found the book "a bit clunky," perhaps in reaction to the numerous elements clomping simultaneously toward an uncertain outcome. It is an understandable assessment, but for all that Vinge's novel is a remarkable achievement on more levels than one. (It is packed with little insider jokes, too; in cryptography, "Alice" and "Bob" are sender and receiver in a covert communication; "Eve" is the classic eavesdropper, and she pops up too.) Like Robert Gu, Sr., the book is not especially likeable in the beginning. But it is well worth persevering with, because Vinge has brilliantly created a rich pocket universe within which we, too, might be living in the foreseeable future.

JOHN MEANEY
PARADOX: BOOK ONE OF THE NULAPEIRON SEQUENCE
CONTEXT: BOOK TWO OF THE NULAPEIRON SEQUENCE
RESOLUTION: BOOK THREE OF THE NULAPEIRON SEQUENCE

When Samuel Delany was nineteen, he set out to write an SF trilogy, something fairly rare in the early 1960s. He had it finished and in print, clunky and poetic by turns, by the time he was twenty-two. The final volume's afterword opens with a disarming and pungent quote from Oscar Wilde: "Anyone can write a three-volume novel. All it takes is a complete ignorance of Art and Life."

Delany and his poet wife had confronted an ambitious question: "'All right, what would *you* put into a novel, I mean a real honest to goodness novel?' The answers came thick and popping: social scope, characterizations, scenes, ideas, experiences we had not read yet but would like to have read." Similar answers must have crowded British writer John Meaney's mind as he planned this elaborate world-building, idea-crammed trilogy, only his second book and destined to run a daunting 1,500 pages (the trilogy must be regarded as one long novel, even though Meaney asserts against the evidence that each can stand on its own feet). Granted, there is less than the usual number of words per page, but the trilogy must be nearly half a million words in length. In an epoch allegedly dominated by slam cuts, instant messaging, twittering tweets and shrunken attention span, this is ambition indeed. But Wilde's minatory diagnosis looms above such purpose like a bird of ill omen.

Meaney comes attended, it is true, by good omens. Stephen Baxter declared that his work has "rewired SF. Everything is different now." He had praise from Connie Willis, Paul Di Filippo and Ian Watson. *The Times* dubbed him "the first important new sf writer of the 21st century." Strangely enough, though, none of the major American publishers were tempted to pick up these books published to such acclaim in Britain. This need not be the warning signal it seems, since as we have seen quite a few astonishing UK writers have been left languishing for years—or, rather, American readers have been deprived of their work for no apparent reason.

In the event, Meaney was picked up by Lou Anders at Pyr, an enthusiastic reader of Meaney's work from the outset; he did a revealing online interview in 2002. Was this, Anders asked, part of the New Space Opera/New Weird "Next Wave" of British science fiction? Meaney didn't hold back: "The Brits kick ass! China Miéville is the Vin Diesel of fantasy. Al Reynolds puts the rock into space opera. We're wild, and we're going for it. None of that post-Imperial angst nonsense. I don't know where the dark explosive energy comes from, but we are the Starbucks generation, with a hyper-caffeinated Zeitgeist." This might sound like the brash posturing of a teenager, but Meaney was already thirty years older than that. Maybe it is the grueling martial arts training. His web site makes a point of his capacity to do the splits, Van Damme-like, across two chairs: "Always an ice-breaker at parties! Or conventions."

But never mind the length of the trilogy, and supple conditioning of the writer, what about the quality? The *Nulapeiron Sequence* is palpably modeled on Frank Herbert's *Dune*, but rather as if *Dune* and its sequels had been written by Dickens, Dumas, van Vogt, and Vargo Statten. Much has been made of Meaney's supposedly imagistic writing; here is a grisly example:

> "Eemur? Can you bring me b—?"
> The metallic ceiling hinged open, extended black and copper claws, and reached down.
> **Run, Tom.**
> He lunged to his feet.
> **Run fast.**
> Blades snicked behind him. (*Resolution,* 27)

Here's another:

> Blue flame.
> *Shouldn't be happening.*
> A distinct barrier, invisible.
> *Not yet...*
> Pushing through.
> Burning, against his chest.
> *I don't have a crystal.* (*Paradox,* 477)

You start to see that there are not really as many words as you might expect in these fat volumes. Luckily, the texture of the novels is not all like that, by any means. Sometimes it is like this:

> **Blood-snow in the golden sea.**
> Multifractal cellular automata.
> Shimmer and coalesce: patterns form as they learn from him and he adapts; the system's matrix-factorisation maps eigen-functions from Tom's brain to mu-space processor-architecture; gestalten-integration solitons pulse between continua. (*Paradox,* 284)

Meaney's syntax sometimes gets lost in mu-space. He thinks "span" is the past tense of "spin", or perhaps this is an attempt to capture the vernacular of the world of the thirty-fifth century. As is the increasingly irritating and ubiquitous particle "lev-", rather like "ato-" or "syn-" in 1940s SF, which you can attach to almost anything, lev-cups, lev-bikes, lev-silk, levanquins, and even a useful medication called "lev-gel":

Her robe dropped away. Revealed, she was white-skinned and almost gaunt: areoles [sic; I hope areolas is meant, rather than spines] prominent on small cupped breasts. Cascading black hair [location unspecified].
The treatment. It's another reaction...
Ice and fire.
Hallucinating? But I saw—
There was a vial of scented lev-gel, and she smeared it on, slowly, across Tom's bare torso....
(*Context,* 20)

But by this point, I must admit I was in fits of laughter, wondering if lev-gel could really be the Viagra of the thirty-fifth century. Unfortunately not, it just made them float up into the air, "entwined, combined, as though their very cells would merge. Drifting, pulsing, until Tom's entire being burst in silver crescendo and flowed outwards eternally, forever" (21).

At that stage, I was already 500 pages in. On page 144 of the first volume, a character had cried out, "I can't do this," and already I had known exactly how she felt. After a full thousand pages, I was weak and weepy, and wanted to go home. Dutifully, though, I started the third volume, *Resolution,* until my resolution failed me. The instant I decided to stop reading these books that were rewiring science-fiction, I felt the kind of relief you usually attain only by the application of lev-gel. But here is the strange thing—having decided to throw in the towel, I found myself sneaking back to the final volume, reopening it, trying another page or two, then another chapter, drawn on to the end, forcing myself past Meaney's "femto-tech" (literally, a million times smaller than molecular nanotechnology,) for building "femtocytic networks" in Tom's brain. It is wonderfully inappropriate in its sheer wrongness of scale, the scale of subatomic particles or degenerate matter. Meaney has a degree in physics and computing, so it is hard to believe that this is a simple mistake of the sort exemplified by his belief that "beg the question" means "put the question," rather than "evade the question."

You are wondering about the story. It goes on and on, starting with young Tom Corcorigan and his parents in the mean lower depths of the entirely underground cultures of Nulapeiron, his father an artisan working metal with a gamma-ray laser (although this culture has had nanotechnology compilers for at least a millennium, which makes rather unlikely the poverty and servitude of its lower classes, ruled with heedless cruelty by the rich Logic Lords of the upper strata), his mother a doomed but beautiful drug addict and dancer soon stolen away by a perverse precog Oracle who also sort of kills his dad. Tom is thus set upon his *Bildungsroman*, obsessed by the kind of fury for vengeance that drives Conan, Gully Foyle and other classic heroes, salvaged from poverty when his keen wits are noticed, but quickly mutilated—an arm lopped off—for a crime he did not commit. By sheer grit, innate brilliance, determination, logotropes, and mysterious helpers including a skinned but living severed head, he himself rises to the station of Lord, murders the Oracle, falls in love with a beautiful unsuitable woman and then with a warrior princess who dies, sort of, learns the secret of phi2dao and other forms of martial artistry, not to mention one finger chin-ups, ventures through fungus-glowing caverns measureless to man, joins a monastic order charmingly devoted to marathon running as their devotion, breaks free of their mind-trap, falls off the wagon for several lost years with the bottle, makes a series of inspiring comebacks, travels quite thrillingly inside genetically engineered battle spiders, exits into the terrifying openness of the planetary surface *and beyond*, and ends up as Warlord of Mars, sort of, but that's not the end, of course, because the paradox of his world and its bitter contextual history (Let my people go!) requires a more bracing resolution, however implausible.

The name of this underworld planet is finally unpacked in the third book, when Tom learns that "Apeiron" refers to the unbounded fractal root systems of plants. Oddly, this would appear to be a false elucidation. Anaximander proposed in the sixth century BC that the substrate of the universe is a primal chaos of opposites, the apeiron. It is surely no accident that the favorite curse of Tom and his colleagues is "Chaos!", when it isn't "Fate!" (Tom's loss of one arm, his one handedness, is perhaps an emblem of broken symmetry or, deeper, perhaps of the profound subatomic asymmetry emblematized by what he drolly refers to as the *kaon-koan*.) In a world of perverse Oracles, who know the veridical future and are thus trapped by their own truecasts, Fate has a terrifying definitiveness to it. It is Tom's achievement as warrior logosopher to see that mu-space, the infinite-dimensioned fractal Ur-cosmos underlying ours, permits a breach in Fate through which one can drive a revolution, not to mention driving away a beastly puppet-master world-devouring Anomaly. In a truly fractal and multiply- connected hyperspace, it turns out, Gödel's theorem loses its bite. Mathematics can at last be made perfect and complete, its contextual paradoxes transcended. It is a nice piece of prestidigitation, Meaney's cleverest move, but I am not sure that he gets much more mileage out of it than if he had posited a Genie with the power to grant any wish that you have the wit to ask for.

Threaded through Tom's saga, one book apiece, are three historical narratives, provided to him in a data-crystal by a murdered Pilot, an almost mythical personage with solid black eyes and the ability to negotiate mu-space without going insane. The first is the foundational tale of Karyn McNamara, early mu-space pilot and ace martial artist (a nested story cut into the narrative, and none the worse for that). The second follows her daughter, Dorothy or Ro, born in mu-space and hence, by a kind of Lamarckian hotwiring, peculiarly adapted to its alien rigors. The climactic volume's intra-tale desultorily pursues her twin sons, who speak in consecutive overlap like Huey and Dewey, and goof about with their brilliant lesbian friend Deirdre at a sort of Top Guns school for natural born mu-space Pilots (now with a Cap-P), and it's all fun and games until bigoted rioters lose lots and lots of eyes, sizzling in their heads after a mob attack against the apparently defenseless Pilots, but really people should know better than to poke xeno mutants with a stick. Brother Dirk escapes finally to a sort of infinite Hilbert hotel, the Pilot redoubt, while brother Kian, savagely mutilated and hence himself a sort of embodied Kian-koan for Tom 1,300 years later, grows towards sainthood. This tripartite back story works fairly well, breaking off in a suitably mythological cloud of unknowing.

The main epic, meanwhile, is enormously brocaded, elaborated, replete with ingenious if strangely familiar variations on exotic aristocracy, suffering underlings, mass minds good and ill, gods in hyperspace, mysterious Arcana. For readers who can tolerate the manga-meets-*X-Men* style in which it is notated, it will provide just the kind of hours of fun that Doc Smith offered their great-grandparents. There is no doubt that Meaney is talented. I just hope next time he discovers how to run his sentences and paragraphs together, or alternatively finds somebody to sketch the Grand Guignol 'toons he left out of his very long comic book.

KEN MACLEOD: *LEARNING THE WORLD: A SCIENTIFIC ROMANCE.*

It is always fun to read a romance featuring smart alien space bats, especially when it is also the coming-of-age tale of a feisty young woman on a generation starship crewed by immortals.

Learning the World is perhaps Ken MacLeod's most frolicsome novel to date. Most of his previous books possessed an unusual flavor, at least by the standards of American science fiction; his worlds and characters were often ferociously socialist, more in-your-face so, perhaps, than the slyly relaxed if lethal bonhomie of the post-scarcity Culture universe developed by his friend and fellow Scotsman Iain M. Banks. The setting has a powerfully communitarian taste to it, but several references to the basic Ricardian economic principle known as "the law of association" or "comparative advantage" point in a different direction. The people of the starship *But the Sky, My Lady! The Sky!* are romantic Austrian-school libertarians, possibly even anarcho-capitalists of an extropian tendency. Meanwhile, the more or less late nineteenth-century space bats of the alien world Ground evince a certain avian if combative collectivity, birds of a feather flocking together.

We are 14,000 years into a future calendar restarted with the settlement of the Moon, apparently after some sort of singularity catastrophe on our planet of origin. "Full burn" or "exponential evolution" is, we learn, the risk any high-technology society faces, plunging a culture up a raging spike of uncontrollable scientific advances that seem literally to burn them out. More modest human societies fling their seed outward in great starships driven by—a typical and wonderful MacLeod throwaway conceit—cosmogonic engines that inflate whole new universes and suck off an infinitesimal fraction of their energy for propulsion, leaving a trail of godlike creative exhaust behind them.

"Learning the World" is the *biolog* of adolescent Atomic Discourse Gale, who does learn it. But the phrase has more resonance than an acknowledgement that this book is in part a *Bildungsroman.* Starfaring humans have had reason for millennia to believe that they are the only intelligent beings in the entire cosmos. Now, the starship finds a world populated by winged beings surprisingly close to, if appealingly different from, men and women (many of whom, in turn, have now adapted quite happily to freefall and can teach themselves only with some difficulty to walk). As our blogger says:

> The most important question is this: what does the existence of other intelligent life tell us about the kind of universe we are in?
>
> ...Today we are in a universe that contains us and lots of cool stuff *and alien space bats.*
>
> That's a different universe.
>
> A universe with a different history, different potentialities, different future from the universe we thought we lived in. We are not living in the universe we thought we lived in yesterday.

> We have to start learning the world all over
> again. (100)

And how do they do that?

> ...we'll only find out by discovering more facts, not
> speculating, no matter how logical that speculation
> might seem. The way to learn the world is to *look at
> the world.* (134)

The shock is far greater, of course, for the people of Ground,
which is also, one might suppose, Sky, since they are equally at
home in either dimension. The clever astronomer/aeronautics engineer Darvin (less Darwin than Herschel or Orville Wright) looks
hard at the world, at the greater celestial cosmos beyond the world,
and is driven past mere observation into theory; that is, into deeper
science. His mentor Orro, the eccentric genius and exiled
Gevorkian—rhymes, no doubt, with "Kevorkian"—teaches that:

> "For a student, life is simple. Study. Make love.
> Eat and drink. Learn. And what you learn...is what is
> *known*.... Now for us scientists, on the other wing,
> life is not quite so simple. Because we learn the *un-
> known*." (57)

That is the joy at the heart of good science fiction, especially
when learning the unknown opens a rusted gateway into what Peter
Nicholls has dubbed "conceptual breakthrough," the driving ambition of classic sf. MacLeod provides a series of charming and sometimes breathtaking conceptual breakthroughs inside his entwined
double narrative. We follow prickly young Atomic, her friends and
lovers, through the rapids of adolescent rebellion or clingy complacency. These rites of passage are interestingly skewed in a world
where minds are linked by machine telepathy, where the very
ground beneath your feet is a spinning drum never at rest, always
plunging farther into space, with the stars at its stern glowing green
with the Dyson sphere bubbles of colonizing human life that surround them, where governance is mediated by the market.

Careful observation is one thing, but understanding is something greater. When Darvin in a fit of brilliance utilizes a discarded
propeller from the engine nacelle of a dirigible, it is revealingly and
touchingly characteristic of a batlike species that he uses it to build a
wind tunnel instead of inventing heavier than air flying machines.

Why a wind tunnel? The better to film and analyze the flapping of a flyer's wings (as, in our own history, Eadweard Muybridge filmed figures running in place) in hope of building a chiropter. Darvin, in his day job, seeks an outermost planet in his solar system, but his photographic blink comparator yields up something else entirely—an intruder from deep space, an incoming starship that threatens the stability of his entire planet's political and ethical balance. Meanwhile, moieties and contesting generational groupings aboard the starship boil up in a conflict that threatens to tear the vessel literally apart.

Understanding is always to some extent socially situated, as is the world we learn. For a fabulist of Marxist tendency, like MacLeod, this insight is self-evident. Denying it is, in effect, what vitiates all too many comfort-food sf tales of nineteenth-century imperial derring-do between the stars. Then again, there are limits to how much conceptual derangement we readers can handle—and most sf *is* purchased for its consumer pleasures. This makes MacLeod's astringency all the more admirable, artistically, but I suspect his efforts to balance that shock of the new with some of the pleasures of the accustomed occasionally lead him astray. The adults of the starship manifest themselves instantly to each other, mediated by virtual reality systems hardwired into them at the genetic level—and yet at pulse-racing moments we see them flipping switches like any dope on board the first starship *Enterprise.* The narrative decision to treat the space bats as if they were just folks next door is admirably counter-xenophobic, and provides some amusing jolts, but it is also a cheat, like Vernor Vinge's spider just-folks in *A Deepness in the Sky.* Arguably, this anthropic kindred-under-the-skin thematics is exactly what MacLeod wishes to teach us about a universe where the Fermi Paradox has been abruptly and unexpectedly exploded, despite all the probabilistic explanations of why humans are unique in the cosmos. Still, for all the charm it imparts, this implausibly cozy perspective undermines the deepest power this blazingly intelligent novel could have wielded.

GARY GIBSON: *AGAINST GRAVITY*

Every reader who has tried writing a novel (with the exception of the late Isaac Asimov) will recognize with a smile, at once grim and delighted, exactly what Scottish freelance graphic artist and writer Gary Gibson captures in the name of his blog: *White Screen of Despair.*

As he announced at its outset, in December 2002, if the celebrated Blue Screen of Death signifies that your computer has crashed, the White Screen of Despair is when your soul has crashed, waiting at the keyboard for inspiration. Hemingway sharpened his pencils, but you can't do that with computer keys. A better way is to warm yourself up to the impossible task by typing random Lewis Carroll gibberish, or endless plot and character notes on a novel that seems to recede like the tide, or heart-rending private diary entries. Or, in the day of the blog, all of the above, disseminated instantly to the worldwide blogosphere—where probably nobody at all is listening, or just maybe the whole world is watching. Not only does this Pilates method get the muscles moving, but if you are charming or outrageous enough, it's a dead cheap method for captivating potential readers of your unwritten book, PR for nothing and fun for free. As long as you don't let yourself get trapped in the work-evading fun, and leave the novel fermenting into vinegar.

Glaswegian Gibson's interesting achievement, provoked by Rudy Rucker's equivalent logs as he wrote several recent books, is to convey a likeable personality starting, in Gibson's case, pretty much at the bottom of the pecking order and catapulted through his own wit and efforts into startling success, with three novels published by the British arm of US science-fiction giant Tor Books and widely praised.

Reading through his apparently unedited blog is probably something every would-be writer needs to do, starting with his early statement of the theme of what was then very inchoate book that would become *Against Gravity*:

> Something about an architect building an orbital colony after some global war in order to provide a way in which the human race might continue if things got any worse. Then a deeper theme occurred to me. Posthumanism is the idea that given appropriate technology, people might change in such ways that they might no longer be what we understand as human. So there's a possible theme there; on one hand, some people want to create a society where they can escape the madness of Earth, but unfortunately, since they're human too, then by definition they take the madness with them. And on the other hand, representing a separate point of view, are posthumans, who by virtue of effectively ceasing to be human, may escape the drives and desires that bring about

most of our failings. In other words, they represent an argument which goes like this; the only way humanity can improve itself in the ways it has dreamed of in utopian ideals, is by giving up those very things which make us human (as we understand the term) in the first place.

By the time the novel had made its way through some six revisions, all of them detailed in his informal history, the orbital O'Neil colony has withdrawn from the focal point of the novel to become an unattainable and probably toxic mystery, where machine minds apparently frolic or seethe, building a time gate to the end of universal evolution and the Tiplerian Omega Point god they expect to find there. The transcendental promise of super-intelligent machines familiar by now from so many singularity tales is poisoned by contagion from a demented human mind, the pure snake ruined by the apple of the tree of knowledge and mad passion. So it is another Frankenstein story, in its way. Utopia is blighted, because, as the blog informs us, "You can put people in a perfect society, but you can't make the *people* perfect."

Not that the people of some ninety years hence inhabit anything remotely akin to a perfect society. The world has been racked by several small nuclear exchanges in the East, and by crop-mutating viruses in the West, turning much of North America into a wasteland. Kendrick Gallmon, an investigative journalist in Edinburgh, is infused with nanites that are working dreadful Augmentations upon his flesh and nervous system. One side-effect of this imposed modification seems to be hallucinations of a dead friend, hard to dismiss because they contain unexpected and useful information. Another side-effect, remarked in the opening sentence, is the Kendrick's heart stops beating without this affront doing him any harm; later, he gives up breathing as well when it seems opportune. In short, he has been turned into a kind of cyborg, as have many of his fellow victims, complete with the sorts of metallic cables growing from his limbs and excrescences coating his skin that we have seen rather too often as special effects, from *The Fly* to *The Outer Limit* reruns. Alfred Bester patented this trope half a century ago in *The Stars My Destination*, and Keith Laumer repeated it ten years later in *A Plague of Demons*, so successfully that it is hard to get much mileage from it any longer—or would be, if so many sf readers were not victims of generic forgetfulness.

An irritation in the typical blog format is the way each entry appears *above* the previous one, so that tracing Gibson's line of development forces you to pull up a month's entries, scroll to the end, scroll up page by page to the start of the first entry, plod back up again to the second entry, and so on until you finally reach the start, and then you can go back and find a subsequent month and do it all over again. Eerily, the novel itself reflects something of this absurd structure, with a more or less continuous narrative broken and contorted by micro flashbacks justified only by the need to delay some revelation, and that in turn interrupted by major flashbacks to Kendrick's incarceration as a "Labrat" eight years earlier in the Maze, a generic and murky secret laboratory/bunker hell out of a hundred lurid gothic horror comics.

Kendrick is driven, in a rather muffled way, by motives ranging from concern over the fate of his former lover, who hates him because he killed her brother (in self-defense, but there you are), bafflement about the ghost and the tiny winged pests with the dead brother's face, various hard types hurting, tricking and betraying him, and the need to claw his way up to orbit to learn what in heaven's name is going on up there, where they seem to have the secret of zero point energy and the Bright are building their stairway to eternity. Is this space opera? No. "I did space opera with *Angel Stations.* Lots of running about, shooting, and blowing up things. I did slightly less running about, shooting and blowing up things with *Against Gravity*, which wasn't really a space opera at all, and was meant to be more 'serious' (stop laughing at the back, there)."

Serious is as serious does. Gibson is terse in his blog about the literary failings of classic science-fiction: "I made the horrible mistake of pulling some childhood favorites from the shelf in a fit of nostalgia...re-reading...Alfred Bester.... Horrible mistake. Horrible, horrible mistake. Book goes back on shelf. Have I learned my lesson? Do I turn away from the execrable fiction of yore? Do I hell? Next down is *The Best of AE Van Vogt*, with one of those Seventies paperback covers that screams second hand bookshop at you. Got halfway through 'Weapon Shop' before doing everything but bouncing it into the wastebasket." He favors Lucius Shepard, and indeed *Against Gravity* does seem a by-blow of *Life During Wartime*. Is his writing up to it? Here are the second and fourth sentences from the opening chapter:

> The pain crashed down on him suddenly and he sagged, unable to prevent his legs crumbling at the knees.... He vomited noisily, bright agony rushing through his every nerve ending, like wildfire surging to attend a tinder-dry forest. (1)

Late in the novel, this lurid journalistic style has not improved (but then, of course, journalists usually do write foul fiction): "Searing pain shot into his brain while bullets continued to zip through the air just inches above his head....Through a haze of agony he became aware of the corpse lying several feet away from him, its head and shoulders reduced to a crimson pulp" (335). That is the problem. Gibson's ambition is evident. "The fiction I favored the most as a kid was the relatively hard stuff (as well as, yes, Dick and Bester and Ellison and Moorcock and Ballard, and all the new wavers and experimentalists). Sometimes the quality of the prose got sacrificed along the way...." Well, yes. The strenuous effort he records his blog is admirable. But finally, too much of his text is pulp, crimson and otherwise, as with a great deal of science fiction, in this century no less than in the twentieth. Happily, that is changing, although in many cases the improvement tends to go hand in hand with a slipstream slide into surrealism or frank fantasy, as with the notable work of skilled writers as dissimilar as China Miéville, Kelly Link, Jeffrey Ford, Kage Baker, Jeff VanderMeer, Lois McMaster Bujold, and John Wright, to whom we now turn.

JOHN C. WRIGHT
THE LAST GUARDIAN OF EVERNESS
MISTS OF EVERNESS
ORPHANS OF CHAOS
THE FUGITIVES OF CHAOS
TITANS OF CHAOS
NULL-A CONTINUUM

John Wright burst into notice with the outstandingly well-received *Golden Age* space opera "trilogy" (a single novel split by his publisher, Tor, into three standard-sized volumes). When he followed it with a fantasy diptych, or perhaps severed single volume, I speculated that he had chosen to move to lusher cash-crop fields. It seemed that his voice had gained authority and variety in his second large novel. Mr. Wright smiled merrily at this notion. Actually the Everness fantasy was written first but had failed to find publication prior to Wright's success with the tale of Phaeton and his really enormous spaceship.

In the land of formula, casuistry and guile are premier defenses against tedium. For formula fantasy—the relentless iteration of the already-read and doted-upon—formula itself, turned back in irony or parody or mocking sport, becomes a weapon of choice in the quest for novelty. It can seek redemption in advance (like a purchased in-dulgence) for the sin of endless return. So for one gang of creepy comic badduns in Wright's fantasy duology, the piratical rule is: "All are innocent when no evidence can be trusted." Masked in flayed human pelts, these seal-selkie pirates are awash in drowned identities, none certain of his own name or station, an absurdist cir-cumstance that plays beautifully into an artful rescue toward the end of this first compulsive half of *The War of the Dreaming.*

Wright's awareness of the twice-told, many-told armature of his revisionist fantasy is keen and undisguised. In one hilarious *faux*-bumbling page and a half aria, his initial hero Galen Waylock tries to explain the situation to a *naif:*

> Now, the Emperor of Night sent ambassadors to the nine races of the nine worlds, including the selkie of Heather Blether...no, wait. You don't need to know that. Um...the Regent of the Sun, Belphanes, at Oberon's command, sent the unicorn as his messen-ger to the King of the Logres. Eurynome the Unicorn established the Rule of the Order of Everness, and opened the gate between Pai's and Morpheus' realm, the realm of nature and the realm of dream. Mor-pheus...well, never mind who he is. (*The Last Guardian of Everness,* 67)

"You're not very good at this, are you?" asks his amused lis-tener, batting her eyelashes (68). But he is very good indeed, since in this absurd listing of the recycled iconography of Wright's syn-cretic secret history of the world, he has managed an enormous indi-gestible datadump that causes us to laugh rather than throw rotten tomatoes.

Wright, as he gladly admitted on his webpage, enjoys pastiche, borrowing feverishly the tones and colors of his favorite writers. Is it accidental that his headstrong youthful hero almost shares the names of Jack Vance's darkly deathless protagonist the Grayven Warlock who, in *To Live Forever* (1956), goes among mortals under the guise Gavin Waylock? In the first volume no justification is apparent for the *hommage,* although Waylock's ancient traitor ancestor, Azrael, the tale's tormented figure of evil, is a Warlock of great if twisted power.

This play of appropriation and spoof gives the book an antic air. At times it feels like an arch collaboration between Samuel Beckett (for comic Godot despair) and Gilbert & Sullivan (pirate silliness), working with Lewis Carroll and J. M. Barrie (the main female character is a somewhat icky-sweet relentlessly cheerful woman-girl fairy named Wendy, who might as well be Alice a few years on; Gavin's apostate dad, all grown up and repudiating magic, as in Spielberg's *Hook,* is Peter). Some of the set pieces—assaults from forces of Darkness ancient and current—more than verge on the slapstick: ice giants crunching along, shanty-singing seal marines, ichor-dripping swords, stone statues to the rescue, you know the sort of thing.

Yet Wright can approach the true uncanny unease, fearful ugliness and lucent beauty of dream. Then the tale of the High House of Everness, with its proliferatingly detailed architecture and detailing, wings forward with inventive impulse, genuinely captivating, a little reminiscent of Orson Scott Card's strangely successful reworking of Russian folklore, *Enchantment* (1999). And yes, there is a Russian wonderworker in this book, too, who like all the rest is more than he seems—a Titan's son, at least, and, it seems for a time, perhaps the Pendragon as well, somehow.

Raven, son of Raven, is Wendy's husband, and his tragedy is to love her too well as she is dying, to purchase back by guilty murder her mortal life at the cost of poisoning their bond. That fairytale motif is characteristic of the moral underpinning of what otherwise might have been a pell-mell adventure to save the world from extinction when Darkness invades the sublunary world and Light threatens a Last War that will obliterate us whichever side wins. (The blurbed story-line is misleading, but to say more about the plot or characters would spoil the unfurling of the tale, which is by turns ingenious, absurd, disturbing, elevated and even moving.)

Whether the morals advanced are worthy or absurd must be decided by the reader, and of course in the moral landscape of most fantasyland trilogies, as China Miéville has noted: "Superheroic protagonists stamp their will on history like characters in Nietzschean wet dreams, but at the same time things are determined by fate rather than social agency. Social threats are pathological, invading from outside rather than being born from within." Here that is not entirely true.

Yes, archetypal challenges and figures from myth and legend strive at the margins of dream, readying the ruination of the waking world. But in some measure Wright's tale invokes a social context to his heroics. An especially odious bit-player observes: "A mob that bites the hand that feeds it, spits on the warrior protecting it: that is all a democracy is…. The best should rule, and the rest should bow." In the *Golden Age* trilogy, a nobility of valor, imagination and ultra-libertarian romantic can-do ran dangerously parallel to that opinion. Here it is rebuked as distinctly contemptible. While there is no lack of heroic deeds of renown without peer, the archangel Uriel in a rosy glow and peals of majestic music reveals that will, judgment and love of virtue surpass courage, prudence, glory and justice, although a Celestial Monarchy does remain at the world's helm. One could not avoid wondering: would Wright pull a Pullman and throw down God and Satan alike by the sequence's end?

The opening volume ends as abruptly as a sentence torn in half. Several characters crucial in the first third and then summarily dismissed—Gavin, grandfather Lemuel—remain, in effect, in hell and nearly incommunicado. Wright takes the risk that his reader's curiosity and pleasure in the tale will excuse this matinee cliffhanger. But as with *Buffy, the Vampire Slayer,* each season's Apocalypse must gamely give way to the next. That is the formula. All anyone can do is finesse it.

The bad news, perhaps, is that while the Dreaming War narrative arc was satisfyingly completed with its second volume, it seemed to open the way to a host of sagas set in Wright's vast syncretic mythos. *Is* this bad news? Am I looking a thoroughbred gift horse in the mouth? Maybe so. After all, a well-devised cosmos is worth revisiting and exploring to its bounds and beyond, especially if fresh characters enliven the stock setting. It is worrying, though. Roger Zelazny managed a fair passage through his first sequence of five Amber novels, then dismally botched the next installments. Isaac Asimov's Foundation trilogy was crammed with pleasing surprises; his bloated return to that universe grew ever more tiresome and embarrassing.

While *Mists of Everness* tears along at the same manic pace, veering between high-toned mysticism and farce, lashings of derring-do and moments of hilarious absurdity, the quotient of scenes where I bit my lip and averted my mortified eye went up. That is very much a personal estimate, of course; others will relish what I found gauche, off-key. Take the sometimes-flighted Wendy, the artless girl-wife of looming Russian Raven, son of Raven (actually, son of Prometheus). She is the daughter, it turns out, of Titania and the Shadow (the fellow with the dark black cloak and hat who, back in the 1930s, knew what evil lurks in the hearts of men), and she giggles a lot when not speaking like this: "We dropped the bomb on the bad guys and saved the earth! It was magic! Look at me flying! Magic! Stop laughing! It is not so wires!" (322). In a burst of 1940s' cheesecake, she strips off in the U.S. President's empty office and sits on her husband's lap, "legs crossed, toes pointed, arching her back, and running her fingers through her long, black hair." This is porn lite for B-24 bomber pilots; sixty years on, it rather thuds in a twenty-first century fantasy, even though the apparently retarded Wendy and her bearish husband immediately make whoopee on the Presidential desk (336). Sorry, but no cigar.

Wright's story is nothing if not replete. The great House of Everness stands between the world of everyday waking, and the larger, mythical, grand and terrible worlds of Dreaming. Once upon a time, Arthur and his knights, with some divine help, expelled the gods, demons, face-thieving selkies, and a host of other monsters, and locked the door. The arch-demon Morningstar broods in the drowned city of Acheron, poised to rise from the frigid depths. The United States government has been infiltrated by monstrous imposters and vile quislings. King Arthur and his heroes sleep, waiting to be woken, as legend assures us, for a final fraught Battle, whereafter, if they win, the world will be wiped away and replaced by something wonderful but inhuman. (This is a recurrent trope in Wright's science fantasies.)

The family of Galen Waylock ("the Parzival of this time" [220]) are the current scions of the Guardianship of Everness's limin or portal. For 1,500 years they have trained in the ways of magic, spells and mnemonics, but Galen's father Peter has rebelled against all this superstitious nonsense and gone for a soldier, losing the use of his legs and his sense of humor in the process. Grandfather Lemuel readies naive Galen, but the green kid bites off more than he can chew, releases his bad mad ancient ancestor Azrael from hellish dream confinement. All manner of terrible things are loosed. Meanwhile, twittering, deathly-ill Wendy and her large Russian spouse fall out when he kills an innocent (Galen, as it happens) to save her life. People rush this way and that. Angels and gods come and go. Mighty battles are fought, by magic and sturdy arm and not without a laugh or two, and a tear, you know how it is.

Anton Pendrake, or Pendragon (but *not* Arthur, as I'd guessed), shows up in Shadow drag, Nobel Prizewinner in physics, newspaper magnate by day, cloaked avenger by night, and says a lot of stuff that blends Ayn Rand with classic pulp fiction: "You will not escape. The fruit bourn by the weed of crime is death" (328), and "Arm yourselves, my fellow free men; do not obey any order that infringes on your rights to free speech, free assembly, free press; do not permit any searches without warrant of your property." It is easy for him to take this stand, because he has a bunch of advanced weapons and miniaturized information devices under his cloak, and he can whip up a cold fusion weapon from first principles. I was reminded of the *Illuminatus!* playground of Robert Anton Wilson and Robert Shea, but Wright's fictional mysticism is not quite Discordian. The theology, not to mention theodicy, seems to be crypto-polytheistic, but with a Supreme Being lurking offstage. The current sky god of the Dreaming is one-eyed Oberon/Odin, apparently once a human, but his estranged wife Titania is older than he: Gaia/Isis, former wife of Ouranos the murdered unicorn, "the Demiurge who dreamed this world into being" (291), And so on. It is a delirious, delicious mishmash of midrash and myth, for those who enjoy cavorting in such. For the rest, it might be a bit baffling but no more so than the cosmogony of *Buffy* and *Angel,* or *Lost*.

Does this trifle pudding (cream, angel food, brandy, cherries) work? Well enough, but the messy mix of whimsy, preachments, bloody battles, dreamy and nightmarish surrealism, all done in a *tour de force* of impersonated voices, has a centrifugal tendency to fray and fly apart. It is very diverting to watch Prometheus, unbound, pulling machine to pieces to see how they work, and making improvements on the fly ("If you curled your rotor blades at the tip, you would avoid the turbulence caused when the outer part of the lifting surface goes supersonic"). The Titan's prophecy that the "machine intelligences that shall supersede mankind will have vastly greater intellect, which they will be able to increase at need" sounds like a segue to the future of the Golden Oecumene. It thrills the child within to see maimed Peter hurling Thor's hammer at supersonic speed, even around corners, and smearing his nasty foes. It is charming to watch a wheelchair drawn into the heavens by supernatural goats, and Titania's own flying chariot pulled by a team of cats (which land, of course, on their feet). Wright gives us adults permission to sit back and let that inner child behave badly and bravely by turns, while speaking in tongues and remembering forgotten mythologies. There are worse ways to spend Sunday afternoon.

* * * * * * *

A bit like C. S. Lewis's *Chronicles of Narnia* updated by half a century, but with more gusto, *Orphans of Chaos*, the opening volume of John C. Wright's second fantasy sequence (*The Chronicles of Chaos*) seemed to me at first reading an imaginative exercise in Christian apologetics, reflecting the author's dramatic conversion from atheism after what he construed as a near-death miracle. "I can see the many dimensions of the world," explains Miss Daw (an unreliable commentator, it's true), "and so I knew what it was that reached down through higher space.... It was a power above Saturn, older than Time, able to restore the dead and recover the innocence I had once and lost.... And now I know that Eternity is beyond even the gods of Olympus. There is a shadow, a hint, of what Eternity is like within this world of time and death and decay; for if there were not, we would have no notion of perfection, no idea of beauty, no love, no hope" (287). This is the quintessence of Lewis's theodicy, as well.

Lewis, like Wright, first made his literary mark with a trilogy of interplanetary adventures, although those were Christian allegories rather than, in Wright's inaugural *Golden Age* three-decker, elaborate and playful investigations of a deep future hypertech libertarian society under dire threat from without and within. What makes that comparison less than entirely fanciful is something young-fogeyish in Wright's voice and tone, especially in his interviews and interventions on e-mail lists; he can be almost comically Colonel Blimpish, invoking the sort of stuffy early twentieth-century punctilio where gentlemen addressed one another as "Mr." and "Sir". Luckily, this affectation is largely put aside in his fiction. If *Orphans of Chaos,* for all its rodomontade, lacks the elegant surreal melody and terrible power of Philip Pullman's great *His Dark Materials* trilogy, still it possesses a measure of audacious syncretism—figures drawn from myth and legend and Wright's own abundant imagination—blended with a sort of headlong whimsy.

My estimate of Wright's intentions was quickly slapped down in his own blog in November, 2005:

> Please keep in mind how slowly the wheels turn in the publishing world. *Orphans Of Chaos* was written many years ago, while your humble author was still a zealous atheist. There are several passages in the book which take organized religion quite lightly.
>
> However, I never pulled a Phillip Pullman. In this book, Christian mythology is treated with the same respect, or lack of respect, as classical mythology.
>
> Because it was not openly and obviously anti-christian, at least one reviewer reading *Orphans* came away with the idea that it was a work of pro-Christian apologetics! This mildly astonishing fact should serve as a warning to people who place too much faith in reviewers: some of them cannot tell the difference between night and day.

> Even back when your humble author hated
> Christianity with all his heart and soul, I did not go
> out of my way to put that hatred on display in my
> works of fiction. I assumed there were be [*sic*] Chris-
> tians in my buying audience, and I had no psycho-
> logical imperative to drive them away. I was writing
> an adventure story.

It is perhaps surprising, given Wright's post-conversion zeal, that he does not seize these hints in retrospect as a sort of proleptic hint at inner yearnings. At any rate, the obvious template comparison might seem J. K. Rowling's unprecedentedly successful (and Hugo winning) Harry Potter saga of magicians' school—but the chronology indicated above suggests that these books were written before Potter appeared. Wright's five protagonists, whose ages range indeterminately between fourteen and twenty-four, if not 2,400 or 24,000 years old, are the only students in a dark and twisted version of the author's own much beloved St. John's College in Annapolis. These talented and pubescent students reprise a curriculum not seen elsewhere for a century: Latin and Greek, the "Great Books"—Aristotle, Aquinas, Newton, Pascal, the old masters of political discourse—and more than a little advanced mathematics. In an interview with Nick Gevers, Wright praised St. John's: "There are no tests and no grades at that school, and no lecture classes. There is never a time when the student is not allowed to speak. There are no secondary texts; we do not read some blowhard second-guessing what the geniuses of history thought; we read the geniuses in the original." It is a little odd, then, to find so diabolical and perverse an avatar of the dear old alma mater used as the setting for this perverse and diabolical coming-of-age tale.

Fairly quickly, we learn that our narrator, Amelia Armstrong Windrose (the children have named themselves, sometimes floridly), and her chums are possessed of curious powers. Is this, then, a school for witches and wizards, bound for some dubious purpose under the constraint of cruel villains? One might readily gain this impression, especially as the two beautiful and stacked teenaged girls are ogled and worse by Mr. Glum, one of the school's more odious factotums. Amelia herself is at last chained and jailed by this creature, and by their lovely music teacher Miss Daw, but not before being spanked by Headmaster Boggin, whose manly, red-haired chest and great wings are usually tucked away beneath his academic gown:

I was breathless; a shy feeling was actually sending tremors through me. All my skin trembled with goose pimples as all my little hairs stood up. This made my skin more sensitive; I could feel every nuance of the texture and fabric of my skirt, which suddenly seemed quite flimsy and thin on my bottom. I could feel the air on my exposed upper legs. I could feel the muscles in his legs beneath my stomach...And there was an even darker, naughtier pleasure trembling beneath the fear and confusion in my body. Because I knew this wasn't a teacher punishing a schoolgirl. This was a man spanking a woman....It was something for me. A bad thing, maybe even a terrible and humiliating thing, but it was mine. (248-9)

Heinlein of Gor, or maybe *The Story of Ow!* While Jack Lewis enjoyed showing the joy of devilish cruelty at work, I do not recall any of the Narnia children over the knee of a masterful mentor.

So who are these ageless children—psychic Colin Iblis mac Fir-Bolg, levitating Quentin, Victor the materialist scientist, Vanity Fair with her command of Chaos, Amelia who is extruded into higher dimensions and finds notes apparently written by her older self? Each seems to inhabit a slightly different reality, each governed, empowered and restricted, as Vanity asserts, by a separate metaphysical paradigm—warlock, scientist, mystic, etc. Are they comic book mutants? Demigods from legend (like the Titans and Shakespearean fairies in Wright's earlier fantasy novels, as the title of the third volume hints)? Do they dream themselves or each other into trouble and out of it? Such questions are swiftly given answers, in set-piece dramatics that allow us to guess, when we are not told outright, who all these odd people are, students, teachers, visitors, the cruel and beautiful, gods and monsters, and why the kids cannot physically escape the boundaries of the school, and their, you guessed it, legendary destinies.

This British public school is located conveniently close to the last resting place of King Arthur, destined to rise from his sleep and save his Christian nation from evil forces and evil men alike. Had the kids botched it? Had they failed in their multidimensional rebellion against lesser pagan gods and monsters, in the cloaked service (as Miss Daw believes) of "the Redeemer...a strange and nameless God...who was, at once, himself and his own son," that "reached down through higher space..." that "power above Saturn, older than

Time, able to restore the dead and recover the innocence I had once and lost" (286)? At the core of the mystery is the matter of hidden or masked identity, lineage, filiation, and, I remain convinced, a religious impulse of a kind very familiar from C. S. Lewis, severally figured:

> Victor... [Amelia reflects ardently] held my hand and told me the secret, the secret too enormous and wonderful to be true.
>
> He told me that this world was not our home; that these people were not our people; that our real parents were still alive; that somewhere, someday in the shining future, we all would escape, and find the place where we were meant to be. Someday, we would find our home. Someday, we would be happy. (*Fugitives,* 64)

Answers to these questions came in *Fugitives of Chaos* and *Titans of Chaos,* which were arguably more rushed yet paradoxically drawn out, everything plus the kitchen sink. The passion god Cupid, would-be emperor of Heaven, observes revealingly that "my Soul tells me there is a greater Love in the universe, a Timelessness beyond time, a supernal Eternity. A Forevermore" (*Titans,* 162).

The trilogy is an erudite mythological soap opera, spectacularly *brainy,* a sort of twenty-first century version of John W. Campbell's famous *Unknown* magazine (1939-43), which launched fantasy conducted by the rationalizing rules of science fiction. It breaches all the rules of commercial fantasy—perhaps the closest equivalent is Alan Moore's cerebral *Watchmen* comic—which might explain why it took a long time to get into print. One cannot imagine this kind of high-IQ confrontation in a Robert Jordan saga (but in Kage Baker, maybe):

> Dr. Fell called down in a dispassionate voice: "I ask you to surrender."
>
> Victor called back in a voice also calm and matter of fact: "Impossible. I can be killed, but I cannot be defeated without some act of consent on my part. I do not consent."
>
> Dr. Fell said, "That strategy limits your available range of options. You lose the opportunity to minimize unfavorable outcomes and maximize favorable ones."

Victor replied: "Only in the short term. Over the span of all possible future interactions, positive as well as negative, a declared policy of no-surrender lowers transaction costs by deterring zero-sum interactions."

Fell: "Your policy renders the present interaction negative-sum."

Victor: "I am taking that into account." (*Fugitives,* 89)

Whereupon they return to zapping each other with lances of fire. Throughout the second half of the final volume, the principals endlessly almost-die, one after another, but again and again are snatched back by clever, intellectually entertaining but empty tricks. Amelia has trouble with her higher-dimensional extrusions, and those of her current divine foe, Hermes Trismegistus:

Like a Hecatonchire, he was a fourth-dimensional being.... And his geometry was bent the opposite way from mine. His space was Riemannian, mine was Lobachevskian. Everything in four-space was farther away for me than it would have been through flat three-space; for him, everything was closer.

A ball of shortcuts through space-time was folded around him like an origami rose, confusing and complex to behold. (*Titans,* 259-60)

This is not remotely Tolkien, nor Le Guin. It is fantasy in the Second Wave impulse of A. E. van Vogt and L. Sprague de Camp, or Keith Laumer done with more expertise, and relentlessly in the final volume. So the trilogy is a notable achievement in myth-making and recycling—but this childhood longing for an illusory Homeland (regarded as cold fact, not utopian aspiration) diminishes its power, it seems to me, even as it enables a dense, tumbling, clever series of set pieces that are yet somehow, finally, no more than...prestidigitation, in wings, manga tentacles, robot bodies, and lacy underwear.

Meanwhile, though, John Wright had different tricks, or different ways to use the same tricks, up his copious sleeve.

* * * * * * *

Marvelous and original craftsman as he is, Wright is unasham-
edly and avowedly indebted to the great germinal masters of the
golden age, especially van Vogt. Happily, he has had the audacity to
write a sequel not just to Alfred Elton van Vogt's *Null-A* novels
(two remarkable and influential [1945, 1948], one execrable [1984])
but, slyly and with immense enjoyment and brio, to many of the
Grandmaster's other universes as well. It is not the first sequel to a
van Vogt novel, but it is the only one to date worth reading.

What follows cannot be a detailed critique, because to a far
greater extent than usual—the novel being a non-stop ideational car-
nival—that would require a confetti of Spoiler Alerts. Instead, I offer a series of sidelong notes, some cryptic, some perhaps far too
personal. If you have not already wallowed in van Vogt's major
novels, especially *The World of Null-A* and *The Players of Null-A,*
what follows will not make a lick of sense. More to the point, you
will have denied yourself some of the most wonderful and absurd
pleasures of the sf mode.

TENDRILS OF THE NIGHT

Despite its New Age crankiness, Alexei and Cory Panshin's *The
World Beyond the Hill* (1989) enthralled me. Although I have seen it
lambasted, I still consider this a resonant book for readers of a certain age and disposition. Its high point was perhaps the Panshins'
argument for A. E. van Vogt's early fiction as a culmination of the
sf golden age: what I call the Second Wave, and which their subtitle
captures as its Quest for Transcendence. That canonical quest has its
dubious side. The July 2007 *New York Review of Science Fiction* ran
two uncompromising reviews of Kevin Anderson's sub-van Vogt
sequel *Slan Hunter* which raised doubts about the great clumsy
original as well. Both reviews were clear-eyed, but Eugene Reynolds more interestingly drew out a horrid suspicion that I suspect
some of us have always felt oppressively lurking beneath our tendrils.

I began to realise that I hadn't been rooting for
Tiny Tim but for Ebenezer Scrooge...smug in his
convictions of the rightness of his world as evinced
by his superior status. Jommy's pleas for the future of
slanity weren't the anguished cries of the victim but
the petulant whine of the conqueror, frustrated from
his dreams of *lebensraum* by all the inconvenient
untermenschen...the dream that van and Anderson are

dreaming, the wish that they are fulfilling, is the Iron Dream, and I'm cheering for the Nazi stand-ins (17).

Yes, an unnerving discovery. Or, to play at a different kind of psychopolitical registration, it is tempting to be Freudian about infantile omniscience/potency wishes. So Sf is really OsF, Omniscience Fiction...hence, perhaps, *Omni*, child of milky, vulval *Penthouse*? The science fiction commentator John Boston commented: "I suspect Campbell's involvement with Hubbard and Dianetics rekindled his interest in, well, call it human potential—the generalized notion that the human mind is vastly more powerful than anyone acknowledges or understands" (private communication). Which of course the Panshins saw as the yearning secret heart of sf in the golden age. Perhaps psi—the tropes of telepathy, teleportation, foreseeing the future—is the engineer's lever inserted into the transcendent. Since I esteem early van Vogt above all his golden age coevals, this sort of reflection makes the agenbite of inwit all the more stinging.

THE PERSISTENCE OF DREAMS

I have also been reading *The Weapon Makers* (as I tend to do every decade or so), and was struck for the first time by the suspicion that in *2001* and its sequel Arthur C. Clarke might have been replaying a scene he encountered twenty-five years earlier. It is one of the classic van Vogtian oneiric moments ("dreamy" or "dreamlike" doesn't quite catch it), and occurs in Chapter 11.

Hedrock the immortal has just been flung superluminally into the depths of interstellar space inside a small escape pod propelled by a new "Infinity Drive." This is a homey gadget, more 1947 than 4791: "He glanced at the Infinity Drive, and it was still in gear. That was the trouble. It was in gear. The speedometer showed impossible figures; the automatic calendar said that the time was P.M., August 28, 4791 Isher. Hedrock nodded to himself...he glanced at the speedometer, it was registering something over four hundred million miles a second." Wearing an insulation suit, he finds himself inside a strange spaceship that proves to contain generically familiar countryside and sparkling streams. Removing his suit, he enters a small metal room containing a control board and a man seated at a chair; it is himself. He leaves the room, understandably shaken, but on impulse opens the door again; the room is empty.

This sort of thing continues, with Hedrock finding his mind merged with various other humans in different places and times.

Abruptly he finds this comforting, if alarming, imagery replaced by the true interior of the starship: a mass of enormous webs upon which stroll the giant spiders who are his captors, alien scientists who examine him dispassionately. He is apparently returned to earth, and finds himself still wearing the insulation suit. He is unsure whether he is really home. Take a stress pill, Dave.

RIDERS IN THE CHARIOT

Like the Herbert *fils*/Anderson *Dune* atrocities, *Slan Hunter* did get some good reviews, and apparently attracted many forgiving readers; yet those books were vile. Their tone-deaf lumpen oafishness had made me dread Anderson's sequel. Justifiably, alas: Horrible, horrible, most horrible. Isaac Wilcott provides an extensive reading of the book's many failings. Even so, of the barely competent prose, I was flabbergasted to see Wilcott claiming that "[Kevin Anderson] is perhaps the most skilled prose stylist working in the English language today, consistently producing the single most readable style I've ever had the pleasure of reading." I found it all but unreadable. Worse than the duff writing, it was the Boys' and Girls' Own Adventure characterization that affronted me.

Could John Wright escape that trap? In the *Golden Age* sequence that made his name, his posthuman characters are as schematic as Ayn Rand's, but his world creation is astoundingly dense and intrinsicate; you are on your toes the whole time following the action and its implications. That trilogy was like van Vogt with an intelligent underpinning of technology and hyper-advanced sciences. So one knew in advance that his capture of van Vogt's voice and intensively recomplicated method might be adequate to the task.

IF JOHN IRVING HAD WRITTEN SLAN

In a BBC program of appreciation following Sir Arthur C. Clarke's death in 2008, the assembled literati focused more upon the failings of his work than upon its visionary or transcendental accomplishments. Doris Lessing noted that he was not Henry James, but that we did not necessarily wish him to be. Quite so—but still, one of my long term hopes is to read some Doc Smith and van Vogt translated into Henry James, Proust, John Updike, just to see what it looks like. (In my novel *Godplayers* I did translate a passage from Tolstoy into Philip K. Dick; nobody noticed.) What follows is adapted as closely as possible from the opening of John Irving's upper middle-brow *Until I Find You* (2005):

According to his mother, Jommy Cross was su-
perhumanly brave because he was a slan, but
Jommy's most vivid memories of childhood were
those moments when he felt compelled to hold his
mother's hand. He wasn't brave then.

Of course we don't remember much until we're
four or five years old—and what we remember at that
early age is very selective or incomplete, or even
false. What Jommy *recalled* as the first time he felt
the need to reach for his mom's hand was probably
the hundredth or two hundredth time.

Preschool tests revealed that Jommy Cross had a
vocabulary beyond his years, which is not uncommon
among only children accustomed to adult conversation—especially only children of slan parents. But of
greater significance, according to the tests, was
Jommy's capacity for consecutive memory, which,
when he was three, was comparable to that of a nine
year old. At four, his retention of detail and understanding of linear time were equal to an eleven-year-
old's. (The details included, but were not limited to,
such trivia as articles of clothing and the names of
streets.)

These test results were bewildering to Jommy's
mother, Patricia, who considered him to be an inat-
tentive child; in her view, Jommy's propensity for
day dreaming made him immature for his age.

Nevertheless, in the fall of 2569, when Jommy
was four and had not yet started kindergarten, his
mother walked with him to the corner of Pickthall
and Hutchings Hill Road in the Forest Hill, which
was a nice neighborhood in Centropolis. They were
waiting for school to let out, Patricia explained, so
that Jommy could see the slan girls. (after Irving, 20)

Compare this with the fabulous concision and rude vigor of van
Vogt's own opening to *Slan*:

His mother's hand felt cold, clutching his.

Her fear as they walked hurriedly along the street
was a quiet, swift pulsation that throbbed from her
mind to his. A hundred other thoughts beat against

his mind, from the crowds that swarmed by on either side, and from inside the buildings they passed. But only his mother's thoughts were clear and coherent and afraid.

"They're following us, Jommy," her brain telegraphed. "They're not sure, but they suspect. We've risked once too often coming into the capital, though I did hope that this time I could show you the old slan way of getting into the catacombs, where your father's secret is hidden. Jommy, if the worst happens, you know what to do. We've practiced it often enough. And, Jommy, don't be afraid, don't get excited. You may be only nine years old, but you're as intelligent as any fifteen-year-old human being."

Don't be afraid. Easy to advise, Jommy thought, and hid the thought from her. She wouldn't like that concealment, that distorting shield between them. But there were thoughts that had to be kept back. She mustn't know he was afraid also.

It was new and exciting, as well. He felt excited each time he came into the heart of Centropolis from the quiet suburb where they lived. The great parks, the miles of skyscrapers, the tumult of the throngs always seemed even more wonderful than his imagination had pictured them but then size was to be expected of the capital of the world. Here was the seat of the government. Here, somewhere, lived Kier Gray, absolute dictator of the entire planet. Long ago hundreds of years before the slans had held Centropolis during their brief period of ascendancy. "Jommy, do you feel their hostility? Can you sense things over a distance yet?"

He strained. The steady wave of vagueness that washed from the crowds pressing all around grew into a swirl of mind clamor. From somewhere came the stray wisp of thought:

"They say there are still slans alive in this city, in spite of all precautions. And the order is to shoot them on sight." (9)

THE BEST WAY NOT TO READ A BOOK

I am one quarter into what I think of as *Null-A Redivivus*. I'm reading a bound, typeset but right-unjustified Advanced Reading Copy with <u>underlined</u> *italic* (rather disconcerting), and clogged with errors. I guess the ARC was dumped straight from Wright's uncorrected text; there's a *lot* of typos and other goofs. I do wish his spelling were more secure. "In tact" for "intact" grates horribly, for example. No matter—I am delighted by the way he is working in all manner of sly references to other orthogonal van Vogtian realities: the non-linear No-Man, the encyclopedic Nexialist, the callidetic forecasters, the Silkie levels of logic, Isher's pivotal genius Walter de Lany, etc. (The instant the great spaceship filled with scientists showed up, I thought, "Good grief, it's the *Beagle*...."—and lo! there on the next page was a Nexialist.)

SUPERCALLIDETICEXPIALIDOCIOUS

I'm at the less-than-midway point and by god, Wright has out-Vogted Van! And similarized his style to many decimal places. The callidetic planet has been shadowed and Gilbert Gosseyn is about to use his extra brain and non-Aristotelian semantic training to memorize it and shift it elsewhere. Not even the Witches of Karres could do that. I continue to be delighted by the (naughty) borrowings from *Isher* and *Beagle* and *Ptath*, and await the arrival of Samuel Lann at any moment. [Later: And what comes at the novel's climax is *mind-bogglingly absurdly more impressive* than any simple routine planetary teleportational heist.]

Truly, in some respects, Wright is better at van Vogt than van Vogt ever was. I'm now halfway through, Leej the Predictress has (at least apparently) replicated the seesaw swing through eternity at the end of *The Weapon Shops*, and the blend of van Vogt bafflegab and real cosmological jargon is remarkable. Wright does make small errors; for example, he speaks of the 3 degree K remnant radiation as if it remains that hot into the vastly remote future; that is, as if it were a constant; actually it will keep cooling with expansion. Or should we regard this as another clue that the Null-A universe is not cognate with ours? Later, he mentions the giant star S Doradus in the "Lesser Magellanic Cloud" (as van Vogt did, in his Mixed Men stories). I'm prepared to read this (along with the "electronic brains" and "atomic piles" and steamy lush Venus) as a necessary accommodation to his 1940s' Ur-texts and their errors and vernacular. But since Wright also cites black holes, maybe he ought to have put it in its rightful place in the Large Magellanic Cloud? [This was corrected after I drew the error to his attention.]

My chief reservation at this point is the enormous amount of talking head material; yes, Wright does now and then nicely reproduce the dreamlike abrupt intrusions that made van Vogt so disturbingly effective, but there is not so much mad relentless action, I think, as in the great golden age narratives. The scale, though, is even more wondrous, which perhaps compensates. (I keep comparing this with the now-forgotten Ian Wallace superman books, *Croyd* and *Dr. Orpheus*, from forty years ago, which are perhaps more vivid in a lunatic way, but less satisfactorily thought through.)

IS SCIENCE FICTION STILL DEAD YET?

The problem vexing me is far more complex and thorny than any of these quibbles. It has to do with the sort of thing science fiction is and whether, if pushed sufficiently far, ideatively re-re-recomplicated, wildly scaled up, it just stops working. You stop caring because, it seems, anything can happen, or be explained away. I need some time to mull this over. (My own fiction is hitting the same crux, as I see by reading several venomous if insensate reader comments on Amazon about *Godplayers*.)

...ONENESS

The Panshins write, in *The World Beyond the Hill,* of the final paragraphs of van Vogt's extraordinary vampire story "Asylum," where "the frightened and resistant subsystem that still imagines itself to be merely William Leigh, Earth reporter, IQ 112 and proud of it, facing its moment of integration into the Great Galactic," stares into a mirror:

> Where it had come from, he had no memory. It was there in front of him, where, an instant before, had been a black porthole—and there was an image in the mirror, shapeless at first to his blurred vision.
> Deliberately—he felt the enormous deliberateness—the vision was cleared for him. He saw—and then he didn't.
> His brain wouldn't look. It twisted in a mad desperation, like a body buried alive, and briefly, horrendously conscious of its fate. Insanely, it fought away from the blazing thing in the mirror. So awful was the effort, so titanic the fear, that it began to gib-

ber mentally, its consciousness to whirl dizzily, like a wheel spinning faster, faster—

The wheel shattered into ten thousand aching fragments. Darkness came, blacker than Galactic night. And there was—

Oneness! (in van Vogt, *Supermind,* 62-3)

Of this epiphany, the Panshins observe: "There is a holistic ending for you! No other modern science fiction story would ever manage to take a greater leap into the arms of transcendent mystery!" (Panshin, 519)

Well, yes, one see what they *mean*...but here's my question: Do any of the magazines these days publish writing as *awful* as that? "His brain wouldn't look. It twisted in a mad desperation, like a body buried alive, and briefly, horrendously conscious of its fate.... So awful was the effort, so titanic the fear, that it began to gibber mentally...."

There's plenty of merely workmanlike stuff getting into print in the twenty-first century, but doesn't everyone published these days do far better, just at the *lexical* level, than van Vogt? Sentence by sentence, word by word? As a sometime sf editor I have seen incompetence by the bucket load, but even that is usually less foul that this quotation. What the worst of today's submissions lacks, of course, is van Vogt's glorious cumulative sense of wonder and dreamlike transcendence.

A REMARKABLE ACHIEVEMENT

I have finished the novel. Is it a success? Yes, yes, yes, but....

In the meantime: in 1960, fanzine editor Earl Kemp commissioned what become one of the most famous documents of sf fandom, a symposium titled *Who Killed SF?* (now available online). James E. Gunn had this surprising assessment—surprising for an academic who would later host the Campbell Memorial Awards:

> On March 31, 1955, I wrote a letter to Tony Boucher, inspired by his comment in *F&SF* that we needed to take a closer look at science fiction, in which I summed up my feelings about this beloved field of ours.
>
> We have been misled—authors and editors—in a search for a spurious maturity. Any maturity is spurious which tries to deny its origins and its childhood,

which tries to change itself into something else. I used the word [*i.e.*, entertainment] in a letter to Jack Williamson in February of 1954:

It seems to me that science fiction has lost something in the last few years; it has gained some things, too, but I wonder whether they quite make up for it. I wonder if what ails the magazine field currently isn't a paucity of excitement, if circulation wouldn't jump tremendously under the impetus of a new serial by van Vogt or Heinlein....Science fiction had something in the 1940s that it doesn't have any more: a vigor, a sweep, a dream, an excitement. Nowadays there is a great deal of maturity, subtlety, cleverness, good writing, but very little excitement....

Why haven't there been any new Heinleins, any new van Vogts? Their talents are not unique. Their excitement about what they were doing, which poured through into their fiction, was not exclusive. The reason, I think, is because the budding Heinlein, the embryo van Vogt, has had his stories rejected by the leading magazines instead of encouragement, and he has turned to other modes....

Nearly fifty years later, there have been new Heinleins (Varley, Haldeman, Palmer, Spider Robinson, plenty of others) but perhaps far fewer fresh van Vogts, even if his quintessential strangeness and excitement does permeate some of the most effective science fiction. When he followed L. Ron Hubbard into the sucking vortex of Dianetics and Scientology in the early 1950s, he found his dreams of supermen, mind training and transcendence manifested in an increasingly tawdry system of collective manipulative delusion, the sort of thing Eugene Reynolds found lurking in *Slan*. I often wonder how much of red-haired L. Ron's syncretic gibberish was derived from van Vogt to begin with, or vice versa. Is it really a coincidence that the Galactic overlord in the Null-A novels is Enro the Red, that the Venusian detective is Eldred? Two principal characters with such similar names is a misfortune; that the names closely resemble both L. Ron (Elron) and Elton (van Vogt's middle name) is either sheer carelessness or telling us something interesting.

At any rate, John Wright has tuned his tendrils to those cosmic frequencies only a Nexialist or a semantic superhuman with at least two and preferably three brains might detect. He has reworked the canon of van Vogtian dreams into a cosmogonic rapture where

Gosseyn (Go-sane) finally takes his inevitable place at the end of time and beyond as, one might say, Godseyn, then comes home to tend his garden. There is meat here for a score of complex critical essays and exegeses. I look forward to reading them, if anyone younger than middle-aged is interested in this lost treasury of dreams.

CHAPTER FIVE

THE MARGINS OF SCIENCE FICTION

GENE WOLFE: IN SEARCH OF LOST SUZANNE: A LUPINE COLLAGE

Mischievous Gene Wolfe's ripping yarns—Wolfe is, in many respects, a good old-fashioned storyteller—are often also baffling, but scrupulously fair in their subtle deployment of clues and cues. Or so we tell ourselves hearteningly, bashing through thickets toward the masked designs and methods of his delicious fictions. Enigma can seem Wolfe's *raison d'être*. Added to narrative sleight-of-hand is the rich color of this erudite engineer's cultural apparatus. His vocabulary is notoriously arcane, where naming the odd or specialized is called for, yet decently plain when straight-speaking is proper. Sf critics of the stamp of Peter Nicholls, Thomas M. Disch, and John Clute gnawed at his multi-volume masterpiece *The Book of the New Sun*. He has an intimate knowledge of history and place, of Dickens and Proust. The opening scene in his first triumph, *The Fifth Head of Cerberus*, begins: "When I was a boy my brother David and I had to go to bed early, whether we were sleepy or not." It is no accident that the overture of Marcel Proust's *À la recherche du temps perdu* (variously translated as *Remembrance of Things Past* and, more faithfully, *In Search of Lost Time*) begins: "For a long time I used to go to bed early." This is not learned dog; it is relaxed cultivation.

But beyond such knowingness, Wolfe is, as I say, a trickster and a tease. Two entire email lists, run by Ranjit Bhatnagar and archived on the Internet, have been devoted to unknotting the mysteries of his work, especially *The Book of the New Sun* and *The Book of the Long Sun*. Find them at http://www.urth.net/urth/ where you can read or subscribe to the URTH list, which has been tempted ever and anon toward the smaller mysteries of Wolfe's short fiction. One of the more alluring stories is "Suzanne Delage," a kind of epiphany or Proustian madeleine that works in reverse, for it dips into Lethe and soaks up evidence of absurd forgetfulness. Here is the start, compressed:

> As I was reading last night—reading a book, I should explain [...]—I was struck by a certain remark of the author's [...] *that every man has in the course of his life some extraordinary experience* [...] but [...] he has forgotten it. [...It] at last occurred to me that there has, in fact, been one thread of the strange—I might almost say the incredible, though not the supernatural—in my own history.
> It is simply this: living all my life, as I have, in a town of less than a hundred thousand population, I have been dimly aware of the existence of a certain woman without ever meeting her or gaining any sure idea of her appearance. (Wolfe, *Endangered Species*, 362)

The woman is Suzanne Delage, daughter of a dear friend of his mother (with whom Mom hunted for colonial quilts), his own forgotten school class-mate. He is reminded of this odd fact by a fleeting encounter he's lately had with "a girl of fifteen or so [...]. Her hair was of a lustrous black, and her complexion as pure as milk; but it was not these that for a moment enchanted me, nor the virginal breasts half afraid to press the soft angora of her sweater, nor the little waist I might have circled with my two hands. Rather it was an air, at once insouciant and shy, of vivacity coupled with an innocence and intelligence, that were hers alone" (367), "'the very image of her mother at that age,'" a friend's wife tells him, "'—Suzanne Delage.'" (Ibid.)

What can this tale mean? The denizens of the URTH list took its scent and were off, led by the scholarly, droll and fearsomely ingenious Michael André-Driussi, author of a major work of Wolfean or Lupine scholarship, *Lexicon Urthus*. I here collage and condense this discussion, with permission of the participants. The recommended warm-up for the event is, naturally, a (re)reading of Gene Wolfe's very brief story.

How many people have discovered the secret origin of "Suzanne Delage," a quiet little story in *Endangered Species*? I figured something out (largely by accident, as per usual) and asked a lot of people if they'd spotted anything intertextual (it really is a needle in a haystack) and then (when none of them had seen it) told them what I'd found:

> She spoke to me of myself, my family, my social background. She said: "Oh, I know your parents know some very nice people. You're a friend of Robert Forestier and Suzanne Delage." For a moment these names conveyed absolutely nothing to me. But suddenly I remembered that I had indeed played as a child in the Champs-Élysées with Robert Forestier, whom I had never seen since. As for Suzanne Delage, she was the great-niece of Mme Blandais, and I had once been due to go to a dancing lesson, and even to take a small part in a play at her parents' house. But the fear of getting a fit of giggles and a nose-bleed had at the last moment prevented me, so that I had never set eyes on her. I had at the most a vague idea that I had once heard that the Swanns' feather-hatted governess had at one time been with the Delages, but perhaps it was only a sister of this governess, or a friend. I protested to Albertine that Robert Forestier and Suzanne Delage occupied a very small place in my life. "That may be; but your mothers are friends, I can place you by that. I often pass Suzanne Delage in the Avenue de Messine. I admire her style." Our mothers were acquainted only in the imagination of Mme Bontemps, who having heard that I had at one time played with Robert Forestier, to whom, it appeared, I used to recite poetry, had concluded from that that we were bound by family ties. She could never, I gathered, hear my mother's name mentioned without observing: "Oh yes, she belongs to the Delage-Forestier set," giving my parents a good mark which they had done nothing to deserve. (Proust, *The Guermantes Way*, Chapter Two, 381-382)

From: Alice Turner, 14 July 1997

Hooray for you! I love it! I had already picked up the MP connection from the first sentence of *Fifth Head*, as I'm sure you did too, from the French names on Ste. Anne, and from Phaedria, who is described almost exactly as Albertine is and with whom the relationship is similar. So I looked through *Fifth Head* to find the Delages without success—it didn't occur to me to go to the source.

From: Michael André-Driussi, 15 July 97

Yeah, that Suzanne is cryptic. Talk about embedded! Talk about sneaky! (Who knows—maybe the German-language version has a citation or some notes that give it all away!)

For me, it really was luck. I mean, I'd already read just about all the Wolfe there was, then I was reading Proust (a project which literally took me a few years) and one day, "Huh. Suzanne...that sounds familiar...." If her name wasn't in the title I probably would have missed it!

From: Jim Jordan, 15 July 1997

Is there a fantasy element in "Suzanne Delage," and if so, where is it? The story feels like *Peace*, so it is probably a ghost story, but how so?

From: Michael André-Driussi, 15 July 97

The *Peace*/Proust aspect is probably the fact that the narrator is sitting/lying in the old house he's lived in all his life, casting his mind about in nostalgia and detective work.

The "fantasy" element that occurs to me is the Wolfe favorite of reincarnation—Suzanne's daughter looks exactly like Suzanne did at that age. This isn't fantasy in the hands of most authors, or in our everyday minds when we use such analogies, yet Apu Punchau = funeral bronze = ("second") Severian...

Which does tie in nicely with the Peter Pan/communist, identity hijacker/history erasures complex of "The Changeling."

From: Michael André-Driussi, 22 July 97

More about "The Changeling":

If Peter Pan looks eight years old in 1964, then his year of birth would be 1956. Papa is worried that he will leave the Palmieris soon since the family fiction is becoming unsustainable—Mama has to claim to have given birth to Peter when she was in her fifties, now. [...]

If Peter Pan has determined that it is time to change families, it might be that he is going to set himself up as the son of crazy Pete— we can imagine the townsfolk saying, "Little Pete looks just like his dad at that age—look at this fourth grade photo from 1944." (Shades of "Suzanne Delage," oooh...)

From: Peter Westlake, 06 May 1998

The fantastic element? I had wondered that when I first read it, so I read it again, twice. On the first reading, nothing. But on the second pass, I came across a sentence that gave me the most extraordinary sensation I've ever had while reading: it "caught my gaze" in the most literal sense imaginable. Does anyone know what I mean? Or am I imagining the whole thing?

07 May 1998

I'll start with a couple of hints.

First, why do we see Suzanne's daughter? I think she's there to tell us what Suzanne looks like. I would have been surprised if she had been a tanned redhead, for instance. We don't meet Suzanne herself because that would be too much like the Stoppard parody of *Waiting for Godot*—"there he is now". It would undo the plot.

Second, the narrator wonders if Suzanne belongs to any cliques. I think she belongs to at least two: the Pie Club, and one other group of people, mentioned in the story.

Final hint: what's the problem with looking for Suzanne in the picture of the Pie Club?

Here's the sentence, and in particular the phrase, that still gives me the shivers:

Suzanne is listed among those "Unable to be photographed".

And the girls in the Pie Club photo are too loosely grouped to be identified easily. But I bet they wouldn't have looked that way at the time...when you could see Suzanne.

From: Craig Christensen, 8 May 1998

I read "Suzanne Delage" again last night and when nothing unmistakable jumped out at me, I re-read it with the story's opening statement in mind. The narrator was struck by the passage he had read which stated that every person has probably had at least one event so momentous and unassimilable that he has wiped it from his memory. I took that to mean that the narrator had not only met Suzanne in his past, but that she was very important to him. I read the "Unable to be photographed" to mean that Suzanne was pregnant then and that the young lady he saw was his own daughter.

The vampire angle never occurred to me.

From: Adam Louis Stephanides, 8 May 1998 16:03:03

I hate to pour cold water on your theories, especially since this story has always mystified me. But if, as you seem to be implying, Suzanne is some sort of supernatural being who doesn't show up in photographs, I think the narrator would have heard about it and remembered it, along with the entire town. And if Suzanne had been absent from the Pie Club photo, instead of just unidentifiable, wouldn't the narrator have noticed that the caption contained one too many names? I think "loosely grouped" means only that the girls are posed as if in the middle of cooking, rather than lined up in rows as is usual.

The best I've been able to do is: if Suzanne's daughter had really been as strikingly beautiful as the story's next-to-last paragraph describes, then the narrator would certainly have noticed Suzanne. Ergo, the daughter is really not so remarkable, and the flowery prose of the description reflects the sentimentality of a lonely middle-aged man. But if that's all there is to it, it is not much of a story. And the way Wolfe writes it, it feels to me that there should be some greater payoff.

From: Peter Westlake, 09 May 1998

> "the narrator would have heard about it."

I did wonder about that myself. But as Craig has just reminded us, the story starts with the narrator reading about the idea that everyone has had some truly extraordinary experience and forgotten all about it. Mirrors might be more of a problem.

Looking again, I see that the narrator isn't quite certain of the name of the Pie Club. So maybe Craig is right and it is the "Pudding

Club" instead! Suzanne's daughter is only about fifteen, so that would mean the story takes place only about sixteen years after high school, and we are told the narrator has retired; but "much sooner than most men," so it might still work.

One more small bit of evidence for the supernatural theory, and the vampire theory in particular, is the way the narrator's mother is so exhausted by her trips with Suzanne's mother, but is always so keen to go again. Not much to go on, I admit.

Another theory is that Suzanne never was at the school, and her mother didn't die while the narrator was at college, but rejuvenated herself and then invented a high school career to account for her appearing on the scene in her teens. Then we really *do* meet her at the end. I'm not entirely convinced by this, though.

From: Peter Stephenson, 09 May 1998

I absolutely agree that "unable to be photographed" is a chilling phrase, coming from Wolfe. I don't necessarily think that means there is any "obvious" supernatural explanation. Wolfe is an expert at straining the bounds of reality so that it still makes perfect sense the way it is. I continue to read the story as I first did: that there is some "non-obvious" supernatural explanation, that the narrator's reality is warped in some way that he simply doesn't ever see Suzanne. The whole universe is conspiring that they don't meet—even by bending the laws a bit. That's what I find chilling. I think (please contradict) this is the naturally Borgesian explanation.

From: David Lebling, 9 May 1998

I like the "universe conspiring against them" explanation, though immortality and vampirism are fun, too.

The "extraordinary thing" is that he has no memory of ever meeting this woman whose life is parallel to his, yet it is beyond the realm of possibility that he never saw her or met her. When he merely glimpses her daughter, who looks just like her, he's bowled over. He *must* have seen and been bowled over by Suzanne at some point in his earlier life.

You could erect an edifice of supposition: who has kept these star-crossed lovers apart for their entire lives? What eventuality does their non-meeting prevent? Is their never-to-be-born child a new Hitler, an Anti-Christ?

This, I think, is the Borgesian reading of the story.

Or maybe she's just a vampire....

From: Alice Turner, 9 May 1998

I tend to go along with Adam's explanation here, but I don't agree that it diminishes the story. I think there is something powerful and poignant about a middle-aged man's shock of realization that his entire life could have been entirely different, had it not been for the coincidences of fate. I think you're all looking too hard for a fantasy element. The godfather of this story is Proust (and for once that is proven, not conjectural), not Kafka or Borges. The flavor of regret is bittersweet.

From: Adam Louis Stephanides, 9 May 1998

I don't know how Borgesian it is, but there's a story by Henry James based on that very premise: that (as best I can recall) there are two people who somehow never meet, despite their moving in the same social circles and having numerous opportunities to do so. The kicker is that after one of them dies, the deceased one's ghost frequently visits the other, and they more or less fall in love. I don't know if this is relevant to Wolfe's story; I suspect not (and I certainly don't believe that Suzanne Delage is dead and the girl the narrator meets is her ghost!).

I suddenly realized that there was indeed "evidence" for this. We are told that Suzanne could not be photographed because of an epidemic of Spanish influenza. It seems possible that this could have been the 1918 epidemic, which did kill a lot of people. And the narrator certainly seems to be in love with the "daughter." But I still don't believe it.

From: Adam Louis Stephanides, 10 May 1998

> "I took that to mean that the narrator had not only met Suzanne in his past, but that she was very important to him."

Lying in bed this morning I came to the conclusion that this was correct and developed a reading of the story. It explains the text; it is consistent with Wolfe's method in other works such as *Peace* and *The Fifth Head of Cerberus*; and on this reading the story is worthy of Wolfe.

As in other works by Wolfe, the narrative seems ordinary on the surface but, when you study it carefully, anomalies appear. First, why is the narrator so obsessed with the "certain remark" he reads, to the point of lying awake trying to remember something extraordinary that happened to him that he has forgotten(!)? And what he comes up with—never having met Suzanne—is not, despite his claim, all that "strange—I might almost say...incredible." (362; page references to the Tor hardcover, in which the story runs from 361 to 367). By implication, the town's population is close to 100,000 (362), and the high school is a large one (364). Later in the story he states that if he had ever danced with Suzanne "the years have so effectively sponged the event from my memory that no slightest trace remains" (366). Together, these suggest that something has indeed happened to the narrator which he has not merely forgotten but repressed, and that his non-meeting of Suzanne is what psychoanalysts call a "screen memory": a false memory covering up a repressed event.

If so, there should be traces of it in the narration. And there are. He tells us that if he had met Suzanne as a child, "I would no doubt have soon come to both love and hate" her (366). This is certainly possible, but why does he say there is "no doubt"? Then, it is odd that he thinks he might have danced with a girl as beautiful as Suzanne apparently was and casually forgotten about it. But it is the description of Suzanne's daughter that is the real giveaway. Firstly, we have this sudden outburst of poesy in a narrative that has up till now been completely prosaic. Secondly, he claims to have observed in her "an air, at once insouciant and shy, of vivacity coupled with an innocence and intelligence that were hers alone." But he only saw her for a few seconds as she "walked quickly past" him! How could he have possibly perceived all that? This passage is in reality not a description of the daughter, but a repressed memory of Suzanne herself bubbling up, triggered by seeing her daughter.

Confirmation comes with his friend's wife's reply: "'But of course you know who she is, don't you?'" (367). If he really did not know Suzanne, why should his friend's wife assume he will recognize her daughter? He did know Suzanne well enough for the friend's wife, an acquaintance but not a friend herself, to remember it, although he—consciously—does not.

To sum up: the narrator did know Suzanne, who may well have been as extraordinary as he describes her daughter as being, and did "love and hate" her. He later "sponged the event from his memory": either because he "considered himself so mundane," or because the end of the affair was too traumatic, and he made himself "mundane" as a reaction. Since then he has led the "dull" life he describes.

I have to admit, when I first read Mr. Westlake's post I thought he was saying Suzanne was not a vampire but a fairy or something of the sort. In that case, I have some other objections. "Her complexion [was] as pure as milk" (367) does not, to my mind, describe a vampire's pallor; and the entire description does not feel vampiric to me. And the vampire theory doesn't explain why the narrator never met Suzanne, or forgot meeting her, since his wife's friend did not forget.

From: Peter Westlake, 11 May 1998

> "The flavor of regret is bittersweet."

That *does* make a lot of sense. In fact, I shall enjoy reading that version of the story very much even if another explanation proves to be the true one, just as I enjoyed reading "my" version. So do you think that never seeing Suzanne is sufficiently odd to fit the notion at the start of the story? Actually, I suppose it is, and the narrator hadn't called it to mind before he read the idea.

It certainly is a powerful and poignant story, and at the moment I think you're right.

From: Peter Westlake, 11 May 1998

I do like Adam's theory, even though I don't believe it is the one the author intended. It does fit the text pretty well, but I think it isn't quite strongly enough implied. At least, I *think* I think that.

I would prefer her not to be a vampire. It just seemed to fit, and to be reasonably Wolfeish.

Not meeting her would just be a coincidence, as it is in Proust; it starts the narrator looking through his yearbooks, and reveals the subtext to the (possibly over-imaginative :-) reader, though not to the narrator.

Of the theories I've heard so far, I like Alice's the best. It makes most sense of the structure of the story—with Suzanne's daughter appearing at the end, a very conspicuous part of the story. I do wonder how many other readings there are, though—we haven't had the one yet in which the Pie Club is really the Pudding Club and they're all off ill having babies at exactly the same time, like the women of Midwich. I'll spare you that one, I think.

From: Peter Stephenson, 10 May 1998

> "a repressed memory of Suzanne herself bubbling up, triggered by seeing her daughter."

You're right that this is a key moment, and seems to be asking for a psychological rather than a fantasy explanation. Actually, it recalls another part of Proust, towards the end, when he meets Gilberte Swann's daughter and recognises in her all the things he once saw in Gilberte. Maybe there's a really telling quotation in *Le Temps Retrouvé* (Time Regained) somewhere.

From: Craig Christensen, 11 May 1998

I looked for Spanish Influenza information, to date when the characters were in high school. Of course I was surprised to learn that the Spanish Influenza occurred in 1918 during the First World War. This certainly doesn't seem to be the correct period for the characters' high school years. Interestingly, several sites made the observation that the epidemic has been almost completely wiped from the world's memory.

I took this quote from:

http://www.pbs.org/wgbh/pages/amex/influenza/trackers.html

Perhaps the 1956 quote by H. L. Mencken is the very quote that sparked the short story:

> "Those learning for the first time of the devastating consequences of the worldwide 1918 Spanish influenza epidemic—or pandemic—typically respond with two questions: How could they have never heard of a world-wide scourge that killed upwards of 30 million people? And, could it happen again? [...] The epidemic is seldom mentioned, and most Americans have apparently forgotten it. This is not surprising. The human mind always tries to expunge the untolerable from memory, just as it tries to conceal it while current."

I think that the mention of the Spanish Influenza is a major clue. The narrator has forgotten knowing Suzanne in the past; he hasn't simply failed to meet her. And his relationship with her was not minor, it was consequential.

I am willing to concede that the young lady may not be the narrator's daughter, but I still like the idea.

I have two questions. What is the reference to Hamlet? And why the long rambling description of quilt collecting? In such a compact story it must have significance.

From: Peter Westlake, 11 May 1998

The fact that everyone has forgotten that flu epidemic is certainly very suggestive. At the very least it's a nice coincidence, and a great find—thanks!

The Hamlet, at least, is easy: "There are more things in heaven and earth, Horatio/ Than are dreamt of in your philosophy."

I wondered about the quilts too. Misdirection? Some very subtle clue? They connect with the late eighteenth century, but I don't know what to make of that, if anything.

From: Adam Louis Stephanides, 11 May 1998

I think my theory is at least as strongly implied by the text as is Weer's ghostly state in *Peace*, which we know Wolfe intended.

The main problem I now have with Alice's theory is that it doesn't account for the strong indications that the narrator has indeed forgotten something. (I don't think you can say he has "forgotten" not having met Suzanne.)

From: William H. Ansley, 12 May 1998

I came up with my own theory, almost against my will. I doubt very much that it's what Wolfe had in mind (if he really had anything more in mind than a nod to Proust) but it does have the signal advantage of making the quilt-hunting significant.

But first a comment: it is very hard to tell when the "present" is for the narrator. On page 363 of *Endangered Species* (pb) he says, "There are a number of pages missing from the class picture section of the earlier book and I seem to recall that these were torn out and cut up to obtain the individual photographs many decades ago."

Assuming he is right about the time frame, this "many decades" poses problems. I would think that at a minimum it would need to be three decades, though "many" usually means more than this. Three is no problem. It would mean (if the pages were torn out of the sophomore yearbook right away) that the narrator could be forty-four $(14 + 30)$ and that Suzanne would have had her daughter at the age of twenty-eight (44-16). Of course, if the pages were torn out of the sophomore yearbook "n" years after it was taken home, we have to add n to the above ages.

If "many" is four, we have Suzanne giving birth at the age of thirty-eight; if five, forty-eight. And "many" could certainly be a higher number than these!

I say the narrator did know Suzanne as a child and as a teenager. They fell in love and, perhaps, planned to marry. But the narrator's mother did find a "American Revolution times" quilt or embroidered blanket at some time before the narrator's senior year and probably after his sophomore year, in high school. It was infected with smallpox. It had been preserved because some colonists intended to use it to infect Indians. (I have read that colonists did this. I don't know if it is true but it seems plausible. Certainly many, many Indians died of smallpox and they almost certainly caught it from European settlers.) Perhaps a smallpox epidemic breaks out. Even if all the inhabitants of the town were vaccinated, it is likely that some would still be susceptible to the virus to some degree. But certainly Suzanne gets the disease and is dreadfully scarred. Other people who come down with it get milder cases and are not scarred noticeably. (This is consistent with what the *Encyclopedia Britannica* has to say about smallpox.) The source of the disease is discovered. The quilt/blanket is destroyed. Suzanne blames the narrator and his family and hates him. The narrator, horrified by Suzanne's appearance, no longer loves her. Or, perhaps, she is not so badly scarred, but he finds that he cannot love her now that she is no longer "perfect" and she hates him for this.

Suzanne can't be photographed because she is sick with smallpox or she refuses because of her scars. The narrator destroys the pages of the sophomore yearbook because he can't look at her old "pure as milk" complexion without being guilt-stricken. (The description of Suzanne's daughter, under my theory, is to let us know what a beauty Suzanne was, pre-smallpox.) Perhaps his own picture is missing because of endearments written on it by Suzanne, that he could no longer bear to read. He forgets all about the smallpox outbreak and so does the town. Suzanne becomes a recluse and so doesn't serve as a reminder. This also explains why he never saw her after high school.

In this context, the fact that the narrator (falsely) remembers a Spanish Influenza epidemic is significant because it was a pandemic disease outbreak that was totally forgotten in a relatively short time, as Craig Christensen's posting noted. This may be a hint that the town could forget its own epidemic.

The sentence: "On the other hand we are neither of us invalids, nor are we blind" also takes on new significance and perhaps some poignancy, since blindness is a common result of scarlet fever and invalidism could be caused by rheumatic fever or polio. Some part of the narrator that remembers is saying "It could have been worse, couldn't it?"

This could also explain Suzanne having a child quite late in life. She finally finds someone to love and marry despite her reclusiveness and disfigurement.

Now this is certainly not a supernatural explanation of the story, but I don't think that is required. It is certainly against all probability, and the survival of variola (smallpox) virus for hundreds of years might be considered a dislocation of nature.

I am aware there are a lot of problems with this idea; perhaps someone else can refine or build on it. Perhaps the fact that I find it at all convincing just demonstrates that I should get more sleep and do less email reading.

From: Damien Broderick, 13 May 1998

As I was reading this morning—reading the URTH list's digest on my computer screen, I should explain—I was struck by the deluge of posts, deliberately left unread until now, concerning the story "Suzanne Delage". It occurred to me to wonder about this thread. Living all my life, as I have, in a genre comprising less than a hundred thousand stories, I had not even been dimly aware of this particular tale. And yet it had plainly excited the witty and astute lupine readers here. I went as soon as it was convenient to my local library and found the copy of *Endangered Species* that, hardly opened except to read "The Cat," I had returned only a month before, and there belatedly met for the first time the enigmatic absence of Suzanne Delage. Or so it seemed, until, with a strange frisson, my first for the day, I noticed that this story had originally appeared in a collection entitled *Edges* (Pocket Books, 1980), co-edited by Mr. Wolfe's agent, Virginia Kidd, and her other most notable client, Ursula K. Le Guin. This was striking enough as a coincidence, for at that time I too was a client of Ms Kidd. Stranger yet was the fact that this volume, in which I had never previously encountered Mr. Wolfe's story, opens with a novella that I believe Mr. Wolfe might enjoy, entitled "The Ballad of Bowsprit Bear's Stead". As it chanced, I had written that story.

I turned for clues to Ms Kidd's introduction to the story. It proved immediately unreliable in a small way, not perhaps a startling discovery in a paperback original which had printed the closing sentences of my own story at the head of the italicized introduction to the next, Carol Emshwiller's "Omens". We are misinformed that Mr. Wolfe had been "working extensively on his tetralogy (*The Rock of the New Sun*)". Nevertheless, it is worth attending to Ms. Kidd's insiderly comment:

"His short story hereunder is a den of iniquity;
no one else could have written it."

I think this is likely. It is less a madeleine than a reverse
veronica, a kind of Turin test. Here are some incidental, glancing
reflections:

Suzanne is not a vampire, I think, nor is she her own daughter
and mother, not quite. I do think she might have no use for men. Is it
implausible that those exhausting trips taken by Madame Delage and
Mother, so eagerly repeated, were spent as often under the quilt as
on it? Was it Mother who later scissored out the photos of the young
woman who (perhaps)—like daughter, like mother, like
grandmother, faithful mirror of the flesh—so resembled her lost
lover? Why did the bitter old neighbor widow so detest Mrs.
Delage? Had she been displaced in the beautiful friend's affections
(or those of someone looking quite similar—wait, wait for it) by
other, younger women, Mother being merely the latest?

Why should this be the occasion of retrograde amnesia? The
conjecture above might be the root of a complex Oedipal agony of
(as it were) biblical proportions. As Adam noted of this confessedly
(or avowedly) dull small-town dog: "'extraordinary experience' he
refers to is not necessarily supernatural, merely a 'dislocation of all
we expect from nature and probability.'"

The provenance of the luscious, fifteen-year-old daughter of the
absent Suzanne? Michael provided the key allusion to Proust, a
writer for whom sexual evasions and masks were not unknown. But
here's another possible layering (if we are prepared to accept that
Gene Wolfe is vatic as well as gnomic, the necessary premise for
many of this list's entertainingly over-interpretative hi-jinks). You
all know, of course, that Ives Delage (1854-1920) was the French
zoologist who (as the *Encyclopaedia Britannica* tells us) "developed
a method for culturing sea urchins following artificial fertilization of
the eggs with chemicals". This might be irrelevant in the work of
anyone with less interest in cloning and reduplication than Mr.
Wolfe.

From: Adam Louis Stephanides, 13 May 1998

> "Spanish Influenza...certainly doesn't seem to be the correct
period for the characters' high school years."

According to Krug's *The Shaping of the American High School,
1880-1920*, extracurricular activities of the type the narrator

describes were found in that period; and I don't see any other details which are inconsistent with it. (The reference to a "fundamentalist church" might be a problem, since the term may not have been in use then; but this could be the narrator himself using anachronistic terminology.) This would mean, of course, that the "present" of the story was itself in the past when it was published, but I see no problem with that. In fact, the initial reference to "those somewhat political, somewhat philosophical, somewhat historical books which can now be bought by the pound each month" doesn't seem to really apply to the late-1970s publishing scene.

Good question about the quilt. I took it as furthering the characterization of the narrator as boring, as well as indicating a possible source for this trait in his mother's conventionality; but it may well have some more specific significance.

The "many decades ago" bit (363 in *ES*) is indeed hard to explain. To me "many" is certainly more than three, and even more than five—I wouldn't say that Wolfe had written many novels with Severian as protagonist—and as William points out, for Suzanne to be sixty-five now is already pushing the outer limits of probability (although Damien's theory would account for that). I use this to support my own theory: not only has the narrator repressed the events to the extent of suppressing that it was he who tore out the pages, but he pushes the tearing-out back in time to an impossible extent.

Assuming that the comment about the "den of iniquity" reflected inside information and not just the editor having nothing else to say, it confirms that there is *something* under the surface. While the Ives Delage cross-reference is indeed suggestive, though, I don't think I can buy the theory as yet; now if you could tie it in with those quilts....

From: Peter Westlake, 14 May 1998

> "Ives Delage."
Astounding!

I don't know which boggles the mind more—that this is a coincidence, or that it isn't. A bit like life on other worlds.

I see that Ives Delage died soon after the height of the Spanish Flu epidemic; but that way madness lies, I fear.

Here and Now:

The conversation lapsed, for the moment. Mr. André-Driussi suggested in passing his speculation that the small town in question is Cassionsville, the scene of *Peace* and several other short stories. I found the exercise enthralling, proving that readers remain, as always, monarchs of the text—and, equally, that the inexhaustible text baits us endlessly with unexplored possibilities. Or maybe just that Gene Wolfe is smarter and cagier than all of us combined.

BRUCE STERLING: *TOMORROW NOW:*
ENVISIONING THE NEXT FIFTY YEARS

I think Bruce can be characterized as a journalist who likes working around the edges of the new, revolutionary ideas...he's full of manic energy. He's out there with a machine gun of ideas spewing bullets in all directions, and he tends to hit an awful lot of targets head on.

Charles Stross, *Locus,* August 2003

I once suggested that the first novel by Charles Stross's sometime collaborator Cory Doctorow was a prime instance of *blogpunk*, a tooth-grating neologism that deserves a non-fiction partner. If Bruce Sterling's futurist writing (I am explicitly not addressing his sf now) is a form of *blogpunditry*, his book *Tomorrow Now* really can be read only as an instance of this short attention span assemblage idea-tumble format. It is sassy, knowing, with short sharp jabs of wit and factlets, tied together (between, as it were, cool sips at the glass or hotlink twitches at the mouse) by a laconic, sardonic delivery that's more stand-up comic than Toffler Associates truffle hound snuffler nosing after the future shock drivers of social change.

His narrative device for holding this explosion inside one heaving skin is Shakespeare's seven ages of Man, from *As You Like It*: infant, student, lover, soldier, mature magistrate, aging scholar, senescent old dodderer. Within this cyclic trajectory, already warped considerably from Shakespeare's paradigm as well-fed, exercised, secure Boomers made 60 the new 40, his sharply observed anecdotes, *obiter dicta,* case studies and artful self-revelations tell us that *things will change* (and how! but not *how*, which is unknowable), yet *not that much.* Why, otherwise, regale us (fascinatingly) with a fifty-page digression on three insurgent thugs—Shameil Basaev, Khottab and Arkan? In a real blog, this would mark a week's abrupt obsession, or a sideways link to a site on paramilitary tactics in the epoch of the cellphone. It doesn't have anything much to do with futurist analysis except, perhaps, to insist that tomorrow will be just like today, only different, yet *not that much.*

It is a book made, in a way, of digressions and asides.

Here is Sterling on how money moves away:

> whenever some uppity national government politically restricts some activity in the name of its people…. The money goes, but you don't get to follow it. If you could, then the money would have no reason to run; it would have to sit where it was with a sense of grim resignation. The money is running from you—from you and your decisions that affect its interests. (191-2)

This is funny, astute, cynical and soundbitey all at once. It reminds me of a *Wired* version of "Adam Smith," the charming money explainer of the 1970s who told us ignorati the sorry saga of pork belly futures, random walkers, chartists and frequentists, and the wily corporate accountants who paved the way for Enron, Madoff, and worse, a quarter century later. Sterling promises us glimpses of the coming half century, but most of his sparky, jittery book deals with the now, the now of a very smart guy whose tendrils quiver with the beat of the noösphere and who found to his delight (one imagines) that "vaporous rantings" were suddenly, in a climate where intellectual property smelled sweeter than frankincense, myrrh and gold, as good as platinum plastic, that "what used to be sophomoric philosophizing around a pizza and a pitcher suddenly became a valuable exchange of marketable information" (223-4). So valuable, even on the far margins of the real money (surging on its toes in its fantastically over-designed and hyper-featured GPS-detecting escapologist's Pumas), that "when April 15 rolls around, I can see, with wide-eyed incredulity, that I command more revenue and resources than 99 percent of this planet's population" (213). Naturally this is an unseemly confession, and Sterling quickly points out, drawlingly, that "If I were to cut and paste my latest 1040 tax form onto the page here, it would be far worse and more shocking than posting nude pics of myself on the Internet" (216).

Of course Sterling is not filthy rich, he is insufficiently obsessed for that, or at least his obsessions, bloggishly, keep changing. He is too interested in the variousness of the ever-changing world, and simultaneously in the slow regular Shakespearean transitions of his life as family man. It is somehow shocking to realize that Sterling (b. 1954) is more than half a century old, nearly as astounding as the idea that sf's cantankerous *enfant terrible*, Harlan Ellison, is in his mid-70s. Will either of them make it far into the next 50 years? It is conceivable that Sterling will, if he socks some of his money away sensibly and drastic change continues to roll, to accelerate.

Curiously, at a time when a Vingean technological Singularity was still the rage in sf (if only as a Large Terrible Obstacle to be skirted as amusingly as one could manage), Sterling dismissed the prospect. His method of avoiding such a cataclysm of blocked prediction, of futurist opacity, is intriguingly double: it won't happen (or won't be such a big deal if it does), and when it does happen it will just be the first of ever more "rapid, massive explosion[s] of following Singularities" (297).

Can both these dicta be correct? Yes, when viewed through jaded mirrorshades. We or our descendants might be posthuman, but it won't do anyone any good because "the posthuman condition is banal.... By the new, post-Singularity standards, posthumans are just as bored and frustrated as humans ever were...still quotidian entities in a gritty, rules-based physical universe...swiftly and bruisingly brought up against the limits of their own condition...." (297). We might have life extension, even recovered youth (as in his splendid novel *Holy Fire*), but it will be granted piecemeal and cost plenty in dollars and pain. It is a curiously mid-twentieth century picture of dolorous surgery and uncertain healing, even though, for Sterling, last century's blind spot was filled rather with gleaming chrome, effortless machinery and slick Stepford social engineering—as well as the looming certainties of Mutual Assured Destruction's "sudden and total flaming extermination," an "exciting sense" that we perversely enjoyed for its "mythic resonance" (259). What Sterling denies explicitly and by repeated implication is that the next fifty years can be anything other than a continuation of the current ontology by other means.

To suppose otherwise, he claims, is to fall into a nerdish, geeky, digeratish delusion that computers and their numerical algorithms can rupture history's chaotic wanderings through the state space we humans have constructed for ourselves in the long 250,000 year nature-denuding catastrophe of the Sixth global Extinction. I am not the most objective critic of this position, having so firmly staked my own assessment, in two pop-sci futurist books and several novels, upon the likelihood of an impending Singularity that one reviewer called it my *idée fixe*. It is not quite that, but I share with quite a few sf writers this working premise: Stross's Eschaton and accelerando,

Egan's Introdus, Banks's Sublime, Williams and Dix's Spike, MacLeod's and Vinge's frank Singularity, my own Spike or Transcension....

Is this no better than the cognitive Monkey Puzzles Sterling warns futurists against in his 2003 Afterword? The coconut is stuck to a greedy primate's clenched fist: "'You know, on me, this thing looks great!'" (319). It is an appealing, appalling image, echoed in its own mirror by a host of previous very silly obsessions and delusions and Conceptoids in the genre: flying saucers, *deros* from Lemuria skulking under the crust, dianetics, psi machines, unidirectional thrust from the Dean Drive, astrological radio interference, messages from archaic space probes... "Only recently," Sterling confesses, "did I become pretty sure that I have already had, in my life to date, at least four of them" (320). Cyberpunk ("the Movement") was the most prominent; hacker anxiety perhaps another. Was his homespun Viridian movement, lately wound up as redundant, a Monkey Puzzle? Other sf writers might find their own temptation in cryonics, nanotechnology, libertarian or socialist utopianism, Gaian religiosity, greenhouse activism, revived nuclear power. The difference, I would argue, is that the singularity perspective is not absurd, counter-intuitive, wistful, rapturous or supernatural. It is just what seems to be happening with the pace, compression and convergence of key technologies, like the global downturn at the end of the first decade of this century. Not to all technologies, of course. Just the driving information generators and handlers.

In a talk to the Long Now Foundation, though, Sterling argued that this picture is not just preposterous but plainly wrong (and Nobel award economist Paul Krugman echoed this in 2009): there is no runaway acceleration in the technology of water management, say. There might be, he allows, in biotech, and in *Tomorrow Now* this is the arena he designates for drastic disruptive change. He mandates a Shaper future (to borrow from the space opera tales, now long superannuated, of his early maturity), not a Mechanist one. Yet even here it seems he will not allow that the brakes might fail. Who would wish, he asks, to be a benighted early adopter engineered kid and adult, and paints a poignant portrait of weird icky modified humans unable even to reproduce with their loved one because of their scrambled chromosomes.

It is a cunning rhetorical move, but I suspect it is simple wrong in both social and biomedical terms. When a few extra or modified genes can be spliced into ovum or blastocyst, carrying the shaping information for enhanced intelligence and dexterity, sensitivity or robust confidence or both, not to mention immunity from routine aging and fated senescence—how many will resist the opportunity? And if the early adopters are less advantaged than their later kin, how does this differ from the ever increasing educational and nutritional opportunities (not always taken up, granted) of postindustrial culture's generations? More saliently still: if our DNA proves adjustable, it will surely grow *more so* with time. Today, if you detest your haircut, wait a few weeks or months and change it; arguably, in the future this will also be true of your codons and epigenome. Oddly, Sterling admits as much; genomically unmodified people will "*swallow* their advanced genetics...let microbes undergo all those hazards" (30). Why should this work for the unmodified but not the botched clones? We never find out.

Perhaps the central question, if I am right, is: how far off is this future? Does it fall within Sterling's fifty-year ambit? I am inclined to think so. Biogerontologist Dr. Aubrey de Grey, the brilliant poster boy of Engineered Negligible Senescence, argues that we'll reach "escape velocity" from inevitable death sooner than that, just by resolving practical research problems that already have been identified. It might not help Sterling, or me, or most of my readers, but it will surely make the latter part of the coming half century tremendously different—far more so than Sterling admits. He concludes in a poetic peroration that "The future is a lovely thing to contemplate, but...it is where we go to die" (300). "Death is merely a necessity" (301). Yes, it *has been* for untold generations, but might not remain so for much longer. Emortality is not in itself a recipe for singularity, for utter opacity—intelligence markedly greater than human is needed for that—but it starts to blur the image in the futurescope.

But here I merely oppose Sterling's (reasoned) prejudice with my own. No doubt this arcane, skiffyish argument will enter the realm of public policy within the next decade or two, as the first fruits of effective cheap nanotechnology, extended healthful longevity, and hypercomputing (simulating folded proteins and unfolded brain functions alike) start to impact Sterling's New World Order and perhaps to heal some of the turmoil and misery of his New World Disorder. Meanwhile, Sterling's darting mind will tear along the peripheries of both worlds, and we will be the better for what he bears back for our inspection, an eager kid in a body that is already grandfatherly by ancestral standards. *Tomorrow Now* is already Yesterday Now, and arguably Tomorrow Lite, but it remains loads of fun and blogsomely tasty.

ROBERT SILVERBERG: *OTHER SPACES, OTHER TIMES: A LIFE SPENT IN THE FUTURE*

Like Shadrach in the furnace, Robert Silverberg has been tested by fire—literally, and not only once, terrifying and dispiriting as that must be, but twice, as one home burned and another was threatened by wildfire. Figuratively, the same is true of his life as a writer. A highly intelligent, curious only child—"too clever by at least half...plagued with allergies...learning none of the social graces" (98)—he was besotted first by science and myth, then by science fiction. He flung himself happily into that romantic conflagration most sf readers will recall from their own childhoods. When he caught alight as a precocious sf writer, he was doomed, in a parable of the commercial history of American genre writing, to burn steadily, then brightly, burn out, smolder, rekindle.

The fever set in seriously, as it has with many, at the boundary between childhood and achieved adolescence. "I had just turned 15," a high school sophomore. A friend tells him about a store in downtown Brooklyn selling old science fiction magazines. Young Silverberg finds hundreds upon hundreds of science fiction magazines old and new. "My allowance was perhaps two dollars a week." Trembling, he asks the prices. Half a dollar or a quarter each. "Reader, I bought them all." And still owns them: "sometimes I look at them even today, though not to read, because most of the stories they contain are crude, practically unreadable things. No matter. The mere sight of them gets my heart beating faster" (15-19).

In a major autobiographical sketch from 1974 ("Sounding Brass, Tinkling Cymbal"), now the centerpiece of this rather jumbled, enthralling collation of a book, he famously wrote: "[T]he essential starting point, for me, is the confession (and boast) that I am a man who is living his own adolescent fantasies" (97). Prodigious, he wrote early and often, selling his first novel in January, 1954, when he was nineteen. It came out the following year (after severe editorial criticism and rewriting), but attempts to place short stories led him to "draw a sinister conclusion." Trifling items sold, more ambitious pieces bounced. Here was the moment of his Fall, the realization that "if I intended to earn a livelihood writing fiction, it would be wiser to use my rapidly developing technical skills to turn out mass-produced formularized stories at high speed, rather than to lavish passion and energy on more individual works that would be difficult to sell" (105).

He developed "a deadly facility." Now and then he attempted the kind of fiction he respected as a reader (he had a degree from Columbia), but selling it was difficult. So he slipped into disciplined, quick-fire production: "carefully-carpentered but mediocre... much [that] was wholly opportunistic trash" (106). Perhaps L. Ron Hubbard and other frank hacks from an earlier generation might have remained untroubled by such *trahison* of his best possibilities, but Silverberg, rebuked by the more ambitious work of his peers, found himself sunk "in an abyss of self-contempt" (107).

As his prolific output grew, he mass-produced entertaining but undemanding fiction for Ace Books, with its "rather squalid format," but he was "too far gone in materialism to care." His typewriter rolled out endless pages in a dozen genres. "I recall writing one whole piece before lunch and one after lunch, day in, day out" (108-109). Aside from the damage to his self-esteem, it was "stupefyingly boring" (110). Silverberg turned finally to non-fiction, with some notable success, leaving the sleazy magazines behind. But in the early '60s, the upheaval known as the new wave began to shake the comfortable pulp certitudes of consumer science fiction— already damaged by the collapse of the sf magazine market in the late 1950s—with dazzling new work by Ballard, Aldiss, Zelazny, Disch, and many others. A newly literate, college-trained young audience responded to such work, even as the old guard grumbled and seethed. Many restrictions fell away; "a trifle belatedly, I joined the revolution" (113).

A millionaire from his flabbergasting toil, Bob Silverberg could now risk a return to more challenging fiction. (He insists on "Bob"—"Robert" was that ill-fitted child, the pupa from which emerged the confident, worldly, fastidious writer.) By the mid-'60s, perhaps a decade after his beginnings, a newer Silverberg was allowed out of the jail into which he placed himself. A cascade of notable books poured from his typewriter, despite a debilitating attack of thyroid hyperactivity. If this was nature's way of telling him to slow down, it did not quite turn out that way. His new abundant prose "was often oblique and elliptical...action was fragmented in the telling, the characters were angular, troubled souls" (116). In the year following his illness, "knowing I was at last writing only what I wanted to write, as well as I could do it," he produced three novels told in his new voice, two long history books, various short stories, and seven non-fiction children's books.

Was this change of heart, this return to purity of intention, welcomed? Not always. As his science fiction grew more complex and sophisticated, and gained awards or nominations, he was painfully afflicted by accusations of pandering to the New Wave. "Having blithely sold out so many times as a young man...I was hurt to find myself blamed for selling out again...when I finally wrote something that grew from my own creative needs...." (118).

Thus, Silverberg's rather lacerating mid-career report, which we read again now more than thirty-five years later. (One principal deficit of this fascinating book is that no provenance is provided for the many essays and snippets that comprise its overlapping, sometimes redundant narrative, although every section or fragment is dated at its end. I'd have preferred to see the date at the *start* of each module, along with the place of original publication.) A postscript from one year later, resigned, somewhat bitter, reports his decision to abandon science fiction at the height of his powers and accomplishment. As royalties and public response alike dried up, "it seems simplest and best to give it up...evidently modern American commercial science fiction is no place for a serious writer. I have learned my lesson; the seriousness has been burned out of me by it...." (127).

As we know, several years later yet another Silverberg rose from the ashes. Still ambitious, still technically expert, he began to build a series of enormous imaginative structures, crowd-pleasers with the complexity of those trilogies and longer sequences that would remake fantasy in the decades ahead, for good and ill. *Lord Valentine's Castle*, set in the vast low density world of Majipoor, combined the sorts of high-level intrigue and ecological detail familiar from Frank Herbert's *Dune* sequence, the picaresque of Jack Vance, the high consequential quest of *Lord of the Rings....* It was a masterful concoction, and did very well. There have been a number of sequels. Was this another act of treason to his deepest ambitions? I had always suspected as much, but his loving and delightfully detailed account of the genesis of Majipoor has made me reassess. Bob Silverberg told me, "Every word of it was deeply felt. Once I'm inside a book, I live it, whatever my motive in marketing it to my publisher may have been. Valentine is as real a character to me as [protagonist of *Dying Inside*] David Selig is, mutatis mutandis."

* * * * * * *

Since then, Silverberg has never returned to the mad pace of his earlier days, but it might be supposed that he has trimmed his sails even as his sales have expanded. In 2009, seventy-four-years old, he was effectively retired—he told me, "I applaud those who go on challenging the norms of mediocrity in our field but I have neither the stamina nor the desire to return to the fray myself"—but that doesn't mean he is no longer writing. These most recent years get short shrift in the compilation, but then so too, in any intimacy, do the years of his marriage to his first wife, Barbara. As an essay in memoir, the emphasis remains squarely on the writing; I wanted to hear more about, say, his friendship with Terry and Carol Carr, but such wishes might seem impertinent. His most recent essays cast back once more to those earliest years of publication, framing for us some of the experience that went into writing and placing fiction ambitious and otherwise. We do see his early encounters with *Astounding/Analog*'s fabled editor, John W. Campbell, and other editors such as Howard Browne, Bob Lowndes, Fred Pohl; learn of his remarkable synergistic collaborations with the late Randall Garrett; suffer his fires and their psychic aftermath.

Inevitably, and justly, the book closes with his ascension in 2004 to the status of Grand Master, the highest award granted by his peers in the Science Fiction and Fantasy Writers of America. Silverberg is candid: "I think that much of what I wrote over those decades was pretty damned good, and the fact that I have now received the Grand Master award indicates that I'm not the only one who feels that way" (169). Much of his best fiction continues in print, although sometimes only in translation. If his recognition and acknowledgement by the literary community in United States has never seemed likely (although the recent canonization of Philip K. Dick and H. P. Lovecraft shows that the critical climate is changing), it must have delighted him to read the recent estimate by Scott Timberg in the *Los Angeles Times* (April 21, 2009) of his greatest novel, *Dying Inside*: "It feels...like Philip Roth." Timberg adds that "Michael Chabon has called it 'one of those rare novels that manages to be at once dazzling and tender.'"

Bob Silverberg is a complex, remarkable man and writer. The banked fires are still burning there, behind the cool prose.

JOHN CLUTE: FANCY DANCING IN THE SWILL TROUGH: A CHORUS LINE

Half a century ago, this is how science fiction reviews looked in *Galaxy* magazine, then one of the two ambitious outlets for English-language science fiction:

> In the present volume, Kimball Kinnison, dreamboat, Second Stage Lensman and whatnot, and his mighty crew of assistants of various shapes and planetary origins is still hunting down the Evil Pow-

ers that are attacking us from outside our Galaxy, and still failing to find the real villains, the Eddorians. They are still ridding the Universe of Boskonians instead, and a good thing, too—the vicious, sadistic drug-peddlers! And, in the end, Kim acquires his Clarissa in holy matrimony—at last! (*Galaxy,* No. 13, April 1954, UK edition, 65)

Thus, the excellent anthologist Groff Conklin, tongue-in-cheek and no doubt dying inside (he mentions E. E. Smith's "style reminiscent of the balloons in the s.f. comic strips," the "thud and blunder").

A year or two later, Conklin observed of Smith's *Children of the Lens*:

> Sure, it's written in a style varying from the irritating to the infantile. Sure, its characters aren't much more than cardboard cutouts.
>
> Even so, you can't escape the fact that the work has appeal. It moves! (*Galaxy,* No. 29, August 1955, UK edition, 83)

In the same issue, he reviewed *Satellite One*, by Jeffery Lloyd Castle:

> When I first began reading his book, I said to myself, "Ochone! Another one of those stuffy British jobs! But when I finally laid it down, I said—out loud this time—"Eureka! The best novel on the first space station yet to appear!"
>
> The moral: don't always let your momentary distaste for a writing style deter you from further reading. (*Ibid.,* 80)

Two decades on, a little more, call it a generation, this is how sf reviewing sounded in *New Worlds*, notoriously:

> Stately, anfractuous James Blish comes down from Fabers, bearing a bowl of scholium on which two novels and a best of him lie crossed. Lyly's *Geology*, euphuistic sod, is sustained gently behind him by the mild ignorant readership. He holds the bowl aloft and intones:

—The world's my Ostrea edulis.
...with a sigh, down the dark winding stairs he comes to us with gifts, this grim scholar, fearful jesuit, reaper of Joyce and biology.... (*New Worlds Quarterly*, 1975, 118)

The first thing we see instantly, smiling, is Clute's knowing trope on the opening of James Joyce's *Ulysses*:

Stately, plump Buck Mulligan came from the stairhead, bearing a bowl of lather on which a mirror and a razor lay crossed. A yellow dressing-gown, ungirdled, was sustained gently behind him by the mild morning air. He held the bowl aloft and intoned:
—*Introibo ad altare Dei.*
Halted, he peered down the dark winding stairs and called up coarsely:
—Come up, Kinch. Come up, you fearful jesuit.
([1922] 1960, 3)

It is an audacious leap (maybe Clute would call that a soubresaut), or was in 1975, and a smack in the eye to sf's mild ignorant readership. Ochone! How many have clue one, at this outset? For that matter, how many knew Conklin's flourished *ochone*, a Gaelic expression of regret and lamentation? Beyond a doubt, Clute at thirty-five, damn near at the brambly verge of that Dantean gloomy wood, was luxuriating in his own cleverness, his studiously flamboyant obscurities, soliciting the appreciative grins, perhaps the self-preening or ingratiating grins, of those few sf readers educated in the larger worlds of canonical literature and perhaps of antiquarian science but louche with it: the company, maybe, who clustered around Michael Moorcock as the New Wave ebbed and you could say just about anything, dare any jape, because who was listening, really? Just the other smartasses. Just us, and how we loved it. I still do.

A third of a century deeper into the gloomy wood, the clotted preciosity Clute once accused Samuel R. Delany of grows in his own diction more elaborate, thorny, anfractuous and deliriously sure-footed, in his enigmatic unwrapping of enigmas the rest of us took for simple legless trunks in the desert of genre. So we find such puzzleheaded candid admissions as Keith Brooke's response to his novel *Appleseed*:

There is a wordiness familiar from Clute's non-fiction. Or, to be fairer, it's not so much a wordiness as a commitment to using the most right word in any situation. This is not an over-written novel, it's an intensely-written one. At its best it's a fantastically effective technique: a spangly word-portrait that has a real sense of wonder bursting off every page. At its worst, it gets in the way, blinding the reader to Clute's wildly detailed imaginings. (Brooke, *Infinity Plus,* online)

The moral, perhaps: don't always let your momentary distaste for a writing style deter you from further reading. Don't let your momentary distaste for seeing the eyes on the same side of the nose deter you from looking at Picasso. No, it is worse than that, because Clute's crab apples of the sun are burnished and placed with appalling accuracy and intent. Or so it seems, so it sounds, so it opens to the attuned eye. Few sf eyes are tuned to the full spectrum. An intelligent reviewer, Rich Horton, approached *Appleseed*

rather in awe at the imagination evident both in the world-building and the prose; and rather in awe at the ambitious conceptualizing. At the same time I concede that I found the book difficult. The writing is extremely dense: line by line a pleasure, but a pleasure which requires some labor to achieve; labor which is perhaps tiring over time. (Horton, *SF Site,* online)

Clute, after all, is "known first and foremost as a critic...for his formidable intelligence and vocabulary, and his enjoyment in wielding both...at the same time interesting and a bit intimidating" (*Ibid.*). Perhaps tiring. A bit intimidating. That arcane, take-no-prisoners precision and pith is shared with few other writers who have toiled in the mode of sf and adjacent workspaces: Jack Vance at his best, although he is mostly gorgeous decoration over routine tropes; Gene Wolfe; Martin Amis, perhaps. There is an eerie suitability in Robert Douglas-Fairhurst's encomium for Amis:

Actually, your first reaction on reading a novel as mind-tinglingly good as *Yellow Dog* is not so much admiration as a kind of grateful despair. Mostly this is because, like all great writers, he seems to have guessed what you thought about the world, and then expressed it far better than you ever could. (*Guardian* review, 2003)

And of course Amis's writing, like Clute's own fiction and much of his criticism, has suffered plenty of head- and fist-shaking. The resonance with Clute's textual dynamic might be a cause for apprehension. Tibor Fischer praised Amis's memoir *Experience* thus: "beautifully written and clever. Amis is the overlord of the [*Oxford English Dictionary*]. No one can mobilise the English language like him. No one."—only to assail his work (indeed, his character): "one of Amis's weaknesses is that he isn't content to be a good writer, he wants to be profound; the drawback to profundity is that it's like being funny, either you are or you aren't, straining doesn't help." (*Telegraph* review, 2003)

Is that what it is, though, in Clute? Bruce Gillespie, a commentator with a beautifully limpid and effective style, told me:

> I'm not too impressed by wordiness born of self-importance.... Clute is ostentatiously self-important, like Amis, but also funny, and well aware of the effect his rhetoric is having on the lumbering reader such as myself. I prefer the approach in direct descent from Edmund Wilson and Gore Vidal—precise and perfect use of words to put the blade in deeper and cause the reader to yelp louder in pain when recognizing the truth of the criticism. No decoration, because violence is intended to the reader's held assumptions, and no reader will put up with such violence if there is any indirection or hesitation. (private communication)

Yes, but.... Not all fancy dancing is evasive; sometimes it is the matador's glacial capework, the intricated readying of the sword thrust (into the reader's prejudice, or into the problematic). Deploying the technical jargon of criticism, its working tools, can resemble straining after profundity, especially when the unusual lexicon is of your own coinage or idiosyncratic borrowing. Clute's more resonant readings plunge his giddy followers into exogamy (the marrying out of genre and discourse), entelechy (the hidden soul of text and world), kenosis (a theological emptying, the fall from godhood to mortality). Sometimes the current runs the other way. When I first encountered Clute's use of "Thinning," the stripping away of density and meaning from an imagined world under ontological attack, I thought immediately that he was invoking the trope of kenosis—I knew he was a fan of Harold Bloom—under a kinder, gentler nickname. Not quite; in *The Encyclopedia of Fantasy*, co-edited by Clute with "John Grant," he wrote the motif entry for KENOSIS: "As an act of BONDAGE, whether or not voluntary, kenosis tends to mark a THINNING of the relevant world" (535). THINNING, meanwhile, "is a sign of the loss of attention to the stories whose outcome might save the heroes and the folk; it is a representation of the BONDAGE of the mortally real" (942). A tang of the biblical there, again suitably given Bloom's own saturation in scripture and Cabbala, as with the profoundly allusive corpora of Clute's favorite writers, Gene Wolfe and John Crowley; and maybe, under the rubbery skin of the motif, just the faintest scent of arch perversity.

The mild ignorant readership of sf and commercial fantasy surely finds Clute's routine armamentarium perverse enough: POLDERS, those fantastical "enclaves of toughened REALITY" (772), CROSSHATCH worlds where different realities meet without merging, although menaced by "an inherent and threatening instability" (237), WAINSCOTS, hidden habitats of those "living in the interstices of the dominant world" (991), as many science fiction and fantasy fans do, perhaps, reviled but mordantly pregnant with the future and the occulted, a sort of PARIAH ELITE (wonderful pun on C. Wright Mills' 1956 trope *power elite*) "which, though despised and rejected by society, remembers and preserves the secret knowledge necessary to keep the world from ultimate THINNING" (745). Yes, perhaps fans are kenotic Slans after all, for "it is always possible that the PE may be the SECRET MASTERS of the world" (*Ibid.*).

* * * * * * *

Curiously, a hint of Clute's bent for explication is discernible in his 1975 review of the horror movie *Them*:

> the intense visibility of [generic] moves, or trope exposure, arguably distinguishes not only the generic film but maybe cinema as a whole from other narrative arts...[The critic's] primary tasks must still be the creation of an adequate working distinction of cinema from the other arts, and the amassing of a vocabulary of moves. ("Trope Exposure," 1975)

For "cinema" read "science fiction" and "fantasy," and one sees here Clute's self-imposed task of the next quarter century: building an adequate vocabulary for his chosen paraliteratures, and then deploying it relentlessly upon both classic and emergent texts. What's especially noticeable in these encyclopedia definitions, and the many pointers to their embodiment in exemplary sf and fantasy texts, is their comparative simplicity and clarity, their availability. As well as allowing himself free funambulating rein in less populous arcades, for many years Clute more chastely reviewed fantastic literatures in metropolitan newspapers such as the *Washington Post*. It is clear that the discipline has sharpened and streamlined his tenor in vehicles where the need for directness overwhelms his impulse for fancy dancing. Still, in the free Internet venue *Science Fiction Weekly* (now *SF Wire,* which alas has apparently deleted all the following reviews and comments) where he owned a regular soapbox excessively titled "Excessive Candour," few of his reviews fail to rasp mild ignorant nerve ends. Maybe this: William Gibson's *All Tomorrow's Parties*

> puts some spine into the reality relaxants that dosed *Virtual Light* (1993) into amiable torpor, and ironizes the lovesong to the insides of the world we are about to enter that made *Idoru* (1996) into a claustrophile's epithalamium...there is some sense that profound novelistic aperçus, bleaknesses of a saving precision of focus, are diddled into genre outcomes.

Maybe this, of Michael Swanwick's *Jack Faust*:

> the scherzo turns into delirium and shadowings of Thomas Mann's *Doktor Faustus* (1947).... Saturnalia beheads the masques of Reason....

You have to love that scrupulous dating of Mann's canonical novel, for the benefit, no doubt, of the on-line readers also anxious to learn from SFW's *News of the Week* that

> Cards, avatars and ratings changes on the beta server will not be transferred to the live server, but Wizards is urging players to continue as normal so that they can identify and address any new problems, the site reported.
> Based on the *Magic: The Gathering* collectible-card strategy game, *Magic: The Gathering Online 2.0*

is a completely revised version of the original online game, which was released in 2002.

and that

> A federal appeals court rejected a lawsuit by *Star Trek: Deep Space Nine* actress Chase Masterson (Leeta) against the dating service Matchmaker.com, ruling that a fake Internet profile posted with the star's image was not the company's fault....

Meanwhile, here is Clute in the same venue:

> insofar as [Margaret Atwood's] utterances [demeaning of sf] manifest an interior occlusion of intellect, they help explain the abjectly bad bits of *Oryx and Crake*, the sclerotic exiguity of its backstory, the miserly belatedness of the future it depicts...the text itself...cannot allow too much reality into its cod-dystopian remit, into its sci-fi-in-bondage gaze upward from the deep past toward the aged props of yesterday. Like some fossil jewel, [the novel] does shine moistly for an instant under the tap, when its author forgets herself before it falls back into the sands of time, which cover it. When we shut the book, it is as though it had never been.

I find myself wondering again—and these are by no means the most minatory passages of Clutean mass market reviewing—if the web browsing readers, savvy as they surely are with multi-level computer quests and multi-person avatar domains, with C++ and Python, with *Duke Nukem* and Randian libertarianism, might skim this in dazzlement but when they click off the site, it is as though it had never been. At least with the other (often very good) reviewers at *Sci-Fi Weekly*—Paul Di Filippo for example—you were provided, in a big sidebar box, a handy A- or B+ or occasionally a C, just in case you could not work out whether the reviewer liked the book or not, and if so how much. Clute's arrangement avoids the rating box and rigid protocol (one imagines a held ironic glance, a quailing editor), rendering it just that little more inutile to the mild ignorant readership attracted to the site for its regular breathless, endless updates on TV and movie sci-fi, actors, directors, collectable action figures.

So what the hell is John Clute doing, fancy dancing amid the supermarket mounds of military sf and superheroes, crapulous derivative fifth-xeroxed copies of copies of jaded sharecrop piffle? Well, I suspect I know what he is doing: on the one hand, making an honest living, drawing upon his vast stock of insiderly erudition; on the other, proselytizing the right stuff, holding high the flag, and good on him for it. What I want to know is how he can get away with it. What do *they* get out of it, picking their way into this commentator widely seen (readers' comments confirm) as impenetrably difficult and showy, like Samuel Delany, yet, unlike Delany, standing now at the very summit of English-language sf reviewing and encyclopedic visibility?

I can easily tell you one of the great satisfactions I get from Clute: he knows where the writers are coming from. Years ago, in *Foundation*, he noticed a small polyphonic space opera of mine that "almost precisely replicates," he observed, "the basic story unfolded in...Verdi's *Don Carlos* (1867), a very great opera whose story is based (how closely I do not know) on the play *Don Carlos* (1787) by Friedrich Schiller" (*Foundation*, 59, 90). That moment of recognition burned inside me with a hard, gemlike flame; in fact, I'd based the tale directly on Schiller, and Clute was perhaps the only person in the world to have noticed, or at any rate to have said so. Arguably, this is an irrelevancy; perhaps all a reader needs to know is how well or ill today's writer has performed, and forget the hommages and roots. But science fiction is plagued more than ever with loss of memory, willful or inadvertent. The more we can clutch up the past into our responses, the richer will be our readings of the imagined future. Clute knows an awful lot (about, it's true, a truly awful lot, plus plenty of the pure quill), and that is a reason to be cheerful when we hear his confident pronouncements in the marketplace.

Clute's own account, weary and shrugging perhaps, is this:

> I think that all readers co-create the works they intersect. Reading is a form of creation. Reading as a critic—for me, at least—is a heightened form of normal reading, during the process of which I try consciously to co-create, through my own metaphors of understanding, the text being encountered. Because I'm very conscious of this, I think my reviews may in turn have a seductive/invasive timbre which is unusual. But this, again, is a question of degree.... Willy nilly, we are all makers.

All this has been a commonplace in literary theory for at least three decades, but the news can still shock any audience hungry for the author's authoritative authorization. So the question comes around again: what do they, mild and ignorant—makers unaware—get out of it?

The obvious answer rises also from theory, not to mention simple marketing nous: no unified audience exists, not even any single unified reader, although the lazy and complacent border the condition. Genre, after all, is a machine for departicularizing the unique, delving for the bone beneath the individual face, the homeobox within the mutant code. It is a recognition of those unlike families of narrative moves. That need not make it a totalizing corset, especially in any genre, like sf and modern fantasy, that isn't a genre but a mode. One size does not fit all, nor do the makers and re-makers intend it to.

So Clute in full entrechat is in the air for us aficionados, probably, and for the redemption of self-flagellating editors, while the tripe is on another dozen or thousand pages for the groundlings and for the twelve year olds getting their first gawking whiff of conceptual breakthrough, alterity, paradise lite. They'll grow up, lots of them, go to college and read (or read about) Joyce and Lyell (of *The Elements of Geology*) and Lyly (of *Euphues*) and brilliant mid-twentieth century scions of thudding "Doc" Smith's Golden Age unreadable glories (which they might read themselves while still 12, lucky dogs), scions like the sublime James Blish or Theodore Sturgeon, muffled in four great gray shawls of scholia, getting it wrong in the details and lastingly right in the blessed soaring shape of the new thing, which (in a 1999 review of Neal Stephenson's *Cryptonomicon*) Clute reminds us, still dancing despite the sucking sounds of the mire under his heels, is now the old thing: "sf as a genre is dead."

CHAPTER SIX

AFTERLIFE AS SCIENCE FICTION

The concept of a life for humans beyond their individual deaths is very old and very widespread—as old and universal, perhaps, as dreaming. Afterlife is often held to be a consolatory fabrication devised out of grief and wishful thinking, an imagined realm where loved ones persist somehow beyond death as if they had traveled to a land beyond the hill or shore, a place where the evident injustices of mortal life are redeemed and set right, with punishment for the wicked and joyful rewards for the virtuous. Despite its evident gratifications, it is arguable (as Professor Gerald A. Larue has pointed out) that the wellspring of this idea is the real, confusing experience of half-remembered dreams. When we sleep, our drowsing minds mingle memory and fancy, placing us or our viewpoint surrogate inside a kind of shifting, surreal virtual reality where time loses its implacable dominion, where the dead walk among us, where strange chimeras are built from fragments of creatures, people, places, motivations and feelings carried over from waking empirical life.

It is easy to see how such imagined worlds, vivid and more various than humdrum narrow reality, might have enthralled our ancient ancestors, undistracted by reading, movies, television, easy travel or frequent visitors. Certainly we know that hunter-gatherers were given to punishing the living for slights or crimes experienced only in dream, in much the way diseases and accidents were widely blamed on sorcery and ill intent. But even if these are the sources of such widespread and poignant beliefs, are they necessarily untrue for that reason? Parapsychology suggests that intentions *might* act on others without any conventional medium of influence, that thoughts might be intercepted even if unspoken. One interesting intersection between such old beliefs and the scientific *Weltanschauung* is the literary (and now cinematic) form of story-telling known as science fiction.

For sf, the known world is all too narrow and restricted. Sf foresees futures remade by new insights, by clever inventions flowing from scientific analysis of the profoundest structures of the universe, from string and brane to atom, gene, organism, society, planet, galaxy and universe. If its narratives freely conjure story-devices at odds with what science tells us about reality—time machines to the past, vehicles or messages faster than light, extravagant psi powers—still they remain faithful to the *spirit* of science. Coherence and plausibility are retained; a story might violate known physics, but it has to provide some sort of quasi-scientific rationale for doing so, or at least play with the net up during its game (as scientist-writer Gregory Benford once put it). So how does this newest of narrative methods deal with one of the most ancient human concerns: the hope for a life of some different and even transcendent kind following our all-too-familiar life on earth?

The massive and authoritative Clute-Nicholls *Encyclopedia of Science Fiction* contains a substantial thematic entry for REINCARNATION but none for AFTERLIFE. This topic does receive an entry, along with an even longer treatment of POSTHUMOUS FANTASY, as well as REINCARNATION, in the companion volume edited by Clute and Grant, *The Encyclopedia of Fantasy* (1999). The distinction reflects the way commercial imaginative fiction has split into the twin modes of *science fiction* and *fantasy*. The former maintains a clearer vocation to realism (although often of a gaudy and inflated kind), while fantasy's adherence is to something more Gothic and shadowy. The metaphors of sf are intended, by and large, to be taken literally; those of fantasy remain somewhat allegorical, parabolic, dreamlike. So it is understandable that the larger part of fanciful fiction dealing with an afterlife is couched in the older forms of frank fantasy, where angels, fairies, ghosts, haunts, vampires, zombies, heavens, hells, demons and gods are part of the familiar landscape, not an intrusion to be rationalized and treated theoretically. It is the ambition of parapsychology (a maligned discipline I have discussed with cautious approval in *Outside the Gates of Science*) to deal with topics such as telepathy and afterlife on the basis that they are as real as the post office and the tourist agency's offerings, if rather more difficult to put on a paying and taxable basis. Is it possible that fantasies of life after life also offer us glimpses of a reality that scientific cultures dismiss due to their elusiveness and similarity to delusion and psychotic or protective self-deceit? If so (although I seriously doubt it), sf's approach to afterlife is probably more salient than fantasy's, even if the pickings are thinner on the ground and perhaps less emotionally appealing or moving.

In Heinlein's early novel, *Beyond This Horizon* (serialized 1942), the quest for proof of a life beyond death is all that makes his future utopia bearable for the jaded protagonist, Hamilton Felix. When that proof is found, ambiguously, it is more of the same—survival as reincarnation. An essence of the dead informs new infants, although memory of a former life is swiftly lost. It is a position interestingly congruent with the claims of Professor Ian Stevenson at the University of Virginia, in his series of detailed studies into cases compatible with reincarnation (*Twenty Cases Suggestive of Reincarnation*, 1980, *Children Who Remember Previous Lives*, 2001, etc), perhaps the more interesting because Heinlein's book first appeared more than sixty-five years ago. Of course, that hard-headed engineer had a keen interest in Theosophical and magical doctrines, and elements of both emerge in many of his stories. In the late novel *I Shall Fear No Evil* (1970), its biblical title speaks directly to the theme, in which a very old plutocrat's brain is transplanted into the healthy but brain-damaged body of a beautiful young woman. They conduct an internal dialogue throughout the novel, and while it is not clear until the end if this is a kind of hallucination or a form of "somatic memory," it seems clear that each has a soul that finally passes into a different kind of realm. That realm seems to be the sort of Ur-state of a partitioned divinity suggested at a key moment in *Beyond This Horizon*, when ill, unconscious Hamilton momentarily merges with a game-playing Mind that seems to shift from one personality to another, and even change games (and universes) at whim.

> It was pleasant to be dead.... The next time he would not choose to be a mathematician. Dull, tasteless stuff, mathematics—quite likely to give the game away before it was played out. No fun in the game if you knew the outcome.... It was always like this on first waking up. It was always a little hard to remember which position Himself had played, forgetting that he had played all of the parts. Well, that was the game; it was the only game in town, and there was nothing else to do. Could he help it if the game was crooked? Even if he had made it up and played all the parts.
>
> But he would think up another game the next time. (1981, 152-3)

This is by no means a conventional religious or mystical premise, not even for an Eastern faith; it is more like the kind of solipsistic *faux*-religious sf apparatus later developed by Heinlein's fellow *Astounding SF* pulp writer, L. Ron Hubbard. From such an uncompromisingly Cartesian perspective, the only thing that exists is an observing, constructing mind, but that mind is not identifiable with any one of us. It is not so much that there is an afterlife following this one; rather, our mortal lives are small fictions or roles played out within innumerable "fictons," or alternative realities (as suggested slyly in *The Number of the Beast*— [1980], where Heinlein is himself, as Author, the Beast under various guises).

None of this implies that science fiction writers have avoided the theme of an afterlife, although it is true that sf is typically reductive, materialist and atheist in orientation. If humans attain transcendence, as in the closing movements of Sir Arthur C. Clarke's *Childhood's End* (1953), it is usually via incorporation into a kind of cosmic Overmind that is not so much divine as immanent in the spacetime structure of the universe. The format of earthly minds—of brains in bodily action, complete with memories and senses—is somehow written into a more permanent and subtle form of matter or energy field. This is precisely the iterated fate of the deathless citizens of Diaspar, in Clarke's *The City and the Stars* (1956). A billion years hence, the citizens of this last and greatest city live for a millennium and then are dissolved back into computer-stored memories, to be embodied again many millennia later, memories returning in maturity. And in Clarke's *2001,* this transformation is reported as the history of the first denizens of the galaxy, and by implication as our own destiny:

> The first explorers of Earth had long since come to the limits of flesh and blood; as soon as their machines were better that their bodies, it was time to move. First their brains, and then their thoughts alone, they transformed into shining new homes of metal and plastic.... In their ceaseless experimenting, they had learned to store knowledge in the structure of space itself, and to preserve their thoughts for eternity in frozen lattices of light. They could become creatures of radiation, free at last from the tyranny of matter.... Into pure energy, therefore, they presently transformed themselves.... Now they were lords of the galaxy, and beyond the reach of time. They could rove at will among the stars, and sink like a subtle

mist through the very interstices of space. (1968, 184)

This is not so much an afterlife as the emergence of a butterfly from a pupa. In Bob Shaw's *The Palace of Eternity* (1969), souls are *egons*, immortal self-sustaining extraterrestrial patterns of energy that attain awareness via rapport with material, planet-bound creatures. "As the physical host grows and matures, his central nervous system becomes increasingly complex...." This development is matched by the egon, which is set free when the host dies. "Equipped with a identity, a highly complex pattern of self-sustaining energy, it is reborn to its heritage of endless life" (1969, 132)

But if something like this were true, why would it give us humans comfort? Because, Shaw proposes, "as far as the host is concerned, death is merely the doorway to this new life—because he is the egon" (*ibid.*). The same idea informed veteran sf author Clifford D. Simak's *Time and Again* (1951); Brian Stableford notes that Simak's "alien symbionts which infest all living things are obviously analogous to souls" (Clute and Nicholls, 1002).

This is a curious inversion of the old legend of the vampire, which sucks the life out of the warm living. (Vampires, of course, are neither dead, "passed across," nor resurrected, but uncannily *undead.*) Indeed, the pop existentialist Colin Wilson has published several garbled but intriguing quasi-sf novels adapting this theme: explicitly as predators on human "life-fields," in *The Space Vampires* (1976), but more metaphorically in *The Mind Parasites* (1967), and *The Philosopher's Stone* (1969), which draw upon the horror mythos of H. P. Lovecraft to construct an eerie secret history of humans as prey to disembodied creatures. Recently, the vampire trope has gained serious traction in the bestseller erotic-romance field, especially in the teen fiction of *Twilight* and its sequels, with vampires not so much clammy and terrifying as vivid and breathtaking (as well as blood-sucking), "a symbolic embodiment of all the dark sexual urges the psyche represses," as Diana Laurence notes.

* * * * * * *

In a long sequence of novels about the immense Riverworld where all postmortem humanity awakens (*To Your Scattered Bodies Go*, 1971, *The Fabulous Riverboat*, 1971, *The Dark Design*, 1977, *The Magic Labyrinth*, 1980, *Gods of the Riverworld*, 1983, etc), Philip José Farmer proposes, like Simak and Shaw, that we are born lacking immortal souls. In his cosmos, compassionate aliens will someday construct a sort of plug-in spiritual module or "watham" for the technologically resurrected dead, who henceforth *will* enjoy the kind of deathless preternatural life once ascribed by Catholic theologians to unbaptized infants in Limbo. Fallen humankind makes a hash of these plans. A somewhat similar notion plays out in several novels by Spider Robinson (*Time Pressure*, 1987; *Lifehouse*, 1997), in which time travelers from the future create a device in the past that captures and sustains the memories of the dying, salvaging all of us from mortal extinction. I used a comparable idea in *The Dreaming Dragons* (1980), where a subterranean Soul Core of perfectly resonant neutronium crystal has archived all the minds of humanity since our evolutionary emergence, and creates for the dead a variety of virtual worlds as their new home.

This general idea was advanced quite seriously in turn by Tulane University physicist Frank Tipler. In *The Physics of Immortality* (1995), he argued in prodigious detail, complete with mathematics and game-theory equations, that a closed universe will evolve toward a Teilhardian Omega Point god state (as in my *The Judas Mandala*, 1982) that will recreate or resurrect every person who has ever lived, and indeed every person who might ever *have* lived, to enjoy an endless paradise packed exponentially into the closing fractions of a second of the extinguishing Big Crunch cosmos. It is a remarkable perspective, and not particularly credible (even less so now that we know the cosmos is doomed to accelerate and cool endlessly rather than collapse in a reverse of the Big Bang's fires), but has been adopted by a number of sf writers such as Frederik Pohl in his Eschaton trilogy (*The Other End of Time*, 1996, *The Siege of Eternity*, 1997, *The Far Shore of Time*, 2000). Again, while these approaches to an afterlife are audacious and based to some extent on recent physics, they are not at all like the traditional images provided by anthropology, theology or mysticism.

Neither is a more plausible medium-term possibility discussed in both sf and futurist studies: the uploaded personality. If a mind is just the brainy body in action, responding to the world, other people and its own memories and conceits, then in principle it might be feasible to make a one-to-one mapping between each working element of the brain and a more durable machine substrate (see http://www.ibiblio.org/jstrout/uploading/). Greg Egan has explored this kind of notion in a number of stories ("Learning to be Me," 1990, *Permutation City*, 1994, *Diaspora*, 1997), as have Fred Pohl (the *Gateway* sequence, begun in 1977), John Varley ("Overdrawn in the Memory Bank," 1976), Charles Stross (*Accelerando*, 2005) and many other sf writers. In some of Egan's stories, future citizens have a "jewel" (or dual) implanted hygienically in their brain at an early age. Each neurological action is detected and copied into the vast storage of the jewel. Finally the internal structure of the jewel has become an exact copy of the brain it shares, running in parallel to its organic original, and the vulnerable brain itself is disposed of, like the vestigial vermiforme appendix.

The upload option, creepy as it must seem at first, promises a kind of immortality, since it amounts to recording a regular backup of your mind-state that can be reinstated if your present instantiation dies. The new you would lack your most recent memories, especially if you died violently. "She started quivering again. The person who had written that final paragraph," reflects the revived or downloaded backup of a character in Ken MacLeod's *Newton's Wake* (2004), "was a person different from herself...Her other self had been changed...by some experience other than approaching death, in some way that her present self could not understand" (211). So of course that sort of machine-mediated afterlife is entirely different from the kinds imagined by religions or other supernaturalist doctrines. What's more, many refuse to accept that a restored copy *is* the lost person; rather, he or she is just another person sharing the original's memories and concerns (see my *The Spike*, 2001, for a longer discussion). At the minimal extreme, an upload is used in sf as a sort of convenient talking book or oracle, the personality of the dead stored indefinitely and accessible, if somewhat mechanical in tone, as in Cordwainer Smith's "Alpha Ralpha Boulevard" (1961).

Meanwhile, interesting, the established Christian churches are less exercised than one might expect on topics such as imminent machine intelligence and perhaps machine consciousness. In a remarkable address in Rome in December, 2004, the president of the Pontifical Council for Social Communications, Archbishop John Foley, declared that the evolution of technology now raises the question whether "it is about humanizing the machine or about transforming man into something inhuman?" The president of the Pontifical Council for Culture, Cardinal Paul Poupard, added that while "the machine seems to be the negation of man and robotics, the annulment of the spiritual dimension" (a fear consonant with Philip K. Dick's sf obsessions), still "God has given man intelligence, which has enabled him to produce ever-more sophisticated machines, and has left him free to make his choices. We are the ones who create our technological reality" and "confront the evolution of a new dimension in which human intelligence is united to artificial intelligence." That is a remarkable admission for a prelate, and one that eventually might help bridge the gap between ancient dreams of an unprovable afterlife, and techno-dreams of afterlife mediated by the kinds of mechanisms imagined so far only in science fiction.

* * * * * * *

What if the whole world of experience is a sort of elaborate and deceitful simulation, as in the movie trilogy begun in 1999 with *The Matrix,* and the little-known Daniel F. Galouye novel *Simulacron-3* (1964) that preceded those movies by decades and was filmed by Joseph Rusnak with Armin Mueller-Stahl as *The Thirteenth Floor* in 1999? This is not inconceivable; already we have quite lifelike and quasi-artificially intelligent toy worlds such as *The Sims*. If our own civilization continues uninterrupted, growing in computational prowess and raw power, our posthuman descendents might choose to run simulations of our present epoch. Suppose they make very many of these, indistinguishable in their fine grain (especially to the simulated inhabitants) from the original world? Well, then, considerations of probability suggest that our own world is most likely to be one of these simulations (see several papers by the philosopher Nick Bostrom at http://www.simulation-argument.com/), and my novel diptych *Godplayers/K-Machines*, 2005-6).

In such a nested cosmos, it is possible that death can close down not only each individual human consciousness but the entire world—not in a redemptive religious Rapture, or cosmic calamity billions of years hence, but at any moment, if the programmer running the sim grows bored with it and deletes the simulation. On the other hand, a kind of afterlife might be found if the same personality templates or algorithms are reused in various quite different simulations, or if particularly delightful or wicked sims are recorded as art works or object lessons, to be archived or replayed at will. Of course, this prospect is nothing at all like the afterlife as reported by spiritualists and explorers of Near Death Experience, but those, too, have been the source of interesting sf, most notably Connie Willis's award-winning novel *Passage* (2001), which offers a plausible but debunking evolutionary explanation for NDE as complex hallucination.

* * * * * * *

In short, the theme of the afterlife has been taken down many odd and hitherto-unthought roads, as well as many that are well trodden. For example, a high-tech but barbarian culture in my own novel *The White Abacus* (1997) maintains that the soul is anchored to the body via the vermiforme appendix, which helps explain the more deplorable excesses of the twentieth and twenty-first centuries when appendectomies became commonplace...In my *Omni* story "Thy Sting" (1987), study of the full genome reveals that many introns, apparently "junk" genetic intrusions, are actually a repository of living ancestral experiences, perhaps non-locally connected to their originals, permitting partial recovery of memories from our forebears. An entire anthology of exemplary sf stories is *Afterlives* (1986), edited by Pamela Sargent and Ian Watson. The editors offer "aliens providing an afterlife and advanced human technology producing artificial resurrection...the "timeless moment," as well as vicious warfare in the godless heavens...the passage between life and death...afterlives that are bizarre, happy, obsolete, inverted, frightening, tragic and comic" (xvii).

That is a neat summary of sf's conceptual approach to afterlife: all and anything, except, generally, the solemn and sacerdotal. Sargent and Watson's useful gathering does neglect a little-known but unnerving "Paratime" oddity by H. Beam Piper, "The Last Enemy" (1950); in a parallel universe, reincarnation continues to segregate people on class and ideological lines. Also omitted is one of the most famous tales of a zombified afterlife, Robert Silverberg's "Born with the Dead" (1974), a literate and chilly portrait of a man obsessed by his dead Eurydicean wife, revived to a passionless or at least incomprehensible state by future medicine; a kind of Orpheus, he chooses finally to join her in living death, and by inevitable bitter irony shares her cool, unattached condition.

This is an ancient dread of life beyond death: that it will be calculating, distant, unemotional, or at best menacing and cruel. It is the vision of death at the heart of Ursula K. Le Guin's *The Farthest Shore* (1991), where death is a remote silent realm akin to an Egyptian frieze, or the more recent aching, awful vision of Philip Pullman in *The Amber Spyglass* (2000), the concluding volume of his immensely rich Miltonic trilogy, *His Dark Materials.* These two are fantasies rather than sf proper, but their methods follow in most ways the prescription of sf: careful creation of variant worlds with their own lawful rules not to be broken by caprice. It is significant that Pullman's sequence describes as a liberation the literal withering and death of God (or god, or Gnostic Yahweh), and the freeing of the trapped dead—each of us has a glum personal Death that accompanies us in life, and beyond the grave—in a sort of redemptive evaporation "into the night, the starlight, the air...gone, leaving behind...a vivid little burst of happiness...." (2000, 364).

Then there are liminal states, ontological disruptions at the margins of death and life, a favorite haunt of Philip K. Dick. In *Ubik* (1969), his characters are frozen in a cryonic half-life after a fatal explosion, their minds gradually ebbing, leaking into each another, fabricating simulacra of realities into which bizarre and blackly comic irrealities intrude. Is this the shape of an afterlife we might yet attain if cryonic suspension is developed further, so that many people wait, after clinical death, in a sort of chilly ambulance to future resurrection? That is certainly the background of a key character in my novel *Transcension* (2002), who is sliced and diced and reconstructed, eventually forming part of the core description of the Aleph, a machine intelligence of nearly supernatural power. It is the Aleph's decision to store all the world's people, if they agree (as most do), in simulated worlds prior to escaping the limitations of our four dimensional cosmos for somewhere roomier and more hospitable. This is an afterlife to rival those of the old pagans, but it lacks the truly transcendental (and paradoxical) character of religious faiths.

Philip Dick's recurrent obsession was a standoff, as he saw it, between the human and the android: between, that is, the poignant existential reality of *qualia* and sensitivity, versus a cold pretence in the form of machines that nag, pester, advise, loom, threaten, displace the human. In some stories, a protagonist learns with dismay that he *is* a machine, even a programmed bomb aimed at real humans. In *Eye in the Sky* (1957), the world is an illusion, or series of illusions, created by several characters at odds with each other at the moment of their death. In the movie *Bladerunner* (1982), loosely based on Dick's fine and complex dystopia *Do Androids Dream of Electric Sheep* (1968), an android-killing operative faces artificial people as complex and passionate as himself. Indeed, there are hints (in the movie, though not in the novel) that he is himself an android loaded with fake memories. If an afterlife is the blessed repose for souls graduating from this Vale of Tears, may an android dream of Ecumenical Sleep?

Might any artificial consciousness—assuming (as a large number of sf texts do) that such beings will be constructed some day—be deemed to have a "soul" capable of salvation and endurance beyond this life? The question might be sophistical, as most unbelievers maintain. Or it might be that a sufficiently complex mental structure, whether organic, silicon or quantum, generates some kind of organized field that might persist after its substrate's death. This notion has been advanced as (unorthodox) science by Professor Johnjoe McFadden (*Quantum Evolution: The New Science of the*

Life Force, 2000), and by parapsychologically informed biologists and physicists such as Rupert Sheldrake and the late Evan Harris Walker. It was a staple of Campbell's *Astounding/Analog* magazine in the '50s and '60s, and influential in other major sf magazines as well, such as *Galaxy,* where Robert Sheckley's *Immortality, Inc* (1959) was first serialized in 1958-9 as "Time Killer." Sheckley's method of immortality amounted to hijacking the bodies of others, a putative form of vampiric afterlife that some spiritualists dub "drop-ins."

That trope is used on a very large scale in Peter F. Hamilton's New Space Opera trilogy, *Night's Dawn* (*The Reality Dysfunction,* 1996, *The Neutronium Alchemist,* 1997, *The Naked God,* 1999), where dead souls erupt to infest the living across many stellar systems and thousands of pages. Perhaps the bleakest image of human afterlife to date (aside from Poul Anderson's "The Martyr," 1960, where it turns out that humans, unlike aliens, simply don't *have* immortal souls) is my own "The Womb" (1998). I draw upon another widespread recent mythos, the UFO abduction narrative, to portray an Earth penetrated by dark matter and dark energy that hosts fetus-like Gray aliens sprung from energy correlates of unborn human neural systems. This heterodox theology is perhaps the concoction of a bogus religious abductee, or it might be the simple and terrible truth:

> "We are of no more significance in the real universe, the invisible, impalpable immensity of dark matter that comprises the true cosmos, than a lump of bloody afterbirth.... The meaning of human life is not afterlife but afterbirth: we are a disposable stage in the production of the Children of Heaven, our Scions, the first casts, the happy miscarriages, the uncorrupted abortions. Those who perish in the flesh before crude matter has infected, corrupted and swiftly corroded their potentially immortal souls.... We produce fetuses with souls. If they're lucky, they die in time. Or the gray doctors come down and harvest them." (117-8, 124).

By contrast, the legacy of shamans, spirit seers, channelers, Raudive electronic voice interpreters, NDE experiencers and ghosthunters remains an insistence that afterlife *is* provable, that evidence is abundant to those with eyes to see and ears to hear. The burden of proof, however, seems to fall back as ever upon subjective criteria of evidence and the reliability of fallible testimony. This realm has been given vivid visual expression in such semi-sf movies as *Flatliners* (1990), where young medical students deliberately induce NDEs and apparently suffer a blurring of their worlds between this and the next. In Natalie Wood's final movie, director and special effects genius Douglas Trumbull's *Brainstorm* (1983), a scanner captures and displays the transition between death and afterlife. A 2005 movie, *White Noise*, draws upon the idea that hissing tape noise might be modulated by the dead to convey barely detectable messages to the living. In *What Dreams May Come* (1998), based on Richard Matheson's novel, a man follows his dead and psychically wounded wife through a harrowing of hell in a quite astonishing blend of bathos and pathos. For Kevin Costner in the silly but oddly haunting *Field of Dreams* (1989), ghosts of eight disgraced Chicago White Sox ball players are summoned when he builds a baseball field in his Midwest farm. *Ghost* (1990) is street-parapsychological in tenor. *Chances Are* (1989) has a dead husband return as the boyfriend of his wife's daughter, who then falls in love with the still grieving widow; in 2004, Nicole Kidman in *Birth* carried this to a creepier level, persuaded that a ten-year-old boy is her dead husband returned. Are these sf? Probably not, or not quite; there is no enabling super-machinery, no rationalization in terms of psi powers. Still, such movies perhaps might not have their impact without the prior immense success of sf tropes in the cinema, and the sf-based special effects that enliven fairytales into the dazzling representational realism of cinema.

* * * * * * *

Back here in our shared empirical world, as Sargent and Watson noted prophetically some quarter century ago, "Nationalist politics as mediated by Islamic clergy has now given us modern religious martyrs, while in the most advanced technological country many millions of fundamentalist Christians view nuclear Armageddon with positive enthusiasm, for those who believe will be 'raptured' to heaven" (1986, xiii). Since that observation, terrorist "martyrs," convinced that they go after death to a banal paradise of seventy-two virgins for every man, have wrought horror in the US's technocratic heartland, and "martyr brigades" strike with their own exploded flesh against foes in Israel, Iraq, and other nations where opposed conglomerates of money powered by faith, and vice versa, battle furiously for supremacy. This kind of dire slow-burn Armageddon is driven by people anguished by mean lives on earth and hoping desperately for a better existence beyond death; it has rarely been treated with any nuance in sf.

The general background assumption of the scientifically informed, after all, has been that a belief in afterlife will wither away as technology serves up utopia. While it is true—despite rumors to the contrary—that more people now live more secure and comfortable lives than ever before in history, with life spans increasing in the privileged parts of the world, a suspicion grows that wealthy Westerners thrive at the expense of the rest, and at the cost of a world rushing into Greenhouse and resource-depletion horror. Reincarnation might prove a less tempting belief as that suspicion hardens. Steely disbelief, though, is a stoic virtue perhaps beyond the grasp of suffering people who defer their hopes to a better life beyond the grave.

Unless mediums and parapsychologists can demonstrate unequivocally that such a domain is real and attainable, its adherents will regard afterlife as something to be hoped for in private faith, rather than by water-tight public evidence, and that is a posture somewhat antithetical to the spirit of science fiction. As more desperados rich and poor blow themselves and their victims apart, we might expect sf to turn away in resolute revulsion from the premise of spiritual afterlife, and emphasize instead the kinds of technofixes described above: cryonic suspension in expectation of eventual medical repair, rejuvenation, indefinite life extension, uploads, a transformative transition to some posthuman condition we can scarcely yet imagine. Death will be defeated, if science fiction is right, so that after life we can expect more life, and after that more, and still more, perhaps to the re-ignition or budding off elsewhere of a drained and failing cosmos.

CHAPTER SEVEN

READING MYSELF ON MARS

Is it improper, undignified, wrong to write about oneself writing? That is the literary, "gentlemanly" convention, it's true, a counsel of huffy propriety that, luckily, my working class upbringing failed to instill. I take heart from Philip Roth's passionate volume *Reading Myself and Others* (1975), where he responds with a sort of earned and lethal patrician amusement to those who gnaw at his work and chosen modes. Needless to say, I make no large claim for the following comments, adapted (or, as Roth put it, "unclogged") from interviews in various media: radio, print, email, on-line. Still, it might be of interest to hear what it is like to be not only a lifelong devoted reader and sometimes viewer of science fiction, sf, "sci fi", but a writer as well, and not only of sf, but of high theory, criticism, and futurism.

A commentator on real science and real technology works rather differently from a fiction writer, let alone a critical theorist. The methods are not entirely partitioned, of course, so the fact that I have been reading science fiction for half a century means I take a somewhat more...louche...approach than some to the remarkable possibilities opened by science and technology. Before anything else, science fiction tries to tell an interesting story—and, in my case, to build some sort of pleasingly ornate postmodern structure as well. In the popular science books *The Last Mortal Generation* and *The Spike* (and a volume I commissioned and edited, *Year Million)*, I tried to confront the reality of accelerating change, which is the correct description of our human world. Since that reality is extraordinary, it makes sense that my fiction and criticism tend to embody an awareness of strange novelty.

Here's how I write fiction: I encourage the basic ideas to percolate through my mind and body, less visualizing than feeling or dancing them (in imagination); then I tell a story by, as it were, *liv-*

ing in the universe I've invented. Quite often that imagined reality is an adaptation of some structure I've taken from somewhere else. *The White Abacus,* for example, is a series of tropes and variations on *Hamlet* and other Shakespearean plays, and on their heightened language—which is rich and humorous and intellectually demanding and all sorts of fun. My incipit: If Shakespeare were alive now, and imagining what it might be like in a thousand years time, what sort of story could he make out of the found materials that *he* used when he invented Hamlet?

When you look at the structures of the play, you find interesting tensions, moral issues, characters that embody them. Then you start to put a futuristic or science fiction spin on it. I have a robot, an "ai" (which rhymes with the personal pronoun "I") in my future world. This ai is named "Ratio," rather than Horatio, which happily conveys the idea of science fictional reason. Ratio provides a narratorial voice that continually observes these strange, passionate, uncontrollable, driven creatures who are humans. I invented a set of nongendered specific pronouns. Se cannot help thinking: These are *very strange creatures*, these humans.

In some ways, that must always be the stance of the science fiction writer, too.

I start with the science fiction megatext—the body of extant work that has been under construction for more than a century, tens of thousands of novels and short stories that have worked up commonplaces, tropes, enabling principles and devices, ways of telling stories, shorthand jargon, the sort of thing one finds in a very debased form in *Star Trek*'s "transporter beams," "warp speed," "dilithium crystals." Compressed specialized shorthand is the only way one can usefully talk about the future because it is the way we talk about the present. We say, "Get in the car and I'll drive you to the mall," not "Let us open the doors and enter this internally combusted device and we will go to places where food is vended by a privatized yet centralized system of distribution." Every writer has to invent his or her own particular little snazzy version of the shorthand, and of course there are points to be won for dreaming up some terrific new gadget or cosmology. Essentially one creates a richly lived-in world by just having people act with comfortable strangeness while using a curious terminology that points to things that don't exist outside the rest of science fiction. Consider the opening of my 1997 novel *The White Abacus*:

> *On the day I was born, the ai Conclave deputized*
> *me to a hu committee on matters of general concern.*

*My meeting was fixed for four hours after my birth,
so I spent that time hexing to the most beautiful
places in the Solar. The spring blooms of the Tuiler-
ies were fragrant in their profusion, lovely as the
Monet murals in the Orangerie. It was warm morning
when I visited the Grand Canyon, and chilly morning
as I stood some minutes later in the green, torrent-
foaming Valles Marineris on Mars, and later still
watched the whole ochre and khaki world, it seemed,
from T'ian-an-men Piazza at the caldera peak of
Olympus Mons, kilometers above the vast planetary
bulge of Tharsis Planitia. From Pluto's observatory
blister the sun was a poignant star, a delicious contrast to its fireball beyond the crater's lip high above
Mercury's icy south polar station. I lingered in the hu
Poetry Preserve at Stratford-upon-Avon: quaint,
meditative, ancient beyond belief, long repaired after
its centuries of industrial ruination. At the end of my
four hours (Saturn's braided rings, burning Venus all
a-tremble from the festung in Beta Regio, Father
Jove turning in majesty just a million kilometers
overhead, as I watched from Ganymede) I hexed to
Melbourne for my committee meeting. Most ai spend
the whole of their first day in a feverish spin about
the galaxy, blipping through hex gates as fast as they
can manage it, blazing with ten thousand impres-
sions. My own wanderday had been truncated for
reasons I barely understood at that time, but I held
no grudge. I was dizzy with love, with the gladness of
Awakening. We love you, love you, they had told me,
opening my eyes, my sensors, my mind, my links.
Welcome to the Real, young ai. Your family greet
you. Radiance and joy!*

Immediately, we wonder about these "hu" and "ai," and about
"hexing," the teleportation device in this world, a kind of field that
flimmers into existence. The word's origin in never explained, but it
might be Holophrastic Exchange. It looks like a net of luminous
*hex*agons, but "hex" also suggests magic—the kind of advanced
technology from which it is indistinguishable. So "hex" conveys the
idea of magic transportation in a nice short word. We know that if
an invention is widely used all the time, it is soon going to have a
short name and "hexing" sounds plausible.

What about the "wanderday"? I suppose strictly that should have been "Wandertag." In our world the young have (or used to have) a *Wanderjahr*, a wanderyear when adolescents can do the whole of Europe wearing a backpack. For my robots who live so fast, who can go places so very rapidly, they have a wander*day*. Mostly they zoom all over the Galaxy, sampling its infinite variety. Ratio, the narrator of the opening passage, decides just to restrict semself to the Solar System so se goes to those places se enumerates. That's followed through in later chapters by a contest in which teams led by Ratio and Telmah, the Hamlet figure, compete to find an emblematic object. As they quest swiftly to all the different planets of the Solar System, driven by punning clues, we follow as the team disperses. I tried to create something impossible for Shakespeare, despite his abundant gifts—a vivid sense of the incredible diversity of worlds out there in our Solar System.

Can a science fiction writer trust readers to be up to speed on this curious lexical task? It is a problem, because if the balance is missed it can become nothing better than a hard, academic slog, homework you wish the dog had eaten. And since it is not an imposed task—unless it actually has been set as homework, a fate that luckily my books have escaped so far—few will bother to keep reading. The solution is, as it were, pre-programming, what I call an "apprenticeship process." Fortunately, most science fiction enthusiasts have started reading sf at the age of twelve; unfortunately, very many "literary" readers miss that crucial establishing phase. I cannot imagine what it is like to be inducted into this whole megatext nowadays. When I was a child in Australia there was no television until I was fourteen, but happily there were sf radio serials and gaudy comic strips and a few sf anthologies and novels in the local library.

It is not, though, as if this is an unwarranted demand. If you want to read sonnets you have to read a lot of sonnets to understand how it works. Historical novels set in the nineteenth century, or the seventeenth century, or classic Greece, or the Shogunate, if they are well done, are replete with unfamiliar and bristly jargon. One of the pleasures of reading them is limping on until eventually you assimilate the stuff and suddenly it crystallizes and you're there. No longer are you being *told* something, you are actually *dwelling* in this virtual space.

That very process is emblematized in *The White Abacus.* People in this future world, by and large, have access to a connection to the *Gestell* a vast collective artificial intelligence system, through which most of the humans in this world are optionally connected, probably by chips in their brains—we never actually find out about that. So I coined the word "aks"—it resembles a typo or regional variant for *ask* and in some ways it is—which simply means "to access the system," the global information system. Arguably the only way you can tell such a story is by finding a small group who live very approximately the way we do today, and then interfacing them with this extraordinary and almost unspeakable larger reality. While most of the universe is an anarchistic collective of hu (humans) and ai (artificial intelligence), my cast comprises a splinter group who resile from that way of living. Rory Barnes and I used the same device in *Transcension,* a post-Singularity novel told by inhabitants of two enclaves, one of Amish-like religious fundamentalists of many different kinds, the other a restricted community that seems at first the very model of a modern Jetsons/Buck Rogers/*Star Trek* future. In the larger strangeness, they are no less eccentric and shy of genuine change.

An inevitable irony is that we, too, readers of the literature of change, cannot live without certainties. We need something to hang on to, and in some respects that is what art does for us—it anchors us in the experience of life, however fanciful its presentation. Some people have complained that in *The White Abacus* (which is full of music) most of the music is nineteenth or twentieth century music. Of course I did gesture at post-here-and-now forms (Miranda@Urth74429 in Coma Berenices, 3885—), but the point is precisely that *we* now live in a world drenched with music, and in order to convey anything of that quality of living in today's world, one has to refer to the actual music we hear or make. What justification for people in the thirtieth century to be listening to our music? I went beyond the point of justifying it; I made it parodic. My imagined hu and ai consider that the finest composers of the twentieth century are the 1930s' Hollywood romantic, lush innovator Erich Wolfgang Korngold, and Miklos Rosza, who wrote the movie music for *El Cid* and *Ben Hur* and other stirring costume dramas. This is pretty unlikely, yes, but people did once regard Bach as trivial, and Haydn and Handel as more important than Beethoven. The conceit orchestrates the telling of the novel, which is a big space opera drama. I hope you can imagine, reading the book, this lurid, bombastic, richly colored music filling the acoustic background.

* * * * * * *

And what of more recent fiction? *Godplayers* was the first of two books that deal in an indirect way with the Conceptoid of a technological singularity. Since life following a singularity is by definition strictly unimaginable, it is necessary to sneak up on one's characters and follow them even when they go into places that seem incomprehensible. By the end of the second book, *K-Machines*, many of the links back to the ordinary realities we already understand are made a lot clearer. But elements of opacity and mystery remain, because I was not writing an allegory. I'm arguing that life in the future will be mind-bogglingly strange, even to the point where it starts to resemble a fantasy scenario.

Godplayers represents mysterious forces shaping the lives of tomorrow's humanity, but then great forces have always controlled our lives. We speak English (those of us who do) because our parents taught us English rather than Mandarin or Urdu, and they did so because that was our community's language. Identity is always, to a large extent, a construct. But it is true that the threat of force wielded by desperate people willing to throw away their own lives and those of others often ends up in official responses that seem to constrict our freedom just as severely. It is possible that advancing inexpensive technology will help protect us against terror—say, if everyone monitors everyone else, using tiny, on-line cameras—but at the cost of losing liberties we have come to take for granted.

It is impossible to know how close we are to such a future, because the real advances must surely be occurring in labs run by the military and (in the spook sense) intelligence communities. What *is* apparent is that Moore's Law—the observation that computer bang for the buck doubles every year or so—has been continuing relentlessly (although some claim it has already peaked.) It is likely that artificial minds will indeed emerge from this escalation, but will be profoundly different from our own, alien and unsympathetic. It is up to the designers to raise their new mind children as we wish to raise our children, with a decent respect for humankind, and vice versa. There seems little doubt that superintelligent machines will emerge, if not this decade or century then eventually. Machines, like bacteria, have the capacity to evolve very fast indeed—faster, because they can scrutinize and augment their own design, something we can't do as yet. Many people are appalled at the idea that we would even wish to try. I hope that the new species of minds will share the world with us, and we with them, although the long contestatory history of evolution on this planet casts doubt on this rosy hope.

It is certainly possible that a powerful but unfriendly mentality lacking empathy for the organic world might simply choose to rework our planet into its own substance. After all, that is what we have been doing for generations. Programmers of such AI systems will have a profound moral responsibility, which as yet they show very little sign of acknowledging. Meanwhile, though, we grow ever more closely linked to our technologies. Google, like the humble calculator or spreadsheet, accelerates the user's capacity to understand and negotiate the world—one reason why science keeps surprising the experts as well as the rest of us. A decade ago, nobody knew that the universe was accelerating ever faster, or that most of the universe is composed of dark matter and energy. Nobody even dreamed it was there. Whatever the coming breakthroughs are, it is almost certain that they will be achieved by people augmenting their natural talents with the prodigious computing power becoming available to us. One change might be the defeat of aging and death. The inevitable predicament is that when such strangeness is unleashed, few will be prepared for it.

* * * * * * *

One of the most striking aspects of living in a representative democracy—Australia, Britain, Canada, America, others across the planet—is that those who present themselves for election are usually lawyers or professional politicians, the very people who likely avoided science at school. These are two completely different mindsets (although effective elite scientists have to master some measure of political savvy). Even those politicians who realize that science is the engine of our society seem to regard its practitioners as irritating and irrelevant much of the time—rather as they do writers, artists, dancers. Our elected representatives seem to find it extremely difficult to understand that science, while immensely disciplined, works best when it can explore freely, driven by imagination and wonder.

If the Spike ramps up in a big way by the middle of this century, there is no telling what the future might offer us, fanciful as such hopes might seem in an era of financial and environmental doom and gloom. If we maintain our nerve and our compassion, we can build a utopia, as the best science fiction hints. The world could do worse than to emulate the traditional virtues of Australian life— the "fair go," suspicion of arbitrary authority, "Jack's as good as his master"—and repudiate deference, paranoia, tribalism.

I spend a fair amount of time these days rummaging about (an Australian would say "fossicking," like a hopeful miner panning for gold) in a variety of disciplines, trying in my nonspecialist way to tie together ideas and images from science, philosophy, culture in general. This is enjoyable, for someone with my peculiar kind of mind, but it can get a bit wearing. Again, that is one of the signals of an oncoming singularity: we are obliged to sip, as they say, from a fire hydrant. So some of the ways I deployed advanced scientific ideas in *Godplayers* and *K-Machines* are deliberately playful, iconic, allegorical, and flung in for the sheer joyous spectacle. Readers ought not feel that they are drowning in this gush of technojargon— sometimes it is meant purely as surrealistic poetry.

I try not to beat the reader over the head with these hints toward an appropriate "strategy of reading," but they are plainly there. Two halves of a diptych, these novels are structured as a sort of rondo using an elaborate multi-dimensional array of Aspects and Attributes (a reference to Roger Zelazny's sf/mythological novels, to which I made plain my indebtedness), astrological and cabalistic drivers, enablers and constraints. I do not *believe* in the truth of these framing devices; I am no astrologer, and not much of a mystic. But one need not believe in God to grasp the virtues of sacred music or painting, its narrative poignancy, its resonance with the bone and gristle and meat of one's life. Consider these epigraphs, hardly there by accident, to *K-Machines:*

> "It's like watching a dance, or listening to music. It's not plot, it's pattern." —Robert B. Parker, *The Judas Goat*

> "There is no end. There is no beginning. There is only the passion of life." —Federico Fellini

The impressionist, thematic nature of the narrative is indexed in the center of the first volume, when sexual climax is paired with just such music, perhaps surprisingly:

> ...we lay in the ebbing flux of acoustic sunlight falling away from the high fog and luminous glory of Alan Hovhaness's *Mysterious Mountain.*

Then, almost immediately, the two-fold unity is spelled out in a passionate yet utterly abstract intellectual epiphany:

> Still the flowering stormed upward and outward, through infinite hordes of number, relation, ordering, bounds, completeness, into Tensor and Hilbert spaces, and Real and Complex manifolds. Finally, at its sunlit capstone, in a torrent of immense generativity, loomed twin rainbowed icy mountain peaks...as if

I witnessed the collision of two immense glacial ice shelves in the white heart of Antarctica, those impossibly abstract glories, their vast doubled structures, merged into the computational unity of—

To say it again: certain words and grammatical constructions we use in sf are specialized instruments for conveying what doesn't already exist. We invent nouns and verbs that do not refer to anything in the real world, utilize terms such as *robot* or *artificial intelligence* that go on to gain a kind of vernacular sense from the media in which our mutable minds swim. This jargon references a shared imaginative world. The printed page, better than any other medium, patches us into this vast encyclopedia of fanciful imaginary knowledge. Words do lend themselves peculiarly to that use, although awe-inspiring visual effects and music can multiply the impact marvelously.

Science fiction is often foolishly or snobbishly dismissed as a kind of Mr. Spock medium par excellence, a dismaying, contemptibly passionless or perhaps autistic construct unlike literature or ordinary movies, say, because its central concern is a phenomenon or a puzzle about the world, rather than the emotional issue of who's going to fall in love with whom, who's going to betray whom. But literature is not opposed to reason. In reality, the more passionate you are, the more your mind accomplishes the ends you desperately wish for, or attempts to avert what you dread.

Good sf invokes both passion and imagination, imagery and thought. So *The White Abacus* reworked ideas Shakespeare explored in Hamlet. Why bother doing that? Because by transposing the problematic of the play into a far future civilization as gaudy and baroque and flabbergasting as I could imagine, all manner of surprising and wonderful new feelings became available to the characters, and through them the readers. Yet at its heart is the same emotional issue and intensity that Shakespeare dealt with.

* * * * * * *

Humankind, or our richest and most adventurous elements, is now in a tentative transitional state that we can call "the transhuman". Sf readers are already accustomed to thinking about the shift away from the evolved hunter-gatherer our genome builds us to be. Now we can consider genetically engineering ourselves. The "posthuman" does not yet exist; it would be some bizarre state beyond transhumanity, where we can literally rewrite our gene codes, plug ourselves into computronium and a global network, a Gessell, to enhance and expand our powers of thought and feeling.

Absurd? Mere "sci fi" mistaken for impending reality? I have a pair of glasses hanging around my neck that I need for reading. That's already a transition from the basic human genomic definition. What happens when you introduce a nano-chip or crafted chromosome into your brain that does the equivalent for your mind that specs do for your failing eyesight? We become co-extensive with technology.

These are the kinds of changes we can expect, whether we like it or not, and not only in fictional form. Do we wish to see humanity prevail? Obviously it cannot, not for long, not as we are currently constituted. There won't be any place for it beyond the Spike, the singularity. Will humanity vanish, then, will it be destroyed (as was hinted in Vinge's fertile novel *Marooned in Realtime)*? No, of course not. Humanity will be transcended at childhood's end. Science fiction has trouble portraying such drastic reorganization. Consider the much-praised movie *Gattaca*. I found it irritating and wrong-headed. If gene-modified humans really *were* capable of superhuman accomplishment, as the narrative insists, the poor little courageous, gritty, damaged human simply could not have "passed." On the other hand, if their genomic boosting were just a Thousand Year Reich fraud, that's no test at all of transhumanity (as Fritz Leiber pointed out acerbically more than half a century ago in "Poor Superman")—because real enhancements will genuinely alter us, or more likely our grandchildren, into something very strange indeed. *Gattaca*, then, was a failure of nerve, or imagination. It can't be that Hollywood scriptwriters are necessarily ignorant of what is possible. How hard, one thinks in despair, to read a few books by Brian Aldiss, Brian Stableford, Wil McCarthy, Greg Bear, or Greg Egan? Very hard, it turns out.

Nevertheless, there is something about the self-defined literary sensibility that still recoils, despite the onslaughts of postmodernism, from the full-blown strangeness unleashed in genuine science fiction. "How vulgar! How meretricious! How infantile! We must restrain our imaginations, as Henry James did, to the scrupulous annotation of what we see around us, or just a tiny step beyond." What's needed, instead of that self-strangulation, is to seize the reins of the imagination and light out for the Territory ahead of the rest, while remaining ruthlessly consistent to your postulate, following through on as many of its implications as you possibly can. Egan is sublime at this. And few people trained primarily in literary texts can decode him, alas. Should we, then, resile into a kinder, gentler version of science fiction? There are now plenty of slipstream novels available, letting us test this alternative. Think of Margaret Atwood or Martin Amis, who can set books in a harsh if simplified future, or redeem a character living backwards from the Holocaust. I love Atwood's and Amis's work, but that is probably not the direction I will pursue myself. I think I'll stay with the pure quill.

* * * * * * *

So how will we or our descendents be, as human beings, if we decide to learn how to avoid death? The worst answer is: The same, only forever. We will play bingo for a thousand years and come home and have TV dinners and eventually get so bored that we throw ourselves under a jet-bus. In fact you won't be able to throw yourself under a bus in a world of immortals because they will be so fail-safed that it will be difficult to kill yourself. No, people will pass through a series of changes. As long as we are not physically failing, if we retain the vigor of youth, we will have the opportunity to learn much and experience even more. We will grow wise. Old people in their seventies and eighties are partly so nice, when they are not crabby and horrible, because their bodies are shutting down and the hormones are leaching away, no longer surging through them. On the other hand, the elderly have been through a lot, they know a lot, they can tell you calm stories about how often today's drama has happened, that they've seen it all before. Now if in fact those insights and recognitions occur to people who remain as physically vigorous as mature youths, we will have an extraordinary, unprecedented situation. Not entirely unprecedented, perhaps; one thinks of Bertrand Russell. All he lost, until close to the end, were some of the physical concomitants of youth.

Frankly, I can't think of anything to be said in favor of death. At the moment, we are stuck with death's pain loss and grief and we have to make as decent a fist of it as we can. It must be acknowledged, though, that death is *the* theme of art. It may be the theme of civilization—it may be that the consciousness of death, the consciousness of the inevitability of decay and death, is what drives us into the kinds of cultural structures we large-brained creatures have developed. In some ways the removal of death as an urgency is going to completely alter the fundamental architecture of culture and art. And to the degree that science fiction is proleptic, prophetic, casting forward into the only half-predictable, it will have to come to terms with the artistic limitations and possibilities of a world without aging and death, and without many children.

That will be a major challenge of art in a different, stranger world. One of the advantages of living in a time where change is always occurring is that we always have novelties to experience and talk about, and hence new ways of doing art. Maybe we will find ways of linking our minds together directly so experiences can be shared in something that makes virtual reality look like a cartoon (which is what it looks like now). When I write fiction now, I am telling a little story that gives readers some notion of how the people of the not-here-and-now might experience their world. The story I tell mimics, in some measure, the story they might tell. But because science fiction is a story told for us by contemporaries, it remains after all crucially time-bound, however futuristic or remote or strange or alienated it might appear to be to readers of conventional fiction. When you look back at the science fiction written in the 1950s, you can tell instantly that is when it was from.

Will Western religions and ideologies cope with the disappearance of mandatory death sentences for everyone? I think Christianity will find a way around it; it has managed, in the past, with all sorts of upsets. Jesus, of course, might come to be seen as the first immortal, one who came back from the dead in a purified, transformed, preternatural body. Granted, endless life might be seen as a wicked desire on our part, wishing to emulate Jesus without having been through the transformation of death. I suspect that some of the other religions with reincarnation built into their center are going to have a little bit more trouble, because if you don't go, you can't come back. But as that old song tells us, "Everybody Wants to Go to Heaven but Nobody Wants to Die." If people were really so eager to go to go to Heaven, into the promised transformed blissful state, one might expect them to be happy, to embrace death, yet people kick and shriek against it. Not everybody, of course. My mother died two decades ago of ovarian cancer, terribly, painfully, but in her Catholic belief, and surrounded by priests and the panoply of Christian iconography, she made the transition fairly peacefully (if to my mind deludedly). All power to her that she managed to die without too much grief. So these are issues that are to be confronted by the people who go through it. Some of us might prove to *be* those people. (Not me, though. I'll fall off the twig too soon, damn it.) Until then, we can explore the terrain in imagination, unleashing as much of the strange as we can stand.

* * * * * * *

A conversation is what I hope to provoke with my books. Let's get people talking about how the future *isn't* going to be the same as yesterday and today, just dressed in silver lycra with jet backpacks. Most of the people who take the singularity prospect seriously, rather than sniggering at "the Rapture of the Nerds," seem to be libertarians, devoted to individual rights as the source of righteous conduct. It is not surprising that they hope to extend their own lives as far into tomorrow as they can, even if that means enhancing and modifying their biology and neurology. Many people shudder, regarding this ambition with horror, calling it "selfish" and "inhuman." I do not believe it is, although it could go that way if the very richest or most powerful people restrict or appropriate the new machineries of change and refuse to let go of them.

I want to see a transhuman future, and expect that when it comes it will pass inevitably into a posthuman one—*not* inhuman or inhumane, but as different from our world as ours is from that of *Homo habilis*—or, finally, from our evolutionary ancestors, the ancient bacteria. We are going to be sharing this planet with a new species, within half a century or less: the ai, the artificial or machine intelligences, probably conscious and capable of rewriting their own mind code. To prepare for *that* epochal conversation, we need to have the most open-minded debate in the history of the world, right now, in fact as well as fiction, before we find ourselves slamming up the Spike, taken entirely unawares.

We can try to stay abreast of strange change by keeping our eyes and ears open, imagination stretched wide but with common sense and rationality fully engaged. There's an appalling amount of wishful thinking and desperate superstitious junk governing the thinking of many people right now; they fall into it with a desperate, eager cry because it is easier and more comforting to rule your life by astrology or the guesses of ancient prophets than to deal with the real universe, fourteen billion years old, cosmically vast, expanding into forever, its life forms evolved by random mutation selected and shaped by nothing more noble than survival. We will do *better* than evolution has managed, because we have hearts and minds able to care passionately, to remember and to cast forward, to plan and to change those plans when we find their flaws.

I am amused by the ways in which for the last thirty years literary theory, which is my own academic discipline, has been discussing the fragmentation of the "subject" (or human self), while cognitive and neurosciences have delved into the modularity of mind and brain—and yet both great discussions have continued in ignorance of each other if not hostility. When people do finally get copied into the virtual space of computers (and let us hope that's "*up*loading," not "*down*loading"—into a more expansive space, not a stifled one) we shall surely find many of these issues resolved quite dramatically. Theory will give way to experiment and experience, as usual.

In the meantime, here is what theory, science, and fiction alike can join to tell us, after all the confusions of the last couple of hundred thousand years: that humankind, risen from ancient slime, is the seed of those great forces that one day shall reshape the entire cosmos. It is a perspective captured memorably in the mysterious phrase that closes A. E. van Vogt's melodramatic novel, *The Weapon Makers* (1943):

"Here is the race that shall rule the sevagram."

BIBLIOGRAPHY

AND SUGGESTIONS FOR FURTHER READING

The indispensable source for basic information and incisive commentary is John Clute and Peter Nicholls, *The Encyclopedia of Science Fiction*, 2nd Edition (London: Orbit, 1993), and supplements. See especially the useful and sometimes pungent entries on CRITICAL AND HISTORICAL WORKS ABOUT SF, HISTORY OF SF, NEW WAVE, and on various relevant authors. Other useful compendia include Neil Barron, *Anatomy of Wonder: An Historical Survey and Critical Guide to the Best of Science Fiction*, New York: Bowker, 4th Edition, 1995; and such landmarks as Hal W. Hall, *Science Fiction and Fantasy Reference Index, 1978-1985*, Englewood, CO: Libraries Unlimited, and Aurel Guillemette, *The Best in Science Fiction: Winners and Nominees for the Major Awards in Science Fiction*, Aldershot, Hants, England: Scolar Press, 1993.

On-line sources are even more convenient, although perhaps less reliable. See, for example,

http://www.dpsinfo.com/awardweb/

Copious information is held at Dr. Jonathan vos Post's

http://www.magicdragon.com/UltimateSF/

which provides Timelines by decade, listing many prominent books and stories, plus the major prize winners. The Science Fiction and Fantasy Research Database compiled by Hal W. Hall is

http://library.tamu.edu/cushing/sffrd/default.asp

Other readily accessible sites record all the Hugo, Nebula, Campbell Memorial, Jupiter, Ditmar, and other Awards to date. An interesting recent essay is "Science Fiction and the Beats: American Literary Transcendentalism," by Norman Spinrad:

http://ourworld.compuserve.com/homepages/normanspinrad/beats.htm

As I write, the World Wide Web has been in existence for fifteen years, routinely used by researchers for more than a decade. It seems entirely redundant, therefore, to provide exact bibliographical details of books that can be found most readily by consulting the Internet Speculative Fiction DataBase (http://www.isfdb.org/sfdbase.html), Google, Amazon.com, Abebooks.com or the Library of Congress catalogue on-line (http://catalog.loc.gov/). This is especially true in respect of sf novels, anthologies and collections, which typically appear in transient paperbacks in many printings. Consequently, the few items I list here are chiefly books where I give page references to a specific edition, or which are difficult to locate. Short stories (from the pulp magazines now mostly inaccessible, but usually gathered in anthologies) can be found most conveniently, in various editions, in their ISFDB listings.

Aldiss, Brian W., ed., *Galactic Empires, Volumes One & Two,* New York: St. Martin's Press, 1976.
Aldiss, Brian W. and Harry Harrison, *Decade: the 1960's,* London: Pan, 1977.
Aldiss, Brian W. with David Wingrove, *Trillion Year Spree: The History of Science Fiction,* London: Gollancz, 1986.
Anders, Lou, Interview with John Meaney, http://www.sfsite.com/10a/jm137.htm
Anderson, Poul, *There Will Be Time,* New York, Signet, 1973.
Ballard, James, *The Four-Dimensional Nightmare,* [1963] Harmondsworth: Penguin, 1965.
— *The Terminal Beach,* [1964] Harmondsworth: Penguin, 1966.
— "You, Me and the Continuum," in *The Atrocity Exhibition* [1969]. London: Panther, 1972.
Banks, Iain M., *The Algebraist,* London: Orbit, 2004.
Barnes John, *Gaudeamus,* New York: Tor, 2004.
Barton, William, "Off on a Starship," *Asimov's,* January, 2001.
Bester, Alfred, "A Diatribe Against Science Fiction" F&SF, May 1961, in *Redemolished* compiled by Richard Raucci, New York: iBooks, 2000.
Blish, James writing as "William Atheling, Jr.", "Making Waves," in *More Issues at Hand,* Chicago: Advent: Publishers, 1970.
Broderick, Damien, *The Dreaming* [originally as *The Dreaming Dragons,* New York: Pocketbooks, 1980] revised, http://www.fictionwise.com/ebooks/eBook561.htm, Fantastic Books, 2009.

— *Reading by Starlight: Postmodern Science Fiction*, London: Routledge Popular Fiction series, 1995.

— *Transrealist Fiction: Writing in the Slipstream of Science*, Conn: Greenwood Press, 2000.

— "The Womb," in Jack Dann and Janeen Webb, eds., *Dreaming Down-Under*, [1998] New York: Orb, 2001, 98-130.

— *The Spike*, New York: Forge, 2001.

— *x, y, z, t: Dimensions of Science Fiction*, Holicong: PA, Borgo Press: 2004.

Brooke, Keith, Review of *Appleseed*:
http://www.infinityplus.co.uk/nonfiction/appleseed-rev.htm

Clarke, Arthur C., *2001: A Space Odyssey*, New York: Signet, 1968.

Clute, John, "Scholia, Seasoned with Crabs, Blish Is" [1973], in Moorcock, 1983.

— "To the Stars and Beyond on the Fabulous Anti-Syntax Drive," in *New Worlds Quarterly* 5, London: Sphere Books, 1973.

— "Trope Exposure," in *New Worlds Quarterly* 9, London: Sphere Books, 1975.

— Review of Neal Stephenson's *Cryptonomicon*, in *New York Review of Science Fiction*, September 1999, No. 133, 13.

Cowdrey, Albert E., *Crux*, New York, Tor, 2004.

Davis, Ray, "Delany's Dirt," in *Ash of Stars*, ed. James Sallis, University Press of Mississippi.

del Rey, Lester, *The World of Science Fiction: 1926-1976. The History of a Subculture* New York and London: Garland Publishing, Inc, 1980.

Delany, Samuel R., *The Jewel-Hinged Jaw: Notes on the Language of Science Fiction* [1977] New York: Berkely Windhover, 1978a.

— *The American Shore: Meditations of a Tale of Science Fiction by Thomas M. Disch*—Angouleme Elizabethtown, New York: Dragon Press, 1978b.

— "A Silent Interview with Samuel R. Delany," *Rain Taxi:*
http://www.raintaxi.com/online/2000winter/delany.shtml

di Filippo, Paul, "Just Like Himself, Only More So."
http://www.infinityplus.co.uk/nonfiction/pdif_rudy.htm

Dick, Philip K., online bibliography:
http://www.philipkdick.com/works_novels.html

Disch, Thomas M., *Camp Concentration* London: Panther, 1969.

Doctorow, Cory, *Someone Leaves Town, Someone Comes to Town*, New York, Tor, 2005.

Douglas-Fairhurst, Robert, Review of Martin Amis, *Yellow Dog:*
http://www.guardian.co.uk/books/2003/aug/24/fiction.martinamis

Ellison, Harlan, *Dangerous Visions* New York: Doubleday, 1967.

— *Again, Dangerous Visions* New York: Doubleday, 1972.

Fischer, Tibor: http://www.telegraph.co.uk/comment/personal-view/3594613/Someone-needs-to-have-a-word-with-Amis.html

Gentle, Mary, *A Sundial in a Grave: 1610*, New York: Perennial/ Harper-Collins, 2005.

Gibson, Gary, *Against Gravity,* New York, Tor, 2005.

Gillespie, Bruce, interviewed by Frank Bertrand, "My Life and Philip K. Dick" http://www.philipkdick.com, 2001

Greenland, Colin, *The Entropy Exhibition: Michael Moorcock and the British "New Wave" in Science Fiction,* London: Routledge & Kegan Paul, 1983.

Harrison, M. John, "A Literature of Comfort," in *New Worlds Quarterly 1,* London: Sphere Books, 1971.

— *Light,* New York: Bantam, 2004.

Hartwell, David G., *Age of Wonders: Exploring the World of Science Fiction,* New York, McGraw-Hill, 1984.

Heinlein, Robert A., *Beyond This Horizon,* [1942, 1948] Boston: Gregg Press, 1981.

Horton, Rich, Review of *Appleseed:* http://www.sfsite.com/07a/ap107.htm

Irving, John, *Until I Find You,* New York, Random House, 2005.

James, Edward, *Science Fiction in the Twentieth Century,* Oxford, Oxford University Press, 1994.

Jameson, Fredric, *Postmodernism, or, The Cultural Logic of Late Capitalism*, Duke University Press, 1991.

— *Archaeologies of the Future: The Desire Called Utopia and Other Science Fictions*, London and New York: Verso, 2005.

Jonas, Gerald, Science fiction, *New York Times*, October 28, 1979.

Kemp, Earl, ed., "Who Killed SF?" http://efanzines.com/EK/eI29/index.htm

Larue, Gerald A., Professor Emeritus of Religion and Adjunct Professor of Gerontology, University of Southern California, "Afterlife," *Humanism Today,* Vol 5, 1989, http://www.humanismtoday.org/vol5/larue.pdf, 3

Linklater, Richard 2006, quoted in Steven Rea, "Animating Dick's paranoid vision." Link no longer available.

Leiber, Fritz, "Poor Superman," in *Galaxy Science Fiction* (as "Appointment in Tomorrow"), July 1951, 134-58.

Lem, Stanislaw, *Microworlds: Writings on Science Fiction and Fantasy,* ed. Franz Rottensteiner London: Secker & Warburg, 1985.

MacLeod, Ian R., *The House of Storms,* New York: Ace Books, 2005.

MacLeod, Ken, *Newton's Wake,* New York: Tor, 2004.

— *Learning the World: A Scientific Romance,* New York: Tor 2005.

Meaney, John, *Paradox: Book One of the Nulapeiron Sequence,* New York: Pyr, 2005.

— *Context: Book Two of the Nulapeiron Sequence,* New York: Pyr, 2005.

— *Resolution: Book Three of the Nulapeiron Sequence,* New York: Pyr, 2006.

Merril, Judith, *The Year's Best S-F,* New York: Dell, especially from the Fifth Annual Edition of 1960.

— *England Swings SF,* New York: Doubleday, 1968

Miéville, China. Cited with links:
http://urchin.earth.li/cgi-in/twic/wiki/view.pl?page=TheNewWeird
Moorcock, Michael, *New Worlds: An Anthology,* London: Fontana, 1983; this includes a complete content listing of all issues of *New Worlds* magazine back to Vol. 1, No. 1, 1946, as well as a sampling of New Wave fiction and criticism from 1965-75.
Mullen, R. D., and Darko Suvin, *Science Fiction Studies,* New York: Gregg Press, 1976.
Nicholls, Peter, *The Encyclopedia of Science Fiction* 1st edition, London: Granada, 1979.
Nielsen Hayden, Patrick—opening epigraph to this book taken from: http://nielsenhayden.com/makinglight/archives/011427.html#011427
Niffenegger, Audrey. *The Time Traveler's Wife,* [2003] New York: Harvest, 2004.
— "An Interview with Audrey Niffenegger,"
http://www.bookslut.com/features/2003_12_001158.php
O'Reilly, Timothy, *Frank Herbert,* New York: Frederick Ungar, 1981.
Poupard, Cardinal Paul, cited in:
http://www.zenit.org/english/visualizza.phtml?sid=62884
Panshin, Alexei and Cory, *The World Beyond the Hill: Science Fiction and the Quest for Transcendence,* Los Angeles: Jeremy Tarcher, Inc, 1989.
Pringle, David, *Earth Is the Alien Planet: J. G. Ballard's Four-Dimensional Nightmare* San Bernardino, CA: Borgo Press, 1979.
— *Science Fiction: the 100 Best Novels,* New York: Carroll & Graf, 1985.
Pullman, Philip, *The Amber Spyglass,* New York: Knopf, 2000.
Roberson, Chris, *Here, There & Everywhere,* New York: Pyr, 2005.
Roberts, Adam, *Swiftly: Stories that Never Were and Might Not Be,* San Francisco: Night Shade Books, 2004.
— Introduction, http://www.adamroberts.com/writing/jupiter-magnified/
Robinson, Spider, *Very Bad Deaths,* New York: Baen, 2004.
Robson, Justina, *Natural History,* New York: Bantam Spectra, 2005.
— *Silver Screen*, New York: Pyr, 2005.
— Interview with Cheryl Morgan, 2003:
http://www.strangehorizons.com/2003/20030421/robson.shtml
Rucker, Rudy. "A Transrealist Manifesto," *The Bulletin of the Science Fiction Writers of America,* #82, Winter, 1983. Reprinted in *Transreal!* WCS Books, 1991, and *Seek!* New York: Four Walls Eight Windows, 1999. Online with other essays on writing at:
http://www.rudyrucker.com/writing/
Russ, Joanna, "The Wearing Out of Genre Materials" *College English*, 33:1, October, 1971.
Ryman, Geoff, *Air or, Have not Have,* New York: St. Martin's Griffin, 2004.
— Interview with Kit Reed:
http://www.infinityplus.co.uk/nonfiction/intgr.htm

Sallis, James. ed. *Ash of Stars: On the Writings of Samuel R. Delany.* Jackson: UP of Mississippi, 1996.

Sargent, Pamela and Ian Watson, eds., *Afterlives*, New York: Vintage, 1986.

Sawyer, Robert J., "Science Fiction and Social Change," *New York Review of Science Fiction,* January, 2005, 11-14.

Scholes, Robert, *Structural Fabulation: An Essay on Fiction of the Future* Indiana: Notre Dame, 1975.

— and Eric Rabkin, *Science Fiction: History, Science, Vision,* Oxford: Oxford University Press, 1977.

— *Textual Power: Literary Theory and the Teaching of English,* New Haven: Yale University Press, 1985.

Scholz, Carter. http://www.bookforum.com/scholz.html; "Invisible man," review of Julie Phillips, *James Tiptree, Jr.: The Double Life of Alice B. Sheldon,* New York: St. Martin's Press, 2006.

Shaw, Bob, *The Palace of Eternity,* New York: Ace SF Special, 1969.

Sherman, Delia: http://www.interstitialarts.org/what/intro_toIA.html

Shippey, Tom, *J. R. R. Tolkien: Author of the Century,* Boston: Houghton Miflin, 2001.

Silverberg, Robert, *Other Spaces, Other Times: A Life Spent in the Future,* New York: Nonstop Press, 2009

Spinrad, Norman, *The New Tomorrows,* New York: Belmont, 1971.

Stableford, Brian, "Reincarnation," in Peter Nicholls and John Clute, *The Encyclopedia of Science Fiction*, [1993] New York: St. Martin's Griffin, revised, 1995, 1001-1002.

Sterling, Bruce, *Tomorrow Now: Envisioning the Next Fifty Years,* New York: Random House, 2003

Sterling, Bruce. "Slipstream." http://www.eff.org/Misc/Publications/Bruce_Sterling/Catscan_columns /catscan.05

Stross, Charles, *The Family Trade: Book One of The Merchant Princes,* New York, Tor, 2004.

— *The Hidden Family: Book Two of The Merchant Princes,* New York, Tor, 2005.

— *Accelerando*, New York: Ace Books, 2005. Citations from the free download: http://www.antipope.org/charlie/accelerando/

Suvin, Darko, *Metamorphoses of Science Fiction: On the Poetics and History of a Literary Genre,* New Haven: Yale University Press, 1979.

Suvin, Darko, *Other Worlds, Other Seas,* New York: Random House, 1970.

Swainston, Steph, *The Year of Our War,* New York: Eos, 2005.

Thompson, Hunter S. *Fear and Loathing in Las Vegas: A Savage Journey to the Heart of the American Dream,* New York, Random House, 1971.

Tuttle, Lisa, *The Mysteries,* New York: Bantam, 2005.

van Vogt, A. E., *Slan,* [1940, 1945, 1951] New York: Orb, 1998.

— *Supermind*, New York: DAW Books, 1977.

Vinge, Vernor, *Rainbows End*, New York, Tor, 2006.

Westfahl, Gary. "Homo aspergerus: Evolution Stumbles Forward." 6 March 2006. http://www.locusmag.com/2006/Features/Westfahl_HomoAspergerus.html

Wilcott, Isaac, Review of *Slan Hunter*, http://home.earthlink.net/~icshi/Reviews/SH-Wilcott.html

Williams, Liz, *The Banquet of the Lords of Night, and Other Stories*, San Francisco: Night Shade Books, 2004.

Wilson, Robert Charles, *Spin*, New York, Tor, 2005.

Wolfe, Gene, *Endangered Species*, New York, Tor, 2004.

Wollheim, Donald A., *The Universe Makers: Science Fiction Today*, New York: Harper & Row, 1971.

Wright, John C., *The Last Guardian of Everness*, New York, Tor, 2004.

— *Mists of Everness*, New York, Tor, 2005.

— *Orphans of Chaos*, New York, Tor, 2005.

— *Fugitives of Chaos*, [2006] New York, Tor, 2007.

— *Titans of Chaos*, New York, Tor, 2007.

— *Null-A Continuum*, New York: Tor, 2008

ACKNOWLEDGMENTS

The opening chapter is adapted from my Guest of Honor Speech at the International Association for the Fantastic in the Arts (IAFA) Conference in Florida in 2005, published as "Transreal Nostalgia in a Time of Singularity," in the *Journal of the Fantastic in the Arts,* Vol. 16, No, 1, 2005.

Much of chapter 2 is adapted from my essay "New Wave and backlash: 1960-1980" in Edward James and Farah Mendlesohn, eds., *The Cambridge Companion to Science Fiction,* Cambridge University Press, 2003.

Much of chapter 3 is adapted from my entry POSTMODERN-ISM AND SF in John Clute and Peter Nicholls, eds., *The Encyclopedia of Science Fiction,* 2nd edition, London: Orbit, 1993, and from my entry "Transrealist Fiction" in *Books and Beyond: The Greenwood Encyclopedia of New American Reading,* ed. Kenneth Womack, Greenwood Press, 2008.

"Fancy Dancing in the Swill Trough: a Chorus Line" first appeared in *Polder: A Festschrift for John Clute and Judith Cute,* edited by Farah Mendlesohn, Baltimore: Old Earth Books, 2006.

The last chapter is derived, fairly distantly, from interviews with Ramona Koval, Australian Broadcasting Corporation national radio, March 1999; Brenda Cooper, on Futurist.com's website, 2004; Alisa Krasnostein, on *ASif.Dreamhosters.com* website, May 2006.

Many of the readings in this book first appeared in *The New York Review of Science Fiction* and *Locus: The Magazine of the Science Fiction & Fantasy Field.*

INDEX

ABOUT THE AUTHOR

DAMIEN BRODERICK, Ph.D., is an Australian science fiction and science writer and critical theorist, and a Senior Fellow in the School of Culture and Communication at the University of Melbourne, Australia, although these days he lives in San Antonio, Texas. His scholarly books include *The Architecture of Babel* (1994), *Reading by Starlight* (1995), *Transrealist Fiction* (2000), and *x, y, z, t: Dimensions of Science Fiction* (2004). In 2005, he received the Distinguished Scholarship Award of the International Association for the Fantastic in the Arts. He has also published a number of award-winning novels.